DREAMS AND VISIONS IN THE BIBLE
AND RELATED LITERATURE

SEMEIA STUDIES

Jacqueline M. Hidalgo, General Editor

Editorial Board:
Eric D. Barreto
Jin Young Choi
L. Juliana M. Claassens
Rhiannon Graybill
Emmanuel Nathan
Kenneth Ngwa
Shively T. J. Smith

Number 101

DREAMS AND VISIONS IN THE BIBLE AND RELATED LITERATURE

Edited by

Jean-François Racine and Richard J. Bautch

SBL PRESS
Atlanta

Copyright © 2023 by SBL Press

All rights reserved. No part of this work may be reproduced or transmitted in any form or by any means, electronic or mechanical, including photocopying and recording, or by means of any information storage or retrieval system, except as may be expressly permitted by the 1976 Copyright Act or in writing from the publisher. Requests for permission should be addressed in writing to the Rights and Permissions Office, SBL Press, 825 Houston Mill Road, Atlanta, GA 30329 USA.

Library of Congress Control Number: 2023947639

Gina Hens-Piazza's essay originally appeared in *Biblical Theology Bulletin* 48 (2018): 10–17. https://doi.org/10.1177/0146107917746577. Reprinted by permission.

Contents

Abbreviations vii

Introduction
Richard J. Bautch and Jean-François Racine 1

Hermeneutics of Readership

Dreams Can Delude, Visions Can Deceive: Elijah's Sojourn
in the Wilderness of Horeb (1 Kings 19:1–21)
Gina Hens-Piazza 13

Envisioning the Visions of the Book of Revelation: A Narrative
Study of Revelation 12
Andrea Spatafora, MSF 27

Interplay between Reading and Intertextuality

What Abram Said He Saw: A Dream Vision and the
Uncertainty of Mediation in the Genesis Apocryphon
Joseph McDonald 49

Violence and Vulnerability: The Vision of Jeremiah in
2 Maccabees
Richard J. Bautch 69

Dreams of Empire: Pilate's Wife in Matthew
Roy Allan Fisher 85

Navigating Dreams and Visions with Affect and Emotion

Why Does Enoch Weep? The Traumatic Vision of the
Book of Dreams
    Genevive Dibley 109

Exploring the Visions in Acts in Their Narrative Context
    Deborah Prince 129

Warning! Cheerfulness Can Be Contagious: A Reading of
Hermas's Emotional Spectrum
    Jean-François Racine 147

Response

Is There a Reader for This Text?
    Rodney A. Werline 177

Contributors 191
Modern Authors Index 195
Subject Index 199

Abbreviations

AB	Anchor Bible
ABRL	Anchor Bible Reference Library
AGJU	Arbeiten zur Geschichte des antiken Judentums und des Urchristentums
AIL	Ancient Israel and Its Literature
AnBib	Analecta Biblica
ANWR	Temporini, Hildegard, and Wolfgang Haase, eds. *Aufstieg und Niedergang der römischen Welt: Geschichte und Kultur Roms im Spiegel der neueren Forschung*. Part 2, Principat. Berlin: de Gruyter, 1972–.
AOTC	Abingdon Old Testament Commentaries
AYBRL	Anchor Yale Bible Reference Library
BETL	Bibliotheca Ephemeridum Theologicarum Lovaniensium
Bib	*Biblica*
BibInt	*Biblical Interpretation*
BibInt	Biblical Interpretation Series
BibOr	Biblica et Orientalia
BibSem	The Biblical Seminar
BLS	Bible and Literature Series
BZAW	Beihefte zur Zeitschrift für die alttestamentliche Wissenschaft
CahRB	Cahiers de la Revue biblique
CBET	Contributions to Biblical Exegesis and Theology
CEJL	Commentaries on Early Jewish Literature
CJos	*Cahiers de Joséphologie*
CNT	Commentaire du Nouveau Testament
Colloq	*Colloquium*
ConBot	Coniectanea Biblica: Old Testament Series
DCLS	Deuterocanonical and Cognate Literature Studies
DSD	*Dead Sea Discoveries*

EJL	Early Judaism and Its Literature
ESEC	Emory Studies in Early Christianity
EvT	*Evangelische Theologie*
FOTL	Forms of the Old Testament Literature
HTR	*Harvard Theological Review*
HUCM	Monographs of the Hebrew Union College
IBC	Interpretation: A Bible Commentary for Teaching and Preaching
ICC	International Critical Commentary
Int	*Interpretation*
ISBL	Indiana Studies in Biblical Literature
JBL	*Journal of Biblical Literature*
JSNT	*Journal for the Study of the New Testament*
JSJSup	Supplements to the Journal for the Study of Judaism
JSPSup	Journal for the Study of the Pseudepigrapha Supplement Series
LCL	Loeb Classical Library
LHBOTS	The Library of Hebrew Bible/Old Testament Studies
LNTS	The Library of New Testament Studies
LSJ	Liddell, Henry George, Robert Scott, Henry Stuart Jones. *A Greek-English Lexicon*. 9th ed. with revised supplement. Oxford: Clarendon, 1996.
LSTS	The Library of Second Temple Studies
MGWJ	*Monatschrift für Geschichte und Wissenschaft des Judentums*
ML.B	Museum Lessianum. Section biblique
NCB	New Century Bible
NovT	*Novum Testamentum*
NRSV	New Revised Standard Version
NTOA	Novum Testamentum et Orbis Antiquus
ORA	Orientalische Religionen in der Antike
OTE	*Old Testament Essays*
OTL	Old Testament Library
PRSt	*Perspectives in Religious Studies*
RB	*Revue biblique*
R&T	*Religion & Theology*
SANT	Studien zum Alten und Neuen Testaments
SC	Sources chrétiennes
SemeiaSt	Semeia Studies

StPatr	Studia Patristica
SRivBib	Supplementi alla Revista biblica
STDJ	*Studies on the texts of the desert of Judah*
StRR	Studies in Rhetoric and Religion
SVTP	Studia in Veteris Testamenti Pseudepigraphica
SymS	Symposium Series
TBT	*The Bible Today*
TDNT	Kittel, Gerhard, and Gerhard Friedrich, eds. *Theological Dictionary of the New Testament*. Translated by Geoffrey W. Bromiley. 10 vols. Grand Rapids: Eerdmans, 1964–1976.
TGST	Tesi Gregoriana, Serie Teologia
WBC	Word Biblical Commentary
WSt	*Wiener Studien*
WUNT	Wissenschaftliche Untersuchungen zum Neuen Testament
ZAW	*Zeitschrift für die alttestamentliche Wissenschaft*

Introduction

Richard J. Bautch and Jean-François Racine

Roughly a century ago, Herman Gunkel (1923, xlii) established prophetic visions as a category distinct from prophetic oracles. In the generations since, biblical scholars have been developing typologies of visions and dreams, often inspired by the form-critical approach associated with Gunkel (Sister 1934; Oppenheim 1956; Long 1984; Flannery-Dailey 2004). This methodology has not been static, however, as novel questions have been continually raised to make the enterprise of analyzing dreams and visions ever more sophisticated. Some studies have articulated a connection between visions and dreams or have sought to differentiate the two phenomena (beginning with Sister). Others have focused on experience or the reality of the visionary event in the life of the seer (most recently, Flannery-Dailey). The present collection stands upon the form-critical work that preceded it, although these essays manifest a wide range of approaches to the text beyond form criticism. Furthermore, the present collection distinguishes itself by focusing on how the reading community interprets the dream or vision in question. This important hermeneutic has not been explored previously in any systematic way. The reading community is central because its construal of the dream or vision plays an integral role in establishing the authority of the text. The question is not simply what an image means, but what is at stake—and for whom—in its interpretation. There are complex hermeneutics in play when different parties "read" dreams and visions in the religious literature of the ancient Near East, including but not limited to the Hebrew Bible and the New Testament.

During the completion of this project, John C. Endres, S.J. (1946–2022), passed away. For several contributors to this volume, John was a teacher, colleague, and friend. May his memory be a blessing to all who knew him.

The following chapters adopt a reader-centered viewpoint in order to focus on the narratees' relationship to the revelatory experience. In these cases, the text incorporates a dream or vision that, by design, performs an authorizing function with an intended reflex: the reading community's interpretation. The revelatory experience is not complete until the reading community interprets what it has witnessed. This hermeneutical thread connects most of the chapters in this book. It is manifest in the studies of Abraham (in the Genesis Apocryphon), Jeremiah (in 2 Maccabees), Enoch, Pilate's wife (in Matthew), the sequence of visions in Luke-Acts, and the Shepherd of Hermas. It is intriguing that, in many of these cases, a close reading of the text suggests that the response of the reading community destabilizes or decenters the intended effect of the revelatory experience and challenges the text's authority. The interpretation of the dream or vision can recalibrate power structures in and surrounding the text. Or, the interpretation might simply ask new questions, a subversive act unto itself. The opportunities that emerge are not limited to antiquity and can apply to today's world, especially where people are suffering injustice or exploitation due to power imbalances. Poignantly, several of the essays here explore trauma as experienced by persons living amid hegemonic structures.

The revelatory experience and the potentially revolutionary interpretation of the same is not a formula that the studies in this volume follow uniformly. Each chapter's organic quality allows it to interrogate the dream or vision freely. The issues of textual authority and discursive politics are rendered differently in each case, depending on the literary and historical contexts and other factors as well. In short, this collection has a *Mitte* or center toward which the essays gravitate in varying degrees and each in its own manner. The *Mitte* can be described as the point where the text's authorizing function meets the community's interpretation of the dream or vision. This hermeneutical intersection represents a new datum in the analysis of dreams and visions.

The studies here are indebted to reader-response criticism in that they work from the perspective of the actual audience without trying to reconstitute the perspective of an ancient audience. Beyond that common denominator, the various chapters adopt one of three methodological stances that in turn serve to delineate the tripartite structure of the book. The book's first section comprises two essays that explore 2 Kings and Revelation and establish in a general way the hermeneutics of readership that inform the subsequent chapters. These essays, respectively authored by Gina Hens-Piazza and Andrea Spatafora, provide a methodological baseline while exploring some of the most iconic visions in the Hebrew Bible and New Testament. Hens-Piazza's essay revisits what has come to be known as Elijah's theophanic vision on Mount Horeb. Rather than be preoccupied by what the experience of God meant, Hens-Piazza instead questions whether the account actually reports a vision of the divine before this esteemed prophet and whether the tradition of Elijah's greatness, stemming from his presumed vision of God at Horeb, has obscured the reader's vision of the greatness of the prophet. Spatafora takes up the visions depicting a woman and a dragon at the center of Rev 12. He shows how the visions serve as rhetorical devices to motivate John's readers to respond to God's revelation, and in this sense the role of the reading community comes to the fore. Readers interpreting these two Johannine visions are led to see that they, too, are involved in the cosmic struggle between God and Satan. John's visual rhetoric invites readers to choose to fight alongside God and the lamb. Together, these initial chapters show how the role of the reading community is active not passive.

In the book's second section, three essays delve into the relationship between reading and intertextuality, especially in relationship to dreams, where the content can help "regulate traffic on the fragile bridge that connects our experiences with our emotions and memories" (van der Linden 2011, 37). In the cases of Abraham and Jeremiah, different aspects of their biblical legacy writ large serve as intertexts that inform the revelatory experience at hand. Joseph McDonald writes on Abram and the symbolic dream that comes to him on the border of Egypt (1QapGen 19.14–23). In the dream, Abram appears as a cedar tree threatened by woodcutters but is saved by a timely cry from a date palm representing Sarai. Prior studies have suggested that the dream serves to explain or justify Abram's questionable behavior in the biblical accounts (Gen 12:10–20; 20:1–18) that stand behind this text. Focusing on the Genesis Apocryphon, McDonald provides overlapping readings of Abram's dream and concludes that all of the readings are both mediated and destabilized by two uncertain mediums: Abram and the reader, the latter of whom McDonald refers to in the first-person ("me"). The text's narrative (and so its authority) is undermined inasmuch as the interpretations of Abram's dream are poorly predictive of much of the coming plot, and Abram's account of his own dream fails to foretell serious threats to Sarai.

Extending the section on intertextuality, Richard J. Bautch interrogates the figure of Jeremiah in 2 Maccabees, where the prophet first appears in 2 Macc 2:1–8. The other relevant passage is located near the end of 2 Maccabees, where Jeremiah comes in a dream to Judas Maccabeus, gives him a golden sword, and commands him to strike down his adversaries. When linked with 2:1–8, the image of the prophet with a sword forms a literary frame that extends the authorizing function of Jeremiah across this text; a gilt sword motivates the troops resisting the Seleucids and spurs them on. The dream's martial interpretation, however, is in tension with other traditions associated with Jeremiah, in which the prophet resists brutality and embraces his own vulnerability. Bautch concludes that the final challenge is to integrate the various intertexts; the reading community must align in some meaningful way the very different traditions of Jeremiah that are elicited by the violent image of the sword in 2 Maccabees.

Concluding this section, Roy Allan Fisher analyzes a dream report in Matthew's Gospel by way of the contemporary (2010) staging of Bach's Matthäus-Passion. As an intertext the performance augments the disturbing dream that Pilate's wife has in the Gospel of Matthew; in an interpretive move Bach recasts the action so that the female character enunciates her own dream as part of the performance. The embodied voice in turn underscores the active role of both Pilate's wife in Matthew's passion narrative and the reading community or, in this case, the hearers of Bach's score. Both parties become witnesses and agents in the retelling of Matthew's Gospel.

The essays constituting the third and final section explore how the reading community employs affect and emotion to navigate dreams and visions in the religious text. In the first essay, Genevive Dibley focuses on weeping in the Enochic Book of Dreams (1 En. 83–90). The figure of Enoch weeps uncontrollably because he has a vision in which it is said that all things come to pass and are fulfilled. Positioned as the final turn of an apocalypse, Enoch's vision along with his reaction to it, in Dibley's analysis, express how the reader has been thrown into confusion. Enoch's sorrow is not consistent with the apocalyptic genre, in which the denouement finds the just vindicated and the wicked vanquished. Typically, there is no cause for sorrow, yet Enoch/the reader weeps. Dibley identifies trauma as the underlying cause of Enoch's tears and notes that incidents of lament in the Book of Dreams are triggered by the traumatic event immediately preceding it. She argues that the God's transformation of the gentiles at the eschaton is one such event, and that the gentiles becoming righteous beings (but not part of Israel) is a dismaying prospect. The redemption of the gentiles prompts readers to question the gratuity of divine righteousness to the point of shedding tears over it.

Introduction   5

Next, Deborah Prince provides a subjective picture of the visions in Acts taken as a whole. She highlights several characteristics including the relationship between the sensory and spatial elements of the vision accounts, the use of vision pairs and a diverse assemblage of visionaries, and the placement of visions at key moments of transition and conflict within the narrative. She demonstrates how these characteristics bolster the authority and reliability of the vision accounts while fostering the process of community discernment of their meaning and purpose, all of which is crucial for guiding Jesus's followers (those within the narrative as well as Luke's own community) at pivotal moments of change and conflict. The unique contribution of this essay is that Prince aligns divine authorization in the visions with the corroboration and discernment of the broader community. Some scholars have recognized a relationship between divine authority and human decision-making but with the emphasis on the individual. Prince shows that the visions in Acts, in their entirety, function to reveal how the community discerns and sanctions God's will collectively.

Closing out the section, Jean-François Racine focuses on the emotional spectrum of the narrator in the Shepherd of Hermas, an aspect that has thus far received scant attention in scholarly literature. Racine's essay provides a thorough map of Hermas's emotions, examines their causes, and identifies how Hermas's diverse emotions throughout the story lead ultimately to cheerfulness. The occasion for cheerfulness and the other salient emotions are the dreams and visions that Hermas experiences through the course of the narrative. In one scene, the character Rhoda appears to the narrator in a dream and states that God is angry at him because of his evil desire for her. Hermas later has a consoling vision in which a different female figure, who represents the church, shows him the construction of the tower, which is a symbol of the church. Racine concludes that the dreams and visions impact not only Hermas at the emotional level but also the reading community at the level of ethics. Readers observe characters who display certain dispositions, behaviors, and patterns of action that convey or collide with the ideal of the good life. Furthermore, readers glimpse the good life in its full extent across the narrative to understand that initial confusion or anguish, such as that which Hermas experiences, can lead finally to cheerfulness through a lifelong habit of moral choices.

To recapitulate the book's organization, the first two essays introduce the hermeneutics of communal interpretation and textual authority with reference to Elijah in 2 Kings and select visions in the book of Revelation.

These initial methodological chapters are followed by the core of the book, which comprises two sections that treat intertextuality and affect/emotion. The book concludes with an afterword by Rodney A. Werline, who offers analysis and perspective on the collection as a whole with a critical assessment of the role that reader-response criticism plays in these essays. Werline locates the present book along a trajectory of landmark studies focusing less on *what* the text means and more on the interaction between the text and the reader, or *how* meaning happens.

In terms of nomenclature, the authors and editors of this volume do not differentiate between dreams and visions. There are several reasons for this. When comparing texts, one finds that seers can have visions while being awake (Exod 24:9–11; Acts 10:9–16) or asleep (Gen 37:5–11; Acts 16:9; Herm. Vis. 1; see Flannery-Dailey 2004, 1–2). Different writers therefore label the same type of experience as either a dream or a vision, and it becomes a matter of semantics, as Hanson (1980, 1408–9) has noted. Furthermore, from a physiopsychological perspective, human sleep occurs in several phases, and dreams often take place in the first phases of sleep, sometimes in a state of semiconsciousness. Thus, certain dreams are more accurately called visions because the seer is in a waking state. These considerations lead to the following definition of dream/vision operative in this volume: "the account of a revelatory experience, mystical or not, fictional or not, involving a visual, or aural, or both aural and visual dimension."

The dream/vision can include a clear message (e.g., the dream of Joseph in Matt 1:20–21) or be symbolic and require further interpretation (e.g., Peter's vision in Acts 10:9–17). Some dreams/visions, like the one Moses experiences in the wilderness at Horeb, qualify as theophanic visions, while the origin of others remains unclear (e.g., the dream of Pilate's wife in Matt 27:19 and the various dreams/visions in the Shepherd of Hermas). Terminology remains the most useful tool to locate dreams/visions, even though some terms can describe more pedestrian realities. In Hebrew, common terms derive from the verbal roots חלם, ראה, and חזה. The latter two verbs essentially mean "to see." In Greek, the most common terms are ὄναρ, ἐνύπνιον, ὅραμα, and ὄψις.

The decision here not to differentiate between dreams and visions also stems from the fact that attempts to identify formal patterns of dreams/visions that apply to all the materials studied in a viable sample size remain inconclusive. For example, the work of Leo Oppenheim (1956, 187) on dreams in texts of the ancient Near East attempted to establish the form of dreams. Oppenheim contended that in the texts he studied, accounts of dreams include formal elements such as a starting frame identifying the dreamer (always a male individual), his location, the circumstances of the dream and the contents of the dream as well as an ending frame that, in some cases, acknowledges the fulfillment of what the dream had predicted. Oppenheim classified dreams in two categories based on their formal composition: message dreams (197–206) and symbolic dreams (206–17). Oppenheim noted that some formal elements could be absent or furtive, an aspect that becomes evident when trying to apply his form-critical pattern to the actual dreams/visions examined in this volume. In this regard, the exercise is like that of Gunkel (1933, 397–415), who was forced to include in his form-critical inventory of the psalms the category of "mixed genre" in order to accommodate all the psalms that did not fit into his schema. A related issue is that Oppenheim's two categories of dreams are based on contents rather than formal characteristics.

Furthermore, Oppenheim's form-critical work, even when refined in later studies (e.g., Flannery-Dailey 2004, 20–24) does not easily move from structure to significance. Since the essays here are interested in the significance of dreams/vision (i.e., how reading communities assign meaning to them), the contributors to this volume did not try to align the dreams/visions under analysis into formal categories or apply a single methodology to all dreams or visions. In many cases, the dreams/visions simply beg for an approach attentive to their particular features.

The need for a diversity of approaches became obvious several years ago when we taught a semester-long course on dreams and visions in the New Testament. Students enrolled in the course quickly realized that the dreams/visions under scrutiny each week were different in length, settings, role, and origin among other features. As a result, the approaches they considered when dealing with a set of dreams/visions one week would not apply to the new set of dreams/visions on the syllabus the following week. The contributors to this volume came to the same realization when discussing each other's essays in annual symposia held over the course of several years. They noted that each account of dreams/visions raised specific questions and called for a different approach not wholly unlike those used in other contexts but with methodological contours unique to the text in question.

In fact, if there is anything common to dreams/visions featured in this volume, it is their eruptive character, that is, they come unannounced, sometimes in a character's familiar environment (e.g., Peter's vision in

Acts 10:9–16). They add the "extra" to the "ordinary" of the characters portrayed in the narratives. They compel the reading community to engage these uncanny aspects of narratives because if they are unfamiliar they are also familiar: not everyone has visions but everyone dreams. Still, not everyone acts upon one's dreams. Characters in these stories do act, often decisively, and the audience comes to know the outcome of their response to dreams/visions that visit them.

In his afterword, Werline notes that the dreams and visions examined in this volume have given rise to a long tradition of interpretation that runs through many centuries. These dreams and visions have served as a Rorschach test for generations of interpreters. While one may profitably consider the sweep of interpretive traditions, the *Nachleben* as it were, the essays of this volume engage questions from reading communities in a way that considers historical context but is not diachronic per se. Often, these questions and approaches emanate from an early reading community, and they highlight in these dreams and visions understandings that underlie certain ancient traditions of interpretation. A contextualized comprehension of both imagery and text is crucial for determining the authorizing function of a dream or vision. An example, noted by Werline, is the image of a cheerful Hermas; emotions are culturally constructed, and one cannot assume that emotions found within an ancient text align exactly with the meaning attached to such emotional displays today.

Werline's afterword makes additional points that, collectively, suggest the way forward for scholars who would continue the study of dreams and visions. The implications and fresh questions that arise from this volume form a horizon of future inquiry. Some of these questions are methodological, beginning with the elaboration of our approach to studying dreams and visions with the focus on the reading community for which it was written. How may we more fully delineate the process by which a reading community interprets a dream or vision in order to assess its authorizing function? What terms serve both descriptively and prescriptively to describe the juncture where the text's authorizing function meets the community's interpretation of the dream or vision? Perhaps a place to start is Werline's notion of wrestling the text, that is, his observation that readers bound together in community are wrestling a meaning out of the text. Wrestling implies an immersive engagement with a dream or vision as opposed to a passing glance. Wrestling includes the possibility of a tag-team approach or communal interpretation that draws on the skills of individuals deployed in coordination. Wrestling also implies a decisive end point where meaning is pinned down or brought under some control by the community. Wrestling, like all metaphors, has its limitations, and discussions of how a reading community draws meaning from dreams and visions will involve new reference points as it goes forward heuristically. Werline elsewhere introduces the phenomenon of a reading community's insiders and outsiders. The fact that communities are rarely monoliths (although they may project themselves in this way) complicates this book's thesis; could there be *other* readers marginalized within the community and inclined to reject (rather than embrace) the common understanding of the dream or vision? Future studies must contend with the diversity manifest within communities both ancient and contemporary along with the data of identity-formation occurring in more complex ways than has been previously considered. Interdisciplinary analysis of the text and its context will shine further light on how the dreams and visions therein were received by readers. It is fitting that this introduction concludes with the horizon of inquiry in view, including as-yet unanswered questions about methodology and the challenge of defining the reading community. This book is a point of departure toward an understanding of how the text's authorizing function meets the community's interpretation of a dream or vision.

Bibliography

Flannery-Dailey, Frances. 2004. *Dreamers, Scribes, and Priests: Jewish Dreams in the Hellenistic and Roman Eras*. JSJSup 90. Leiden: Brill.

Gunkel, Hermann. 1923. "Einleitung." Pages ix–lxx in *Die großen Propheten*. 2nd ed. Edited by Hans Schmidt. Göttingen: Vandenhoeck & Ruprecht.

———. 1933. *Einleitung in die Psalmen: Die Gattungen der religiösen Lyrik Israels*. Edited by Joachim Begrich. Göttingen: Vandenhoeck & Ruprecht.

Hanson, J. S. 1980. "Dreams and Visions in the Graeco-Roman World and Early Christianity." *ANRW* 23.2:1395–427.

Linden, Sander van der. 2011. "The Science behind Dreaming." *Scientific American* 22:24–37.

Long, Burke O. 1984. *1 Kings: With an Introduction to Historical Literature*. FOTL 9. Grand Rapids: Eerdmans.

Oppenheim, A. Leo. 1956. *The Interpretation of Dreams in the Ancient Near East: With a Translation of an Assyrian Dream-Book*. Transac-

tions of the American Philosophical Society 46.3. Philadelphia: American Philosophical Society.
Sister, Moses. 1934. "Die Typen der prophetische Visionen in der Bibel." *MGWJ* 78:399–430.

Hermeneutics of Readership

Dreams Can Delude, Visions Can Deceive: Elijah's Sojourn in the Wilderness of Horeb (1 Kings 19:1-21)

Gina Hens-Piazza

The Old Testament prophet Elijah holds a prominence place within several religious traditions. Much of 1 and 2 Kings (1 Kgs 17-21; 2 Kgs 1-2) centers on his prophetic career, and his greatness is also attested by other Old Testament allusions to him (2 Chr 21:12; Mal 3:23). Elijah plays an important role in the Passover Seder, during which a cup of wine is set on the table, the door of the home is opened, and everyone stands to welcome the prophet. Similarly, at every bris a chair is set aside for the prophet to attend. Havdalah, the ceremony that concludes the Sabbath, also features the prophet. Part of its closing hymn appeals to God that Elijah might come during the following week along with the messiah, son of David.

Elijah's importance continues in Christianity. Some disciples and followers of Jesus thought he was Elijah (Matt 16:14; Mark 6:15; 8:28; Luke 9:8, 19). John the Baptist was also asked whether he was Elijah (John 1:21, 25) and is also said to have gone before the Lord "in the spirit and power of Elijah" (Luke 1:17). Elijah and Moses, respectively representing the prophets and the law, were key witnesses in the transfiguration story (Matt 17:3-4; Mark 9:4-5; Luke 9:30-33). While in Nazareth, Jesus alludes to the encounter of Elijah and the widow to illustrate the rejection of a prophet in his own country (Luke 4:25-26). So, too, Paul references Elijah's prophetic experience on Mount Horeb (Rom 11:3).

Elijah also receives recognition in Islam. The Qur'an and certain Islamic traditions credit Elijah as a great and righteous man of God. Within this tradition, Elijah is painted as a courageous and powerful preacher against the worship of Baal (Q As-Saaffaat 37:123-126). Muslim scholars believe that Elijah came from the family of the prophet Aaron. It is thought that

Elijah was granted prophetic office after the deaths of the great prophet Aaron and King Solomon. Muslims believe Elijah was a prophet commissioned by Allah to preach to the people of Israel. In addition to his religious significance within Judaism, Christianity, and Islam, the prophet also holds cultural importance as well. In Macedonia, Serbia, Bulgaria, and Romania he figures prominently in various folkloric traditions. Known as "Elijah the Thunderer," he is held responsible for summer storms, hail, rain, thunder, and dew by various local groups within these societies.

Given the prophet's importance within different religious traditions and cultures, it is not surprising that some religious orders consider him their founder and mentor. The Carmelites, for example, founded in the thirteenth century, are a contemplative Roman Catholic fraternity who live out their charism in the midst of the people. They consider themselves the successors of the hermits who lived in the spirit of Elijah on Mount Carmel, and the words spoken by the prophet at Mount Horeb form the motto of the Order: "I am very zealous for the LORD, God of Hosts" (1 Kgs 19:10). Hence, the Carmelites venerate Elijah as their model, both as a servant of the word of the Lord and as one who had a profound divine experience at Horeb.

Given the frequency of his appearance across various traditions, Elijah deserves such notoriety. But sometimes the elevation of a historical figure to the status of hero or mentor can blind us to the fault lines that mark their authenticity as human beings. The iteration of a seemingly impeccable character can put an unhelpful distance between these individuals and the lives of ordinary people. Their elevated traditional status can obscure their struggles, failures, and personal self-doubts and even encourage reading past hints of basic human weaknesses. Often romanticized as flawless, their influence becomes remote. As a result, the religious or even spiritual inspiration they might provide for believers becomes compromised. Hence, the idealization of such religious figures risks the potential loss of any real or sound impact that their person or story might exert.

Elijah in the Wilderness of Horeb

Much of the importance afforded Elijah down through the centuries stems from what is read and interpreted as the climax of his career: his encounter with God on Mount Horeb (1 Kgs 19:1–18). This episode, on the heels of Elijah's victory over the Baal prophets on Mount Carmel (18:20–40), is considered the pinnacle of Elijah's prophetic cycle. Without qualification, the representation of Elijah at Horeb, both within Bible translations and across scholarship, takes for granted his visionary encounter with God on a mountaintop. The NRSV subtitles this segment as "Elijah Meets God at Horeb." The Jerusalem Bible's entry for these verses reads "Elijah at Horeb—An Encounter with God." And the NIV registers the account under the heading "The Lord Appears to Elijah." Scholarship also assumes that Elijah, like Moses, was granted a vision of God. Much conjecture exists as to how to translate what was reported as the theophanic encounter. Though the Hebrew here (1 Kgs 19:12: קול דממה דקה) has been variously translated as "still small voice," "sound of silence," and "tiny whispering sound," most interpretations assume the prophet encounters God at this narrative moment. Hence, scholarly analyses exercise the bulk of their efforts not by questioning whether there was a visionary encounter, but by interpreting the meaning of the encounter. Gwilym Jones (1984, 333) assumes the prophet's experience of a vision of God and suggests this encounter conveys to the prophet that God speaks not only in outward signs, as in cult, but also through a quiet presence that he translates as "a still small voice." John Gray (1970, 410) also takes for granted the theophany and focuses solely upon interpreting its meaning. According to his translation of 19:12, "the still small voice" reveals God in "an intelligible communication rather than in the spectacular phenomena." For Gray, this marks "an advance in man's [sic] conception of God as personally accessible and intelligible ... within the framework of human experience" (411). More recently, Terrence Fretheim (1999, 110), who translates 1 Kgs 19:12 as "sound of silence," interprets it as "a pregnant moment of calm" before God discloses the divine self directly to the prophet. In their literary study of the Mount Carmel tradition, Alan Hauser and Russell Gregory (1990, 70) note that Yahweh's response in a "still small voice" coincides with how God takes care of the prophet earlier in 1 Kgs 19:4–5 when he wishes to die: instead of doing something spectacular, the Lord provides nourishment for the prophet. In both instances, the Lord supplies what the prophet needs. Marvin Sweeney (2007, 232) also assumes the experience of theophany and suggests its unique description intends to "demonstrate the impossibility of describing Yahweh's presence." All of these interpretations take for granted that what is reported in the Horeb episode as the קול דממה דקה signals a theophanic encounter. Hence, their analyses assume a visionary experience and only debate what this visionary encounter meant.

This study revisits what has come to be known as Elijah's theophanic vision on Mount Horeb. However, it departs from the above preoccupation with what the experience of God meant. Instead, it questions whether the account actually does report a vision of the divine before this esteemed prophet. Moreover, it attends to how the experience of a dream under the broom tree (1 Kgs 19:4–8) that precedes the alleged vision may have deluded both the prophet and subsequent readers of this account. Finally, it considers whether the tradition of Elijah's greatness, stemming from his presumed vision of God at Horeb, has actually obscured our vision of what constitutes his greatness.

The Nature of Visions

Visions are ecstatic experiences and frequently serve as means of revelation. Surprisingly, they occupy a small place in the Old Testament. In the traditions of the ancestors, one type of vision is commonplace in these early stories: "Yahweh appeared and said" (Gen 12:7; 17:1; 26:2, 24; 35:9). In these instances, the emphasis falls upon the ensuing speech rather than upon the vision. In stories about Moses the vision aspect represents a more persistent component. The vision of the burning bush is a revelation about the divine reality. The bush burning but never being consumed discloses that God has the power to destroy but does not. In Exod 33:18–22, Moses is permitted to see Yahweh's back but not Yahweh's face after requesting to encounter God. Here the vision is thought to grant this great ancestor a glimpse of God while protecting him from the dangerous consequence of a direct view of divine presence.

In an effort to categorize such accounts, form critics have offered a definition of these different visions. Called vision reports (*Visionsbericht*), they are broadly characterized as narratives that "recount what a prophet or seer hears and/or sees in an inner perception" (Long 1984, 263). These vision reports are often cast in autobiographical style and can have sounds, voices, movements, and dialogue that draw the individual into the drama of the encounter. Some visions, like the one Moses experiences in the wilderness at Horeb, qualify as theophanic visions. Unlike Amos's vision of the fruit basket (Amos 8) or Ezekiel's vision of Jerusalem (Ezek 8–9), which are essentially visions of human realities or events, theophanic visions feature an experience of God. A combination of particular elements characterizes such an encounter. First, there may be a description or alert of Yahweh's approach. Second, natural upheavals such as wind, fire, or storm often accompany the announced or revealed coming of the divine. Though not a formal feature of the theophany report, a notable change or even transformation in the individual experiencing the visionary encounter is often included. For example, Job, who steadfastly maintains his innocence and his knowledge of how God acts, retreats from this posture after his theophanic encounter with the divine (Job 42:1–6). As an indication that Job has been changed due to this theophanic experience, he is not only restored everything he lost but is restored everything twofold (42:10–17). Hence, at the end of the story, he is in a changed state different from how he was in its beginning. Isaiah ben Amos, the prophet of Jerusalem, also has a theophanic vision in the temple. In the process, we hear him identify initially as one in a wretched state living among a people who are defiled: "Woe is me! I am lost, for I am a man of unclean lips, and I live among a people of unclean lips" (Isa 6:5). However, an about-face occurs in this encounter after Isaiah proclaims that he has looked upon Yahweh, the Lord of Hosts. Suddenly and enthusiastically he moves beyond his proclaimed unworthiness and confidently agrees to be God's messenger: "Here I am. Send me" (Isa 6:8). Thus, a discernible transformation or alteration in disposition is noted here as well. The prophet moves from an admission of unworthiness to a self-proclaimed worthiness to serve. Scarce in occurrence, as well as manifesting a great deal of variability, reports of theophanic visions warrant careful scrutiny before coming to interpretive conclusions about what is or is not being reported.

Three Journeys and Then a Fourth

In the first three chapters of the Elijah tradition (1 Kgs 17–19), the prophet embarks upon several journeys. The "coming of the word of the LORD" initiates the first three journeys. However, the fourth jaunt stems from Elijah's own scheme. First, in 1 Kgs 17:2–3 the word of the Lord summons him to go and hide himself in the Wadi Cherith. Thus, "He went and acted according to the word of the LORD" (17:5). Hidden away in this safe haven, he receives protection from Ahab's campaign to murder Yahweh's prophets. But he also enjoys a bountiful feast of bread and meat supplied by the appointed ravens and fresh water from the wadi in a time of drought. Next the word of the Lord instructs him, "Get up and go to Zarephath" (17:8–9). There he will be the divine agent that transforms the circumstances of a widow and her son from utter impoverishment and hopelessness to faith and abundance. The word of the Lord summons Elijah a third time, directing him to yet another destination: "Go present yourself before Ahab" (18:1). A spectacular victory for the prophet against 450 of Baal on Mount

Carmel ensues, followed by the rise of a tiny cloud over the Mediterranean that ends the drought.

Upon hearing Ahab's report that Elijah has not only been victorious over the prophets of Baal but has also slaughtered all of them in the Wadi Kishon, Jezebel issues a death warrant against Elijah (19:2). The queen's oath to make "his life like the life of one of them" sets the prophet in motion: "He was afraid; he got up and fled for his life, and he came to Beer-sheba, which belongs to Judah; he left his servant there" (19:3). Thus, Elijah's fourth journey begins in the wilderness of Sinai. However, this time the word of the Lord is conspicuously absent from the travel plan. Instead fear, rather than the word of the Lord, instigates this journey and navigates Elijah's actions (19:3).

The prophet's seclusion intensifies as he moves beyond Beer-sheba. Having departed from his servant, Elijah journeys alone into exile: "But he himself went a day's journey into the wilderness and came and sat down under a solitary broom tree" (19:4). A day's journey geographically separates Elijah from all other people. The vagueness of "a solitary broom tree" emphasizes the lack of a concrete destination. The first three journeys initiated by the word of the Lord yielded abundant sustenance in the wilderness (17:6–7), new life for a widow and her son (17:15–16), and then a victory on a mountaintop (18:38). By contrast, Elijah reports only despondency and desperation on this fourth self-initiated hike. Further, his seclusion and desperation prompts a dire plea: "It is enough, now, O Lord, take my life, for I am no better than my ancestors" (19:4). In this self-inflicted isolation of the wilderness, Elijah now requests to die. The repetition of the word "life" (19: 2, 3, 4) is revealing. The prophet who fled for his "life" (19:3) now wishes to die yet does not want to be killed.

Dreams in the Wilderness

After wishing for death, the prophet lies down and seeks consolation in the unconsciousness of sleep. Entering a dream state that in the Hebrew conception hangs midway between life and death, the prophet moves into further isolation. Characteristic of a dream report, the narrative departs from its previous geographical moorings and becomes highly symbolic. Dream reports (*Traumbericht*) recount principal elements of a dream experience in either first- or third-person style (Long 1984, 248). Although the verb "to dream" is missing, other elements suggesting sleep are present and the use of the particle הנה often serves as a characteristic demarcation that a dream is being described. As the narrative reports: "Then he lay down and fell asleep under a broom tree. Suddenly [והנה] an angel touched him" (19:5). While the NRSV here renders the particle as "suddenly," the Hebrew is better translated as "and behold" and suggests that a dream is now about to unfold.

Two encounters structure the dream report (19:5–6 and vv. 7–8). The first part of the dream opens with, "and behold a messenger [מלאך] touched him" (19:5). Translated as "angel" in the NRSV, the same Hebrew word (מלאך) is used for the messenger who earlier delivered Jezebel's death threat to the prophet (19:2). Psychologists reveal that "Dreams help us process emotions ... especially negative ones that increase worry and anxiety" (van der Linden 2011, 36). Similarly, Elijah's dream-time slumber allows him to confront the daytime anxieties that have driven him to the wilderness. In the dream, the messenger's invitation for him to get up and eat suggests elements that make up the concerns of the individual alone in the wilderness. In 1 Kgs 19:6 the word "And behold" (והנה) once again introduces the remaining part of the dream. At Elijah's head are a cake baked on hot stones and a jug of water—a rather sumptuous fare for the wilderness but certainly possible for a dream by one tired and hungry from such a journey. But the despondent prophet will not be easily revived by food and drink. Thus, he eats, drinks, and lies down again, suggesting that the dream continues. Characteristically, the iterative quality of dreams manifests with the reappearance of the messenger. This time the messenger is identified as "the messenger of the LORD" (19:7). Again, the messenger coaxes the prophet to get up and eat, but this time with a motive. "Get up and eat and drink for the journey will be too much for you" (19:7). Elijah's slumber ends with the mysterious intrigue or questions that dreams often evoke. In this case, when he awakes the question lingers for both the prophet and for the reader: what journey?

Dreams help "regulate traffic on the fragile bridge that connects our experiences with our emotions and memories" (van der Linden 2011, 37). Hence, for Elijah images of the past intermingle with a replay of snippets from his experience in the present. In his dream, the feeding before his journey reaches back to previous events. A miraculous feeding prefaced Elijah's journey to Sidon. There, a widow miraculously fed the prophet before his encounter with Ahab at Samaria (17:7–16). In addition, parallels with an even earlier tradition begin to resonate here. Events from the Moses tradition coincide with the contours of the prophet's dream and his current circumstances. After Moses killed an enemy in Egypt, he fled into the wilderness to escape those who sought his life (Exod 2:11–15). On another occasion, Elijah's great ancestor came to a bush and encountered a divine messenger (Exod 3:1–6). In yet another story, Moses wished for his own death in the wilderness when he was overcome with the burden of his commission (Num 11:15); again, God fed Moses and the people in that desert setting (Num 11:31–32). As images from Elijah's dream, memory, and experience continue to resist the anchor of real time, these Moses-Elijah parallels become more vivid and more explicit. When the prophet finally awakens, as if inspired by his dream, he seemed to have overcome his despondency and sets out on a new plan, a plan suggested by his dream—another journey! "He ate and drank; then he went in the strength of that food forty days and forty nights to Horeb, the mountain of God" (19:8).

Upon arriving at the mountain, Elijah enters "the cave" (המערה), where he spends the night (19:9). The inclusion of the definite article suggests the cave is specific. It sustains the analogy with the rock-like enclosure at Horeb associated with Elijah's great ancestor Moses. Moses was instructed to stand in "the cave" to shield himself from the glory of God (Exod 33:22–23). Such parallels cultivate expectations of an upcoming Moses-like theophanic vision for Elijah. Yet, a fundamental difference separates Elijah from his ancestor. As prophetic intercessor, Moses journeyed to the cave in the wilderness to plead on behalf of the people. By contrast, Elijah flees to the wilderness on his own behalf. Recall, "He was afraid; he got up and fled for his life" (1 Kgs 19:3).

The formulaic introduction, "Then the word of the Lord came to him" (1 Kgs 19:9) suggests an upcoming prophetic commission for Elijah or perhaps another revelation. Instead, only an inquiry is issued. Though his retreat to the cave at Horeb after journeying forty days and forty nights is analogous to that of his ancestor Moses, Elijah's sojourn is questioned. The brief and straightforward query, "What are you doing here, Elijah?" (19:9) contrasts with the prophet's extended response:

> And he answered, "I have been zealous for the Lord, the God of Hosts; for the Israelites have forsaken your covenant, thrown down your altars, and killed your prophets with the sword. I alone am left, and they are seeking my life, to take it away." (1 Kgs 19:10)

First, Elijah proclaims his fervor and devotion for the Lord, the God of Hosts. Then he recites a litany of allegations against the opposition.

Surprisingly, he does not name Jezebel or Ahab, who have determined to kill him. Instead, he reports that the Israelites have abandoned the covenant, broken down altars, and slain the prophets. This too is curious because the preceding account on Mount Carmel ended with all Israel falling down in worship while proclaiming, "Yahweh is God, Yahweh is God" (1 Kgs 18:39). Apparently, still desperate to make his case for being where he is, he ends with the assertion that he is the only prophet left and they want to kill him.

The poetics of his answer disclose a contradiction surrounding the idealized portrait of Elijah as faithful follower of the Lord. He professes his extreme zeal for the Lord at the beginning of his reply. But the conclusion of his response betrays his ongoing concern for himself: "I alone am left and they are seeking my life, to take it away" (19:10). Elijah's flight from Jezebel was instigated by a concern for his life. His despair in the wilderness motivated a request that his life be destroyed. Now Elijah explains his retreat to Horeb as an act of self-preservation: "They are seeking my life, to take it away" (19:10). Concerns for his own life seem to have motivated this fourth journey and now figure again as an explanation for this journey to Horeb. Thus, the prophet's zeal for the Lord is enmeshed with zeal for his own life.

Anticipation builds toward a theophanic encounter as the climactic and concluding parallel between Elijah and his ancestor Moses. Characteristic of the theophanic vision report, there is an alert to Yahweh's approach. Elijah is instructed to go stand on the mountain "for the LORD is about to pass by" (19:11). Congruent with other accounts of theophanic visions, Elijah experiences a display of natural upheavals that conjure fear and awe at the Lord's approach. The ensuing parade of familiar theophanic images—a great wind, an earthquake, and fire—foster expectation of a divine appearance (Exod 19:16-18; Judg 5:4; Pss 18:8-16; 68:8-9; 77:17-19; Isa 29:6; Nah 1:3-6). And yet, the familiar, threefold sonorous cadence—"the LORD was not in the wind," "the LORD was not in the earthquake," "the LORD was not in the fire"—does not produce a vision of the divine. The stateliness of nature contrasts with the tumult it creates. Ironically, this parade of violent upheavals concludes with an ambiguous quietude.

As noted earlier, the translation of the Hebrew in 1 Kgs 19:12 (קול דממה דקה) has long been debated, although recent clarification has emerged from the Qumran manuscript. In both the Dead Sea Scrolls and postbiblical Hebrew and Aramaic texts, the word דממה can only be derived from the Hebrew root דמם "to be silent," rendering the expression קול דממה דקה

"the sound of sheer silence" (Reymond 2009). However, Bible versions that predate this research still vary in their translation of this expression. The NRSV correctly regards it as "a sound of sheer silence" (1 Kgs 19:12), implying that this sound is either imperceptible or undetectable. This combination of contradictory words, *sound* and *silence*, fashions a chilling anticlimax in the place of the anticipated theophanic vision. According to the report, nothing is seen and nothing is heard.

The text goes on to read: "When Elijah heard it, he covered his face in his mantle and went out and stood at the entrance of the cave" (19:13). So, what did Elijah hear? Before the threefold tumult of nature, Elijah was told by the word of the Lord to go stand at the entrance of the cave. Congruent with his fear and concern for his life, he does not move until after the קול דממה דקה "sound of sheer silence." Still inside the cave, what he hears is the cessation of the tumult—the sound of sheer silence. Nature's commotion—in the form of wind, the earthquake and fire—had ended. Only when the prophet hears the "sound of sheer silence," assuring him that the threatening uproar is over, does he move to the entrance of the cave. Now he prepares for a vision like the one experienced by his ancestor Moses.

Elijah's anticipatory response to that which he expects to experience mirrors that of other great religious figures about to experience a vision with a revelation: "He wrapped his face in his mantle" (1 Kgs 19:13). Muhammad envelops himself in his cloak when he is about to receive his first visions in a cave on Mount Hira. Similarly, Moses covers himself when the Lord agrees to show to him the divine glory (Exod 33:20). But once again, a subtle difference disrupts the parallel between Moses and Elijah. In the Exodus account, the Lord covered Moses so he would not die, for as the Lord warned "no one can see me and live" (Exod 33:20). By contrast, Elijah covers himself. This gesture continues Elijah's ongoing concern for his own life as well as demonstrates his expectation of a revelatory vision. But what Elijah prepares for is not what he encounters. Instead, though Elijah does finally hear something, it is only a familiar voice repeating a familiar question. "What are you doing here, Elijah?" (1 Kgs 19:13). Once again, Elijah's location in the wilderness is questioned. In verse 9, the voice is identified as the word of the Lord. Thus, it is the same voice that has been continually beckoning Elijah. The word of the Lord made itself known to the prophet at Wadi Cherith (17:3), at Sidon (17:8), and on Mount Carmel (18:20). Once again, the same persistent word of the Lord that summoned Elijah to make three previous journeys asks the conflict-riddled prophet what he is doing in the wilderness. Despite the prophet's determination to abandon his responsibilities, the Lord still tends to the fleeing prophet and refuses to abandon him.

The points of contact with the Moses-like divine encounter begin to collapse here. No grand theophanic vision erupts on Horeb for Elijah. Even the symbols associated with Moses as covenant mediator are negated. The wind, earthquake, and fire are all devoid of divine presence. Moreover, the elusive "sound of sheer silence" only signals that the disruptive natural events have ceased, enabling the hesitant prophet to finally approach the daylight at the entrance to the cave. When questioned this time about the reason for his sojourn, the prophet's monotonous repetition of his earlier response also corroborates the lack of any vision or encounter:

> And he answered, "I have been zealous for the LORD, the God of Hosts; for the Israelites have forsaken your covenant, thrown down your altars, and killed your prophets with the sword. I alone am left, and they are seeking my life, to take it away." (1 Kgs 19:14)

While a transformation of some kind is characteristically associated with a theophany, nothing has changed for Elijah, nor has Elijah changed. The best he can do is repeat himself. Elijah's despondency after hiding out in the desert and feeling riddled with conflict persists. Moreover, the prophet is stuck in his self-righteousness. The verbatim iteration of his previous reply serves as evidence.

In what follows, a divine commission arranges for the succession of both kings and prophets (19:15–16). The characters at the opening of the story are about to be replaced. Aram, headed by Hazael, will replace Phoenicia (hence Jezebel) as the northern threat to Israel. Jehu's dynasty will overthrow Ahab's house. Finally, Elisha will replace Elijah as prophet. The replacement of Elijah by Elisha artistically climaxes the threefold mandate. Elijah will be relieved of his prophetic post. And amid this turmoil, his sojourn in the wilderness ends with a sharp note of correction. Though Elijah claimed to be "the only one left," the word of the Lord concludes by challenging the prophet's false claim. There are others residing in Israel who have remained faithful to the Lord. In fact, the Lord has preserved seven thousand faithful who have never worshiped Baal (19:18).

Conclusion

The tradition of Elijah as religious champion and spiritual hero receives qualification at Horeb. In the wilderness, Elijah appears in conflict with himself and with his God. He flees for his life, but requests that his life be taken in the wilderness. He seeks refuge from his despair in deep slumber under a broom tree. However, though his sleep revives him, his dreams delude him. He gets up and sets out on another journey of his own design. He prepares, perhaps presumptuously, to encounter God as Moses did in the same place where this great ancestor was granted his theophanic request. Covering himself to save his life, he experiences no vision but simply a "sound of sheer silence." When he does hear something, it is the same word of the Lord inquiring again as to why he is in the wilderness. Prophecy cannot be carried out in the seclusion of the isolated environs of nature. Despite the threats to his life, he must go back. In the course of a threefold commission, Elijah is commanded to replace himself as prophet. As a final chastisement, the word of the Lord makes clear that Elijah is not the only faithful follower.

Elijah's notoriety across several religious traditions and even in popular culture suggests his well-established status as a spiritual rock star. We gravitate to such heroes, often exaggerating their greatness and idolizing them. Sometimes we dream we could even be like them in all their courage, virtue, and greatness. But heroism does not equal perfection, nor is it one dimensional in makeup. True heroes share our disquiet and struggles. They also falter and sometimes fail. They see visions and they dream dreams. And like us, they also can succumb to delusions of grandeur resident in both experiences. Their successes may help motivate us to strive beyond boundaries of fear and self-doubt. Yet, how they respond to weaknesses and even their failures may be of far greater significance. The burden and scars that mar the prophetic hero Elijah become apparent in the wilderness. Such self-awareness left him dispirited and despondent. Yet the greatest trial he had to face was still ahead. How would he respond? Would he confront some of his fears and the sacrifices required of him? Or would he remain mired in self-deception prompted by a dream and the pretense of a vision?

In the end, Elijah responds to the divine summons with obedience. He leaves the wilderness in order to anoint his successor (1 Kgs 19:19–21). It takes immense courage to reverse direction and retrace the steps of a journey one was never summoned to make. And perhaps it is in doing this that Elijah rises highest as a model and mentor.

Bibliography

Fretheim, Terence E. 1999. *First and Second Kings*. Louisville: Westminster John Knox.
Gray, John. 1970. *I and II Kings*. 2nd ed. OTL. Philadelphia: Westminster John Knox.
Hauser, Alan J., and Russell Gregory. 1990. *From Carmel to Horeb: Elijah in Crisis*. BLS 19. Sheffield: Almond.
Jones, Gwilym H. 1984. *1 and 2 Kings*. 2 vols. NCB. Grand Rapids: Eerdmans.
Linden, Sander van der. 2011. "The Science behind Dreaming." *Scientific American* 22:24–37.
Long, Burke O. 1984. *I Kings with an Introduction to Historical Literature*. FOTL 9. Grand Rapids: Eerdmans.
Reymond, Eric D. 2009. "The Hebrew Word דממה and the Root d-m-m I ('To Be Silent')." *Bib* 90:374–88.
Sweeney, Marvin A. 2007. *I and II Kings: A Commentary*. OTL. Louisville: Westminster John Knox.

Envisioning the Visions of the Book of Revelation: A Narrative Study of Revelation 12

Andrea Spatafora, MSF

Apocalyptic writings can be considered visionary literature par excellence because they are not accounts of actual, verifiable events but are composed almost entirely of sequences of visions by a seer. The character of apocalyptic visions is unique. Quite frequently, the images are jarring inasmuch as a lamb appears standing *as if slain* (Rev 5:6) or a beast resembling a leopard but with a bear's paws and a lion's mouth arises out of the sea (Rev 13:2). These juxtapositions create surreal depictions that do not represent anything seen in reality.

This leads to the question of the nature of these visions. What is the source of these strange images? Is the seer awake, conscious, and in control during the vision? Or is he unconscious, asleep, or in a trance or ecstasy? If the former case is true, then are the visions a literary creation, part of a genre intended to transmit a divine message, that presents the seer's theological vision of God, Christ, and salvation history? Or are they simply a description of what the author sees while in a trance?

John has an otherworldly experience during which he receives a revelation from God. However, the visions as they are presented in Revelation are carefully crafted literary pieces that translate into words this ineffable experience of the divine word. The visions serve as rhetorical devices to motivate John's readers to respond to God's revelation. They are intended to persuade God's people that they are involved in the cosmic struggle between God and Satan. John's rhetoric invites his readers to choose to fight alongside God and the lamb. I propose to demonstrate this by examining the vision of Rev 12 using narrative criticism, looking in particular at characters, space, and point of view.

Delimiting the Pericope

Revelation 12:1–18 is found within the section on the three signs. The first two signs that appear in this vision follow the blowing of the seventh trumpet and its accompanying manifestations. The beginning of the vision (12:1) is marked by the presence of the verb ὤφθη, the passive form of the verb ὄψομαι (to see), and means "to appear." The next vision begins at 13:1 with the use of the verb εἶδον, "I saw," and the appearance of the beast from the sea. In 12:18 the dragon takes his stand on the seashore. Thus, 12:18 serves as the conclusion of the pericope and transitions the reader to 13:1. The one vision flows into the next.

A Narrative Study of Revelation 12

The narrative study of Rev 12 includes several elements: the identification of the rhetorical devices used by the author, the analysis of symbolic language, the examination of the setting, the exploration of characters, and a study of the text's point of view.

Revelation 12:1–18 includes several instances of significant verbal repetitions. The term σημεῖον (sign) introduces the woman and the dragon at the beginning of the pericope (12:1, 3). The term is used in the singular one other time (15:1) to indicate the first appearance of the seven angels with the cups filled with God's wrath.[1] The sign of the woman who is to give birth evokes Isa 7:14, the promise of the child Immanuel, as well as Isa 66:7–9, which announces the birth of the new people of God brought forth by the female figure of Zion. What unites, however, the three signs is imagery found in Exodus: the woman who flees in the desert and is nourished there evokes the Israelites, who are fed in the desert with the manna and quails. The reference to eagle's wings is also a reference to God's rescue of Israel from Pharaoh (cf. Exod 19:4; Deut 32:11). As suggests Pierre Prigent (2000, 287 and 291), the dragon evokes the image of Pharaoh pursuing the Israelites, and the appearance of the seven angels' cups is followed by the vision of the conquerors of the beast, who are standing by the sea of crystal singing the canticle of Moses (cf. Exod 14:30–15:22). The three signs announce the new exodus, the definitive liberation of God's people from the power of the devil in the paschal mystery.

---

1. The word σημεῖον is used four times in the plural to indicate the phenomena performed by the dragon in Rev 13:13, 14; 16:14; and 19:20.

The verb "to throw" (βάλλω), both in the active and the passive voices, is found numerous times in this passage. In the first and third scenes of the passage, the dragon is the subject of the verb: in the first scene (12:1–6) he throws one third of the stars onto the earth, and in the third scene (12:13–18) he throws a river of water from his mouth in pursuit of the woman. In the middle scene (12:7–12), however, it is the dragon who is thrown down from heaven onto the earth. This use of the verb βάλλω suggests that the power of the dragon is limited because he himself has been thrown from heaven.

Another important repetition of vocabulary includes the noun "war" and the verb "to wage war" (πόλεμος and πολεμέω). Most instances of the vocabulary of war are found in the second scene where the dragon and his minions contend with Michael and his angels (12:7 [3x]). In the third scene, however, the dragon wages war against the other children of the woman. The war in heaven has its counterpart on earth.

Finally, in the first scene the woman and the dragon are described in similar but opposing terms. The woman is depicted as having a crown (στέφανος) of twelve stars on her head (12:1) while the dragon has seven diadems (διαδήματα), one on each head (12:3). The term "crown" is used as a symbol of victory, suggesting that the woman will be victorious over the dragon.[2]

Another important rhetorical device is the framing narrative. As the term suggests, one narrative forms a frame around another narrative that interrupts the flow of the first narrative, forming a pattern of A, B, A'. This device is also called intercalation or sandwiching. James L. Resseguie (2005, 54) indicates that both the framing narrative and the embedded narrative can comment on each other either by establishing a comparison or a contrast. John begins with a depiction of the conflict between the woman and the dragon: the dragon attempts to devour her child, but when the child is taken up to heaven the dragon turns in pursuit of the woman, who flees into the desert. This narrative is interrupted with the account of the battle in heaven. This ends with the defeat of the dragon and his expulsion from heaven. Following the heavenly hymn of victory, the narration of the struggle between the woman and the dragon resumes with a description of the dragon's actions against the woman. The reader learns

---

2. With the exception of Rev 9:7, the crown is always associated with God or with his faithful and is a symbol of royalty and of victory, as suggests Prévost (2012, 64–65).

here that the events in heaven precede the events on earth because "when the dragon saw that he had been thrown on earth, he pursued the woman." In this case, the embedded narrative of the war in heaven between Michael and the dragon gives meaning to the people of God's struggle with the devil. Humans participate in the cosmic battle between good and evil, between God and the evil one.

In Revelation, the cosmos, animals, human reality, colors, and numbers are all invested with symbolic meaning. As Ugo Vanni (1988, 55–58) explains well, almost every term has hidden or sacramental meaning beyond what is apparent. John's creativity is further evident in the way he relates the panoply of symbols in sometimes complex ways in various contexts. For example, numbers have symbolic value: seven, for instance, is a symbol of fullness. John makes varied use of the number seven. Sometimes he uses it with a positive meaning, such as the lamb with seven horns and seven eyes in Rev 5:6. Contrarily, in Rev 12 John describes the dragon as having seven heads, thus representing the ultimate expression of evil.

Among various tropes, John makes frequent use of similes and metaphors. As I have previously remarked (Spatafora, 2008, 25–26), simile and metaphor are closely related: both compare two distinct realities. Similes make explicit comparison by the use of the prepositions "like" or "as," whereas metaphors make indirect comparison. I. A. Richards (1965, 99–100, 117–38) speaks of "tenor" and "vehicle" to explain the metaphor: the tenor is the reality represented and the vehicle is the reality by which it is represented. According to Resseguie (2005, 63), these terms can be applied equally to the simile and the parable.

In Rev 12, John first sees the woman, whom he describes with three metaphors: "And a great sign appeared in heaven, a woman dressed with the sun and the moon under her feet and with a crown of twelve stars on her head" (12:1). The figure appears to be human, but at the same time her clothing and her crown and the moon under her feet are not realistic descriptions of a woman. These details suggest she is more than a human being. The dragon is a mythological creature, but John has added further symbolic details: seven heads, each with a diadem and seven horns (12:3). The woman giving birth to a child (12:2) is an extended metaphor because this is no ordinary birth: the child who is about to be devoured by the dragon is taken up to the throne of God (12:4b–5).

The second scene (12:7–12) is also an extended metaphor: the struggle between good and evil, represented as a war between angels and demons, which ends with Satan and his devils being precipitated from heaven onto earth. The reference to the blood of the lamb in the hymn by the heavenly voice at the end of the cosmic battle is also metaphorical: "They conquered him because of the blood of the lamb" (12:11). The paschal lamb is the vehicle to express Christ the Savior.

John uses a number of metaphors in the last scene of Rev 12. In 12:14 the woman is given eagle's wings to fly into the wilderness to flee from the dragon (also referred to as a serpent in vv. 14 and 15). The dragon spews a river of water from his mouth to submerge the woman in its flood (12:15). The earth is personified as a mouth that can swallow the water from the dragon's mouth (12:16). The Christian struggle with evil is portrayed as a war with the dragon.

The diverse rhetorical devices John uses serve to persuade his readers that God's people are involved in a struggle with evil. This struggle is part of a wider cosmic struggle between God and Satan. John's rhetoric invites his readers to choose to fight alongside God and the lamb. Such an interpretation, on the basis of the text's rhetoric, is amplified when this narrative study of Rev 12 considers additional elements such as its setting.

The setting of a narrative is significant because it lends to the atmosphere and can reveal dimensions of the characters or aspects of the plot. Settings can accentuate the values of the characters and of the narrator. Setting in New Testament texts include spatial, geographical, topographical, architectural, temporal, social, cultural, and religious indicators as well as props, such as crowns and diadems, and even minor characters.

The most significant setting in Rev 12 is the spatial setting, the alternation between heaven and earth, between the transcendent and the human spheres. The narrative begins with the apparition of two signs in heaven: the woman and the dragon. The dragon sweeps one third of the stars down to earth. As soon as the woman gives birth to the male child, the setting changes to earth where the woman, pursued by the dragon, flees to the desert. In 12:7, the setting changes back to heaven, where John describes the battle between Michael and his forces against the devil and his forces. Finally, in 12:13, the setting changes once again to earth where the dragon pursues the woman and all her other children.

Heaven in the text is more than simply the firmament; it is symbolic of the divine world. It is significant that the central scene (12:7–12) takes place in the divine sphere. The setting determines and interprets what happens in the human world. Although placed in the center of the narrative, the events in heaven precede the struggle of the dragon and woman on earth. The fact that the dragon and his forces, after being defeated by

Michael and his angels, are dispatched to earth anticipates the outcome of the earthly struggle.

Within the earthly space, topographical setting is of great import. The desert features prominently in the narrative in 12:6, 14. The desert evokes the exodus experience, the place where Israel not only wandered and struggled to be faithful (e.g., the incident of the golden calf, the testing at Meribah and Massa) but also where they were protected and nurtured by God. John states that the woman flees to the place that God has prepared for her in the desert. She is protected by God in her struggle with the dragon.

Another significant topographical setting in the Bible is water and the sea. In 12:15 the dragon emits a river of water from his mouth in order to submerge the woman. Water is the dragon's instrument to overcome the woman and defeat her. But as Resseguie (2005, 98) remarks, not unlike the transformation of the Red Sea from a barrier and a place of death for Israel in Exodus, the river is swallowed by the earth, allowing the woman to reach the desert in safety.

Temporal settings in the Bible can be either chronologically or typologically symbolic. In Revelation numbers always have symbolic value. Seven, as noted above, is the number for fullness and completeness. Half of seven, three and a half, is related to incompleteness and short duration. In Rev 12, there are two references to time. In 12:6, the woman remains in the place prepared for her in the desert for 1,260 days. In 12:14 she flees into the desert to remain there for a time (καιρός), times and half a time.[3] The two temporal references are equivalents: 1,260 days corresponds to three and a half years or forty-two months. In fact, John alternates between these three expressions.[4] The temporal setting reveals that the time of struggle for the woman is of limited duration; she will ultimately be victorious because the power of the dragon is broken.

According to Resseguie, minor characters also constitute part of the setting. They are part of the background to the main action carried out by the protagonists. In Rev 12, Michael's angels and the dragon's angels are

---

3. The Greek word καιρός normally indicates the right time for action, the right season, the proper time, or an opportune time rather than chronological, measured time. In this context, καιρός represents the time of trial and struggle but also the time of protection.

4. John uses 1,260 days in 11:3 and 12:6; forty-two months in 11:2 and 13:5; and three and a half years in 12:14.

an example. They are mentioned as part of the cosmic battle, supporting either Michael or the dragon. In a sense they fill up the background of the canvas as Michael and the devil fight it out. Gina Hens-Piazza (2020, 7), however, would disagree with this minimalist view of minor characters. She rejects the term "minor characters" and prefers to refer to them as the "supporting cast" of a narrative, attributing to them a greater role than mere background: "Embedded in the text, these characters constitute the scaffolding of the story world. Though they provide the infrastructure upon which to build the narrative, their involvement often means effacement. Full development of the protagonist appears contingent upon the utilization and delimitation of these supporting cast figures." The angels can be interpreted as more than the background of the narrative canvas; they are essential to the story. Without them, there would be no cosmic spiritual struggle involving the forces of good and evil in which humans are called to participate.

Props constitute another rhetorical element. Resseguie (2005, 105) defines them as "the type of detail that could easily be omitted and no one would notice." They are items that appear to be a gratuitous detail or part of the background of the narrative. Clothing often serves as a prop. Clothing appears to be an inconsequential detail but actually reveals important details about the characters and their inner state or being. In Rev 12, the woman is described as being clothed in the sun. The metaphor suggests that she is radiant with celestial splendor. She belongs to the divine sphere. This interpretation is supported by the other props: the crown on the woman's head and the moon under her feet. Regarding the former, the woman's crown has twelve stars. In the vision of the glorified Son of Man in Rev 1:9–20, the stars represent the angels of the seven churches. The stars represent, therefore, the transcendent and in the vision of the woman the number twelve evokes the people of God: the twelve tribes of Israel and the twelve apostles, the foundation of the people of the new covenant. Second, the moon symbolizes the calculation of time and, more specifically, the months. The woman has a certain power over time and even transcends it.

The dragon is depicted with seven heads and upon each head is a diadem. Like crowns, diadems are related to royal dignity and authority. In this case, the diadems are symbolic of the dragon's authority, but this authority is contrived by attempting to rival that of God and that of the woman.

The male child to whom the woman will give birth will shepherd the nations with an iron rod. The rod is a shepherd's staff used to guide the sheep. In this case, the adjective "of iron" evokes Ps 2:9 LXX, which proclaims that the Lord's anointed will rule the nations with an iron rod (ἐν ῥάβδῳ σιδηρᾷ). This prop is central to the identity of the child.

The setting of Rev 12 alerts the reader to the fact that the woman belongs to the transcendent world and that she is involved in combat with the dragon; their struggle is an extension of the cosmic struggle between Michael and Satan. The desert where she finds refuge evokes the exodus, a time of testing but a time of God's protection as well. The 1,260 days, as well as the one time, two times and a half time, indicate that this time of trial will be limited. The setting is a rhetorical device that reminds the readers that they are presently involved in the cosmic struggle with evil and convinces them that they must not fear because this is only a brief time of trial and they are protected by God.

Characters are at the heart of a narrative. They are the protagonists. Narrative analysis examines how the narrator constructs the characters. This is true both for fiction and nonfiction, because even in nonfictional stories, as Resseguie (2005, 121) explains, the author makes choices about how he or she will depict the characters: "Thus to a certain extent, literary characters, whether real life or fictional, are given life by an author and re-created in the reader's imagination. How can we realize the character that the author intended us to see? What should we look for?"

Cornelis Bennema (2014, xi) claims that characterization is the least developed dimension of narrative studies: "There is currently no consensus on how to study character in either literary theory or biblical studies. Nor is there a comprehensive theory of character." E. M. Forster (1927, 78) put forward a classification of characters as "round" or "flat." Round characters are complex with several, even contradictory, traits and can develop during the narrative, while flat characters are defined by one trait and are static. Forster's classification has dominated narrative studies, although it has been subsequently nuanced or honed. A major development has been to classify characters according to a scale of complexity. Building on the work of Yosef Ewen, Bennema (2014, 86) has contributed significantly to this development. He proposes that characters be considered according to three scales: a continuum of complexity, a continuum of development, and a continuum of penetration into their interior life. In a final step, Bennema suggests the results from these three continua be collated in an aggregate continuum that measures the total degree of characterization as (1) agent, actant, or walk-on; (2) a type, stock, or flat character; (3) a character with personality; or (4) an individual or person.

A character's traits that make up her characterization by the author are revealed through "showing" or "telling." Showing indicates everything that is learned about the character indirectly, such as what he or she says or does or by what the other characters say about him or her. Telling denotes what is learned directly from the narrator.

We have already seen how a setting can reveal information about a character. This includes the spatial setting in either heaven or on earth; the topographical setting, namely the desert; and props such as clothing. We will focus now specifically on the question of characterization. To this end, we will make great use of Bennema's 2014 monograph, entitled *A Theory of Character in New Testament Narrative*.

The study of the characters in Revelation is particularly complex because of their unique nature. In most cases the characters are otherworldly and are often depicted by means of a variety of symbols or through the use of similes and metaphors. For example, Christ is represented by the symbolic figures of the Son of Man (1:13; 14:14), the lion of Judah (5:5), the lamb (5:6–14; 6:1, 16; 7:9, 14, 17; 12:11; 14:1, 4, 10; 17:14; 19:7, 9; 21:9, 14, 22, 27; 22:1, 3) and the white rider (Rev 6:2; 19:11–21). Each of these figures contributes to the overall understanding of Christ and conveys a particular trait of Christ. The individual figures, in turn, are depicted symbolically: for instance, the one like a Son of Man has hair white as wool, eyes like a flaming fire, feet like burnished bronze, a voice like the sound of many waters, and a double-edged sword protruding from his mouth. This means that in our study of the characters of Rev 12 we need to be attentive to their symbolic significance and their relationship to other characters to determine if they are one symbol among others to speak of a particular reality.

In light of the otherworldly nature of the characters of Rev 12, the characters cannot be approached in the same way as the human characters in most biblical narratives. They are not complex characters with ambiguous traits and they do not reveal growth or change. At the same time, I do not believe that they are simply stock characters. Rather, there is a depth to them. Their characterization resembles that of God. Writing about God, Meir Sternberg (1985, 323) affirms:

> The rhetoric of solidarity indicates a more oblique line of unfolding, whereby the narrator first pretends to assume his reader's knowledgeability and then slips in the necessary premises, under dramatic guise and often with corrective or polemical intent, as the need for them arises.

For another thing, it would be equally bad policy to reduce God to a series of epithets, as if he were one's neighbor rather than a unique and enigmatic power, knowable only through his incursions into history. Suggestion again proves more effective than statement and open-ended showing than finite listing, because this reveals enough to make the divine order intelligible and impressive while concealing enough to leave it mysterious, transcendent, irreducible to terms other than itself.

This applies equally for the otherworldly characters of Revelation.

Narrative criticism has traditionally studied characters within the narrative without appeal to any outside sources. Bennema (2014, 61–67) contends that this is not sufficient for the study of nonfictional texts, such as the gospels. Furthermore, characters in biblical texts are not always described explicitly; much of their characterization is inferred. Although one risks no longer understanding the characters as they are depicted in the narrative, the lack of explicit information means that the reader must supplement this with pertinent sources. Revelation represents a particularly challenging composition because it is not a fictional work, but at the same time it is not like the gospels or Acts, which make direct reference to real historical figures. We will return to this point later as we examine the characters in Rev 12.

The first sign John sees in heaven is the woman (12:1). That he identifies her as a sign is significant. Her importance extends beyond face value; she is a symbol, a portent. The fact that the sign appears in heaven implies that it comes from God or is related to the transcendent. This is confirmed by the depiction of the woman's extraordinary clothing, her crown consisting of celestial bodies, and her position standing upon the moon. The sun and light would have evoked immediately in the reader the idea of the divine. Furthermore, the reader would have recalled the stars in the hand of the Son of Man in the opening vision of the book, and the number twelve would have invoked the twelve tribes of Israel and the twelve apostles.

What John describes next appears to contradict his initial portrayal of the woman as a transcendent being. She is pregnant and is suffering with birth pains (12:2). This appears to place the woman in the earthly sphere. The woman gives birth to a male child who is to rule the world with a rod of iron (12:5). The figure of the woman giving birth to the male child evokes Isa 66:7: "Before she was in labor she gave birth; before her pain came upon her she delivered a son." The verse is part of a song of Zion that announces the birth of the messiah. As noted above, the male child who will rule all the nations with a rod of iron also evokes Ps 2:9. Speaking originally of the Davidic king, M. Eugene Boring (1989, 153) suggests that Ps 2 took on a messianic interpretation in Judaism and in early Christian tradition. We can conclude, therefore, that the child is Christ. This leads to the question of the meaning of the vision. Some exegetes have suggested that it refers to the Bethlehem birth of Jesus. Others, however, like André Feuillet (1962, 272–310) have suggested that the vision depicts the "birth" of the resurrected Christ and his glorification. According to Prigent (2000, 297–98), the author of Revelation, like the author of the Fourth Gospel (cf. John 16:19–22), understands the church as a woman who gives birth to the new man, the resurrected Jesus. Vanni (1988, 247) proposes a similar interpretation: the woman represents the church giving birth to the glorified Christ, who will bring history to its fulfillment. The church can be said to give birth to Christ because she brings Christ to the world. Vanni sees a similar thought in Eph 4:13, which speaks of a growth of the body of Christ until it reaches its complete maturity, and, in particular, Gal 4:19 in which Paul describes himself as giving birth to the Galatians.

After giving birth to her son, the woman flees to the desert where she is protected by God (12:6). As noted above in the section on setting, the desert evokes the exodus and the reference to the 1,260 days indicates a brief period of time.[5] When the narrator focuses again on the woman in 12:13–17, he recounts her experience of flight from the serpent. The woman does not triumph because of her own strength or ability: she is given an eagle's wings and is nourished. The passive voice with no subject suggests that it is God who does this. The woman is also aided by the earth, which swallows the river of water that comes from the mouth of the dragon. In the end, the dragon is unable to overtake the woman, so he turns to make war against her other children, the faithful Christians (12:17).

John does not identify the woman explicitly, but the identification of the male child and the woman's other children allows the reader to ascertain the identity of the woman. She is the people of God, the church, as also contended by Prigent (2000, 292–93), Vanni (1988, 227–51), and Pavol Farkaš (1997, 210–16).

---

5. The 1,260 days is also an allusion to Dan 7:25 and 12:7 where a time, times, and a half time indicates the period of the persecution of Antiochus Epiphanes. They represent the brief period that precedes the complete inauguration of the kingdom of God. They represent the contrary of eternity.

The second sign John sees is the second character of the vision: the dragon (12:3). John begins by describing him as great and red. He has seven heads, ten horns, and on each head sits a diadem. In Revelation, red is associated with evil: the beast from the sea is scarlet and the prostitute is dressed in purple and scarlet. The head, as the uppermost part of the body containing the brain and sensory organs—namely the eyes, ears, nose and mouth—symbolizes leadership as in the expression "to be at the head" of something. The leadership of the devil is evidenced in the seven heads as well as the seven diadems. Furthermore, his great power is depicted through the ten horns. The devil's action also expresses his power: he sweeps a third of the stars on the earth (12:4). All this creates the impression of great power. At the same time, however, the devil is not omnipotent: he is able to sweep only one third of the stars. Fractions in Revelation signify partiality. The limits of the devil's power are also manifest in his inability to devour the woman's child (12:5), his defeat by Michael and his angels and his expulsion from heaven (12:8-9), as well as his inability to overtake the woman in the desert (12:13-16). The voice in heaven confirms the ultimate powerlessness of the dragon by proclaiming that he has been thrown down from heaven and that the believers have conquered him by the blood of the lamb and by their own testimony (12:10-12). The dragon, however, is full of rage and persistent. Although he has been defeated by Michael and his angels, he wages war against the woman and her other children.

While the woman's identity remains shrouded, John reveals the dragon's identity directly. He is named the ancient serpent, the devil, Satan, the deceiver of the whole world. The dragon recalls Jer 51:34 where Nebuchadnezzar is described as a dragon as well as Ezek 29:3-5; 32:2-8 where Pharaoh is called a dragon and Dan 7:7 and its vision of a beast with ten horns. The figure of the dragon is also associated with the primeval sea monster in Job 7:12; Ps 74:14; and Amos 9:3 called Leviathan, which the LXX translates as δράκων, as well as Rahab found in Isa 51:9. The designation "ancient serpent" evokes the Gen 3 narrative, where the serpent deceives Eve into taking the fruit from the tree of the knowledge of good and evil. John also states explicitly that the dragon and the serpent are figures for the devil or Satan, who is the personification of evil. The designation "deceiver of the world" reflects the devil's primary handiwork: deception and falsehood.

At the center of the narrative is the battle between the dragon and his angels against Michael and his angels (12:7-9). John does not describe

Michael. The fact that he is the only angel mentioned by name suggests that he is at the head of the heavenly host. His name, meaning "Who is like God," however, would evoke references and images from other writings that would contribute to his characterization for the readers of Revelation (Dan 10:13, 21; 12:1; see also Ps 113:5; Isa 44:7; and Jer 49:19).

Michael is mentioned only five times in the entire Bible (three times in the book of Daniel, once each in Revelation and Jude). In Dan 10:13, 21, the prophet sees a heavenly figure that has been sent to him with a word. The figure refers to Michael as one of the chief princes who has helped him in his struggle with the princes of Persia and Greece. In Dan 12:21, Michael is referred to as the great prince and the protector of the people. Jude 9 alludes to a tradition where the archangel Michael did not judge the devil but commended him to God's judgment. Michael acquires a more prominent role in Jewish and Christian extrabiblical apocalyptic literature. It is, however, the meaning of Michael's name in Hebrew—"Who is like God?"—that evokes his role as the instrument of the all-powerful God: the answer to the question inherent in Michael's name is the confession that no one is like God.

God is a discrete but active character. The most detailed description of God occurs in Rev 4, which constitutes the prologue to the visions of history. In Rev 12, God is mentioned four times (12:6, 10 [2x], 17). The male child is taken to God and his throne, indicating the glorification of the messiah who shares in the divine authority. God is the protector of the woman; he prepares a place of refuge for her in the desert. God is, by implication, the all-powerful sovereign and judge because the devil accuses the faithful before God. The children of the woman are defined as those who keep the commandments of God and the testimony of Jesus. The subtle references to God illustrate that God is in control and has defeated evil. His kingdom is a reality and will be fulfilled in the eschaton.

In Rev 12 the heavens, earth, and sea are personified. In the hymn proclaimed by the loud voice in 12:12, the heavens are invited to rejoice because the dragon has been thrown down whereas a warning is addressed to the earth and the sea because of the dragon's presence. The earth, however, also fights against the dragon in 12:16, coming to the aid of the woman by swallowing up the river of water from the serpent's mouth.

A few characters are simply mentioned in this passage: the lamb, Michael's angels, the dragon's angels, the faithful (in Greek, the brothers), and the rest of the woman's children. The lamb plays a major role in the overall narrative of Revelation. As mentioned in the hymn in 12:11, it is by the lamb's blood that he has defeated evil and brought salvation. The angels in both armies play a supporting role to Michael and the dragon. The faithful—the children of the woman—are characterized by their fidelity to God's commandments and to the word of Jesus. They have conquered alongside the lamb because of his saving death and because of their own witness to him.

The two characters developed in Rev 12 are the two signs: the woman and the dragon. Since they are not human characters, they do not possess cognitive, behavioral, or emotional qualities. Nevertheless, they possess a degree of complexity. The woman first appears as a heavenly creature, resplendent with divine light and standing outside of time. At the same time, she is also involved in a struggle and is a fugitive in need of protection. She is both a heavenly and an earthly reality. There is a greater complexity not at the level of the image or the vehicle, but at the level of the tenor, of that which is represented, the church. In Revelation, there are numerous symbols used to define the church: the twenty-four elders, the 144,000, the immense crowd, the temple, and the two witnesses. The same can be said for Christ, who is portrayed as the one like a Son of Man, the lion of Judah, the root of David and the white rider as well as the male child and the lamb.

The dragon appears to be all-powerful, as symbolized by his seven heads, seven diadems, and ten horns. He can sweep one third of the stars down onto the earth. At the same time, however, he has been thrown from heaven and has been defeated by the blood of the lamb and by the faithful. Consequently, the faithful are also in a dual situation: they have already conquered the dragon but yet are still subject to his persecution.

Revelation 12 hints at a development in the state of the woman and of the dragon. The crown of twelve stars can be correlated with the stars in the hands of the Son of Man in 1:20. In the vision of the Son of Man the number seven refers to the seven churches who are representative of the whole church, whereas in the case of the crown the number twelve alludes to the twelve apostles who are the foundation of the church. As maintains Vanni (1988, 237), the crown, which symbolizes the woman's transcendent character, anticipates fulfillment in the eschaton in the appearance of the new Jerusalem. In the case of the dragon, his downfall from heaven prefigures his final destruction in the abyss. One cannot speak of an inner life as such for the woman and the dragon because they are not human characters. One can infer a desire for fidelity in the woman and a determination in fleeing from the dragon. The dragon, who is identified as the devil, Satan, the ancient serpent, and the deceiver of the whole world, is the ultimate expression of evil.

Every author writes with a certain ideological perspective or point of view and with a particular system of values. Characters are evaluated from the point of view of the author. As notes Bennema (2014, 90–91), this relation to the point of view creates either sympathy or antipathy toward the character in the reader. Alain Rabatel (2009, 82) argues that sometimes the narrator allows one of the characters to express a point of view that is not in agreement with his own, for example, through the use of irony.

In order to evaluate biblical characters, Bennema (2014, 93) suggests first determining the point of view expressed in the narrative: "before evaluating a character, we must determine what we are evaluating and how; that is, we need guidelines or criteria for evaluation. For instance, what is the central theme against which we might evaluate characters?" The purpose of Revelation is expressed explicitly in the first three verses of the book: "The revelation of Jesus Christ, which God gave him to show his servants what must soon take place; he made it known by sending his angel to his servant John, who testified to the word of God and to the testimony of Jesus Christ, even to all that he saw. Blessed is the one who reads aloud the words of the prophecy, and blessed are those who hear and who keep what is written in it; for the time is near." John affirms the divine origin of the content of the book. John considers his book a prophecy (Rev 1:3; as well 22:7, 10, 18–19). The book reveals the interpretation of human history from a christological point of view (this is repeated in Rev 22:6–7). This prophecy recounts how Christ comes into human history and urges its readers to hold fast to the expectation of the ultimate manifestation of God's victory. Believers are called to be faithful to the words of the book. There is a dualism in John's message: reality is seen in terms of good and evil with no half measures or grey areas. People must choose between good and evil, between God and Satan. The characters, therefore, must be read in light of the prophetic nature of the book. They are understood in light of Christ's saving presence in human history and in light of the urgency of our response to Christ's word.

The woman is a prophetic sign that discloses the church's role in giving birth or bringing Christ to the world. In so doing, she participates in the cosmic struggle with evil but is protected by God. Divine protection does not mean that the church can escape the assaults of the evil one. As Resseguie (1998, 185) contends, the church must undergo the exodus experience in order to enter the promised land of the eschaton.

The dragon is a countersign that speaks to the presence of evil in the world. He represents all that is opposed to God. John indicates subtly the dragon's point of view in Rev 12:4b: "The dragon stood before the woman who was about to bear a child, *so that he might devour her child as soon as it was born.*" The dragon's struggle with God is manifest in his intention to devour the messiah. His fate, however, is already sealed even if he still manifests power in his assaults on the church. This is seen from the dragon's point of view: "So when the dragon saw that he had been thrown down to the earth, he pursued the woman who had given birth to the male child" (12:13). The dragon is cognizant of his defeat; he realizes that he has been defeated, but he uses what power he retains to fight the woman and her other children.

The minor characters in Rev 12 are seen from the point of view of John's dualistic understanding. The male child, Christ, shares in God's glory while Michael and his angels are God's instruments in the cosmic battle with the dragon and his angels. The earth is also instrumental in protecting the woman and is part of God's sheltering of the woman.

The plot of Rev 12 contributes to the overall plot of the book by anticipating the final outcome of salvation history. The radiant woman dressed in the sun presages the church's final transformation into the bride and the new Jerusalem. The dragon's expulsion from heaven by Michael foreshadows his final ejection into the lake of fire and sulfur.

The Nature of the Visions

Now that we have completed our narrative study of Rev 12, we turn to our original question about the nature of the visions of the book. What does the narrative study contribute to an understanding of the essence of the visions?

Scholars are divided over the nature of apocalyptic visions. For some like Micahel E. Stone (2003, 167–80) and Joseph Ratzinger (2000), their accounts of ecstatic experience are translated by the visionary through culturally conditioned language and traditional literary form. For others, like Rowland, an apocalyptic vision is the result of a seer's ecstatic experience. Rowland contends that apocalypticists, like the author of Revelation, reinterpreted scriptural texts through visionary meditation, seeing again what the original seer saw in a new context (Rowland, Gibbons, and Dobroruka 2006, 48). Which of these positions does the text of Rev 12 bear out?

Although there is no agreement among scholars with reference to the overall structure of the book, almost all recognize the importance of certain defining elements such as the series of seven letters, seals, trumpets, and cups. The septenaries of the seals, the trumpets, and the cups would appear to be a conscious way of organizing the visions relating to the progress of human history. Furthermore, the visions of the glorified Christ and the heavenly court are strategically placed to introduce the prophetic oracles to the seven churches, the visions of history, and the visions of judgment and the eschaton as a deliberate way of emphasizing that God is sovereign, and everything depends on God.

John employs a number of rhetorical devices in Rev 12. The rhetorical devices we have examined include the repetition of vocabulary such as σημεῖον and the terms for war (πόλεμος and πολεμέω); the use of framing narrative (12:1-6 centered on the woman and the dragon; 12:7-12 centered on the battle between Michael and the dragon; 12:13-18 centered on the woman and the dragon); the use of symbols and tropes, including the symbolic significance of numbers (7, 10, 12); and setting (topographical setting of the desert and water and temporal setting, the 1,260 days). John chooses these for their effect on the reader and hearer to convince believers that they are involved in a veritable war with evil and that this struggle is part of a greater transcendent reality, the outcome of which is already decided. The idea that God has overthrown evil encourages the pilgrim church journeying toward the new Jerusalem.

Certain elements of characterization also reveal John's literary activity. The male child is identified by the allusion to Ps 2:9, which is a detail provided by the narrator (telling) rather than a visual descriptive detail (showing). The narrator also interrupts the narration by informing the readers that the woman's place of refuge has been prepared by God and that she will be nourished there for 1,260 days. The narrator also intervenes in the characterization of the dragon and the children of the woman. Besides the physical description of the dragon (showing), John identifies the dragon overtly: he is the ancient serpent, the devil, Satan, the deceiver of the whole world. The children of the woman are named as those who keep the commandments of God and hold the testimony of Jesus. These instances where the narrator tells rather than shows the reader something about the characters are overt signs of John's work; he is not simply describing something he sees but is, at the very least, interpreting it.

I would go further and argue that the book presents itself as a literary work, composed with great care and not simply recounting ecstatic visions. This is not to deny that John received a revelation, that is, a prophetic message from God about divine salvation. But it would appear that John artfully composed his work using a literary genre with which his readers were acquainted. He draws primarily on the Old Testament, reinterpreting it in a new context to express the revelatory message. I therefore concur with Russell (1964, 122) who writes: "Some of this symbolism no doubt had its origin in the fertile imagination of the apocalypticists themselves through their experience of dreams, visions and the like. But for the most part they were using stereotyped language and symbols that belonged to a fairly well-defined tradition whose roots went back into the distant past." This is born out of the bizarre, fantastic nature of the visions, which are impossible to imagine literally. Rather, John expresses the ultimately inexpressible divine reality through symbolic images in order to encourage believers in their fidelity to God's word and to Christ's testimony.

Bibliography

Bennema, Cornelis. 2014. *A Theory of Character in New Testament Narrative*. Minneapolis: Fortress.
Boring, M. Eugene. 1989. *Revelation*. IBC. Louisville: Westminster John Knox.
Farkaš, Pavol. 1997. *La "donna" di Apocalisse 12: storia, bilancio, nuove prospettive*. TGST 25. Roma: Editrice Pontificia Università Gregoriana.
Feuillet, André. 1962. *Études johanniques*. ML.B 4. Paris: Desclée de Brouwer.
Forster, E. M. 1927. *Aspects of the Novel*. New York: Harcourt, Brace.
Hens-Piazza, Gina. 2020. *The Supporting Cast of the Bible: Reading on Behalf of the Multitude*. Lanham, MD: Lexington.
Prévost, Jean-Pierre. 2012. *Les symboles de l'Apocalypse*. Paris: Bayard.
Prigent, Pierre. 2000. *L'Apocalypse de saint Jean*. 3rd ed. CNT 2.14. Geneva: Labor et Fides.
Rabatel, Alain. 2009. "A Brief Introduction to an Enunciative Approach to Point of View." Pages 79–98 in *Point of View, Perspective, and Focalization: Modeling Mediation in Narrative*. Edited by Peter Hühn, Wolf Schmid, and Jörg Schönert. Narratologia: Contributions to Narrative Theory 17. Berlin: de Gruyter.
Ratzinger, Joseph. 2000. "Theological Commentary to the Congregation for the Doctrine of the Faith, The Message of Fatima." June 26, 2000. https://tinyurl.com/SBL06103a.

Resseguie, James L. 1998. *Revelation Unsealed: A Narrative Critical Approach to John's Apocalypse*. BibInt 32. Leiden: Brill.

———. 2005. *Narrative Criticism of the New Testament: An Introduction*. Grand Rapids: Baker.

Richards, I. A. 1965. *The Philosophy of Rhetoric*. The Mary Flexner Lectures on the Humanities. Oxford: Oxford University Press.

Rowland, Christopher, Patricia Gibbons, and Vicente Dobroruka. 2006. "Visionary Experience in Ancient Judaism and Christianity." Pages 41–56 in *Paradise Now: Essays on Early Jewish and Christian Mysticism*. Edited by April D. DeConick. SymS 11. Atlanta: Society of Biblical Literature.

Russell, D. S. 1964. *The Method and Message of Jewish Apocalyptic, 200 BC–AD 100*. OTL. Philadelphia: Westminster.

Spatafora, Andrea. 2008. *Symbolic Language and the Apocalypse*. Ottawa: Novalis.

Sternberg, Meir. 1985. *The Poetics of Biblical Narrative: Ideological Literature and the Drama of Reading*. ISBL. Bloomington, IN: Indiana University Press.

Stone, Michael E. 2003. "A Reconsideration of Apocalyptic Visions." *HTR* 96:167–80.

Vanni, Ugo. 1988. *L'Apocalisse: Ermeneutica, esegesi, teologia*. SRivBib 17. Bologna: Dehoniane.

Interplay between Reading and Intertextuality

What Abram Said He Saw: A Dream Vision and the Uncertainty of Mediation in the Genesis Apocryphon

Joseph McDonald

Fear. Lust. Talking trees. What remains of columns 19-20 and the top of 21 of the Genesis Apocryphon preserves a highly engaging, much-expanded retelling of the traditions that underlie (approximately) Gen 12:8-13:5. In the first person, Abram relates how he wandered at God's behest and built Hebron (19.7-10), how he set out for Egypt in a time of famine (19.10-13), and the contents and aftermath of a symbolic dream that came to him on the border of Egypt (19.14-23), which is the main focus of this study. It is often asserted that this dream, in which Abram appears as a cedar menaced by woodcutters that is saved by a timely cry from a date palm representing Sarai, helps to explain or justify Abram's behavior in Egypt. The dream's apology, however, seems incomplete when evaluated against subsequent events such as Sarai going into hiding for five years and her eventual discovery, abduction, and two-year imprisonment (19.23-29; 20.8-9, 17-18). Meanwhile, Sarai's lie about her relationship with Abram does forestall an attempt on Abram's life (20.8-10), and Abram eventually bests Egyptian healers at their own game, curing Pharaoh of an illness sent by God as punishment for taking Sarai from Abram (20.16-29). Both Abram and Sarai are extravagantly compensated, and after Sarai is restored to Abram the newly wealthy family returns to Bethel (20.29-21.4).

This essay poses overlapping readings of Abram's dream, drawing upon the complementary and sometimes intersecting approaches of narrative-critical, spatial, and media studies. First, scrutinizing the dream in its narrative context, I argue that the dream's imagery, and Abram's interpretations of it, are inadequate or misleading as explanations of the larger plot, especially as regards Sarai. Everything in this tale is "according to

Abram," and his testimony may be suspect. Then, I turn to the work of Henri Lefebvre on the "production of space," reading the dream as an assumed or asserted divine communication, but one whose interpretation still teeters on the edge of Abram's sketchy reliability. Next, I consider problems of mediation and the dream as an image, as conceived in the work of W. J. T. Mitchell, and draw attention to the large number of media and mediators, including the manuscript of the Apocryphon itself, that intervene into its interpretation. Attempts to visualize the dream, finally, lead me to revisit Cheryl Exum's provocative readings of the sister-wife tales through the lens of René Girard's "mechanism of triangular desire." In the end, I suggest that all of my readings are both mediated and destabilized by two uncertain mediums: Abram and me.

Abram's Dream in its Narrative Context[1]

Here is Abram's account of the night of his dream and its aftermath, as translated by Daniel Machiela (2009, 70–71):

> [14] Now I, Abram, dreamt a dream in the night of my entry into Egypt. I saw in my dream that there was a single cedar and a single date [15] palm, having sprout[ed] together from [one] roo[t]. And m[e]n came seeking to cut down and uproot the [ce]dar, thereby leaving the date palm by itself. [16] But the date palm cried out and said, "Do not cut down the cedar, for the two of us are sp[rung] from o[ne] root!" So the cedar was left on account of the date palm, [17] and they did not cut me down.
> Then I awoke in the night from my sleep, and I said to my wife Sarai, "I dreamt [18] a dream, (and) on acco[unt] of this dream I am afraid." She said to me, "Tell me your dream, so that I may know (about it)." So I began to tell her this dream, [19] and I said to [her], "... this dream ... that they will seek to kill me, but to spare you. Therefore, this is the entire kind deed [20] th[at you] must do for me: in all cities (?) that [we will ent]er s[a]y of me, 'He is my brother.' I will live under your protection, and my life will be spared because of you. [21] [... t]hey [will s]eek to take you away from me, and to kill me." Sarai wept because of my words that night [22] [...] when we en[ter]ed into the dist[ri]ct of E[gypt ...] And Pharaoh Zoa[n ...] t[he]n [...] Sarai to turn toward Zoan [23] [... and] she worried herself [g]reatly that no man should see her (for) [fiv]e years. (1QGenAp 19:14–23)[2]

---

1. Portions of this and the following sections draw on McDonald 2020, 146–55.
2. I have not sought to reproduce Machiela's spacing precisely. Unless otherwise noted, subsequent translations of Genesis Apocryphon are my own.

The relation of dreams and their interpretations features prominently in this portion of the Apocryphon.³ Here, Abram casts his dream as an arboreal allegory, with himself represented by the cedar and Sarai by the date palm.⁴ This pairing has parallels in the wider Jewish tradition, though these do not fully explain the dream's imagery. Psalm 92:13 (Hebrew), which asserts that "the righteous one sprouts like the palm tree, grows like a cedar in Lebanon," has been linked by the rabbis to the biblical episode of Abram and Sarai in Egypt (Gen. Rab. 41.1; Tanḥ., *Lekh* 5; Zohar to Gen 12). As Marianne Luijken Gevirtz (1992, 238–39) points out, however, none of the relevant passages maps the two species to Abram and Sarai respectively. A better parallel might be that suggested by Eva Osswald (1960, 21 n. 17) who notes similar imagery in the Song of Songs where the male's appearance is likened to cedars (5:15) and the female's attributes are compared to the features of a date palm (7:8–9 [Hebrew]). Still, this sheds limited light on the symbolism of Abram's dream, as it lacks any hint of danger or mention of a personified tree's speech. Both of these elements appear in the tradition, as Gevirtz (1992, 234–37) notes: felled trees function as metaphors for disaster and death (Dan 4:10–15), and speaking trees and plants feature in disputation proverbs common in the ancient Near East (Judg 9:8–15). But while all these may be common motifs, Abram's dream seems to aggregate them in an ad hoc manner that reflects the demands of the narrative and not cultural set pieces. Similarly Tomáš Vítek (2017, 142–43) argues, primarily with reference to Greek materials, that allegorical dream elements were generally not fixed symbols as late as the Hellenistic and early Roman periods and instead took their meaning from their particular contexts. Penelope's dream of an eagle killing twenty geese, for example, patently refers to Odysseus slaying her suitors (*Od.* 19.535–558), but not because geese are typically symbolic of suitors. Gevirtz (1992, 232–33, 237, 239) suggests that the differing human uses of cedars and date palms—cedars must be cut down to be of use while a felled date palm's primary utility is at an end—prompt the choice of imagery in a natural, pragmatic way.

---

3. Outside the Abram, Sarai, and Lot cycle, see (at least) columns 7 and 14–15.

4. If the proposal in Machiela (2009, 71) is correct, Abram's identity as the cedar is also explicit in his relation of the dream (19.17: וְלֹא קְצָצוּנִי, "and they did not chop me down"). The allegorical mapping of the trees is likewise encouraged by the respective genders of the nouns; compare also the potential fate of the date palm (19.15: וְלְמֹשְׁבָּב) with the predicted fate of Sarai (19.19: למשבב).

This may help illuminate the action of the dream, though the metaphors in question mostly disintegrate in the plot to come.

The Dream's Conceptual Inadequacy

Abram's relation of his dream to his narratee raises serious questions about its explanatory power or, on the other hand, about Abram's candor. Sidnie White Crawford (2008, 118) relays the scholarly consensus in contending that "there can be no doubt to the reader that [the dream] is sent by God and foretells future events." But the action of the dream maps poorly against the plot of the rest of Abram's tale. When three powerful men of Egypt seek him out, according to his later account, they are after his wisdom and esoteric knowledge, not his death (19.24–26). Moreover, by the time Pharaoh reportedly does seek to kill Abram, the king has already sent men and taken Sarai away (20.9)—an order of events that fits with Abram's second attempt at explaining the dream in 19.21 but not with his initial recounting here in 19.15. In 20.8–10 Sarai—the date palm—not Abram, is the primary focus of the men. Even further, while the date palm is spontaneous in its defense of the cedar in the dream (19.16), Sarai's intervention on Abram's behalf was scripted years before (19.20; 20.10). But the central difficulty with Abram's dream is that he wakes up much too soon.[5] The failure of the cedar tree to say anything in its own defense seems to track with Abram's later presentation of the scene in which he is spared or left behind due to Sarai's voicing of the script Abram sets for her in 19.20: Sarai says "he is my brother," while Abram is apparently the silent beneficiary of her intervention (20.10). Yet Pharaoh's rebuke of Abram in 20.26–27 implies Abram's active and ongoing participation in the ruse: "why did you keep saying to me that 'She is my sister'?" Most importantly, Abram and Sarai's encounter with the men of the land is not resolved with the sparing of Abram, the cedar, as his relation of the dream suggests. Instead, Sarai, the date palm, is herself uprooted (cf. 19.15) and taken away to languish in captivity for two years (20.8–11, 17–18). So is the dream's communication incomplete? Or is Abram less than fully truthful?

---

5. It is possible that the literal force of ואתעירת (19.17: "I was awakened"; Fitzmyer 2004, 187) implies an untimely return to full consciousness.

Abram's Reliability and Perspectival Limitations

The question of Abram's reliability as narrator shadows his entire tale. Inconsistencies between the dream and the plot are significant clues, but all rests ultimately on Abram's identity as a first-person narrator. Abram claims to have been intimately involved in most of the events that he is relating, but as Shlomith Rimmon-Kenan (1983, 100–103) explains, "personal involvement" in a story is one of the "main sources of unreliability" in a narrator, and narrators who "are also characters in the fictional world" are "on the whole more fallible." At the same time, Abram exhibits another rather converse indicator of narratorial unreliability as defined by Rimmon-Kenan, which is a "limited knowledge" of some affairs that he nonetheless undertakes to relate, such as the content (and poetic form!) of the Egyptian courtiers' paean to Sarai in 20.2–8.

With his every word—our only path into the story world—Abram is making claims that must be evaluated. And Abram, as a human character within the tale he's telling, is at all times potentially subject to all of the limitations—of perspective, knowledge, and descriptive power, among others, not to mention a weakness for portraying oneself in a favorable light—common to humans telling stories about themselves.

The Dream's Interpretation(s)

After Abram wakes up, according to his account, he expresses his fear to Sarai, who urges him to share the content of his dream with her (19.17–18). After presumably relating the dream's action to Sarai, Abram offers an initial interpretation, urges a response, and predicts its result in rapid succession. The dream signifies, says Abram,

> that they will seek to kill me, but you to leave behind. But this is the whole favor that you need to do for me: in every city that we come to, say about me that "He is my brother." And I will live with your help, and my life will be saved because of you. (19.19–20)

Most of this explanation fits the outlines of the initial narration of Abram's dream reasonably well. But events to come will expose Abram's interpretation as completely inadequate or at least shortsighted. The phrase "the whole favor" or "kindness" (19.19: כול טבותא), for example, implies something like "this is all you need to do," and Abram's double expression of the expected benefit to him, coupled with the reader's knowledge of the content of the dream, suggests that the preservation of Abram's life will mark a happy end to the matter. But Sarai's deceptive testimony to Pharaoh is only the beginning, for her, of a deeper stage of oppression as she moves from living in fear to bodily captivity. Sarai will not be left behind but will instead be abducted in violence (20.9–11).

There is a sizeable lacuna at the opening of 19.21 extending at least a third of the line. Perhaps some reference to Sarai's initial reaction once stood here, for what survives after the gap represents a somewhat different reading of Abram's dream than the one offered in 19.19. It is almost as if Abram is having another go at it: "they will seek to take you away from me," Abram says—employing עדי "to remove," instead of שבק "to spare" or "leave behind"—and, only then, they will strive "to kill me." In its verbal conception and order of events, this explanation fits the later plot (20.8–9), but on the same two counts it strains to make sense of Abram's dream as recounted in 19.14–17.

In any case, Abram's second interpretive attempt shares the flaw of the first. The broader context leaves it unclear—and this is not helped by the lacuna—whether the force of Abram's remarks here is "if you don't pronounce and perpetuate this lie, they'll try to take you away, and kill me," or "when they attempt these things, you can save me by saying this." The false statement seems to serve as a prophylactic in Abram's recommended course of action in 19.20, while the content of the dream in 19.16 suggests that the lie should only be invoked in an emergency. The complex of predictions implies then—at least as the text stands—either that the whole mess can be avoided by concealing the truth, or that Abram can be protected by Sarai's well-placed falsehood. The latter more closely suits the action to come, but both options fail utterly to foretell the consequences for Sarai. "They" will still "seek to remove" her, and they will, in fact, succeed. In a sharp irony, it is only the revelation of the truth, and not a scripted lie, that finally begins to resolve the crisis (20.8–9; 22–32). Once again, the adequacy of the dream's message and its interpretation—and perhaps even its basic congruence with the truth—is in doubt.

Space, Place, and Dreamspace

Notions of space, place, and geography are special concerns of the narrators of the Genesis Apocryphon. The purposed division of the earth among Noah's sons and grandsons in columns 16–17, some of which seems to be foretold in the context of an elaborate dream (columns 13–15), demonstrates this. Abram too claims to receive divine communication in a possible dream that tells him to survey and tour the extent of the land promised to him and his descendants (21.8–10). Dreams and space, then, show significant links in this narrative, especially as dreams help to actuate the divinely ordained division of space.

In the remains of first portion of column 19, space, place, and their traversal are key subjects of Abram's narration. The first legible words feature Abram locating himself in a particular place, perhaps Bethel: "I called there on the name of God" (19.7; compare 21.1–4). God's response, as Abram relates, arrives "during the night," which may suggest the divine provenance of his later symbolic dream that likewise occurs at night (compare 19.8 and 14), and God tells him to "wander," referencing another place (the holy mountain). What follows is a minor travelogue and a mention of Abram's literal construction of a place (i.e., Hebron) followed by a vacat (19.8–10). Following the vacat, Abram speaks of a famine in "this land"—later specified twice as "our land"—and details his, Sarai's, and Lot's journey to and over the Carmon River (19.10–13). "Look," Abram says, "now we have gone out of our land and entered into the land of the sons of Ham, into the land of Egypt" (19.13). This is followed by a sizeable vacat at the beginning of 19.14, after which Abram begins to relate and interpret his dream of the night he entered Egypt. Yet, in 19.22 Abram seems to speak again of entering Egypt (though this is very fragmentary and tentatively reconstructed).

So Abram's dream of the cedar and the date palm comes to him in a borderland, a liminal space; he and his companions have somehow crossed over Egypt's boundary (19.12–13) but have not yet entered into it (19.22). The visceral distinction between "our land" and that of others, "the sons of Ham" (19.13), heightens the tension of being suspended in the middle, an in-between that tracks with the nature of dreams as I have experienced them: neither here nor now but somehow both here and now in my bed at four in the morning. This is also compatible with the way in which Abram (as Noah before him) presents the dream experience: these events blur boundaries, mediating not only between wakefulness and sleep but also between present and future, heaven and earth, divine and human. Here as everywhere, however, it is essential to remember that everything is being mediated by Abram himself as the narrator. First, Abram (the character living prior to his narratorial incarnation's textualized formulation of his earlier experiences) sees a dream and then wakes to tell Sarai about it.

Later Abram (the narrator of this part of the Apocryphon) talks about the seeing and then tells about the telling.

Lefebvre's Moments of the Production of Space

The work of Henri Lefebvre on the "production of space" can inform both a reading of Abram's vision in a dream and, perhaps, readings of other visions and dreams in biblical and allied literature. I rely here on the discussion of Lefebvre in Eric Prieto's *Literature, Geography, and the Postmodern Poetics of Place*. Some of Lefebvre's basic concerns are conducive to the task. Prieto (2013, 90) describes how seemingly self-evident binaries such as "subject and object, mental and material, imagined and real"—foisted upon us, from Lefebvre's Marxist perspective, by social forces that rely on domination and the estrangement of humans from the products of their labor—prevent us from constructing "authentic (meaningful and productive) relations with the space around us." Moreover, the "artificial partitioning of spatial experience," a natural byproduct of these binaries, "makes the problem of representation a central concern" for Lefebvre. The dichotomy of "imagined and real" has particular pertinence to an analysis of dreams and visions, while the problem of "representation" is relevant to any narrative or media inquiry.

Lefebvre famously suggests a conceptualization of space that involves "three interdependent levels" or "three levels or moments of the production of space, none of which is separable from the others and none of which can be entirely liberated from the uncertainty of mediation, be it of the senses, of the dominant social structures, or of the individual consciousness" (Prieto 2013, 90). Though these distinctions—Prieto refers to the "division" of space, but his own treatment suggests that the ideas are heuristic ways to think about space—are "notoriously obscure" and a full discussion is impossible here, some useful notes may be gleaned. A glance at other discussions (Merrifield 2006, 109; Bauer 2019, 207) of this "spatial triad" underlines the crucial role of the reader in its interpretation.

Lefebvre's first category, "spatial practice" or "perceived space," involves space as produced by an individual in society and in dialectical fashion. A person is shaped by her spatial circumstances yet also shapes the space in which she lives (Prieto 2013, 91–92). In other parts of the Apocryphon, such as the broader context of Abram and Sarai's Egyptian stay, Abram's later survey of the land (21.8–19; cf. Noah in 11.11), and the earlier division of the earth among Noah's offspring (16.8[?]–17.24[?]), this may have substantial heuristic value. Abram's initial "wandering" at God's direction, for example, involves a profound shaping of physical and human space as Abram, the *Ur*-urban planner, founds and constructs the city of Hebron (19.9). After dwelling there for two years, moreover, Abram's lived spatial circumstances lend decisive shape to the course of his life and that of his family, as a local shortage of resources and rumors of plenty elsewhere prompt their emigration (19.10–11). In a close reading of Abram's dream vision, however, this level of space production is of limited use, as his dreamspace is imaginary and not tangible even by the terms of the story world.

Lefebvre's other two categories are more suggestive here. The second, "representations of space" or "conceived space," is an abstraction that has to do with conceptual arrangements of space that originate in spheres of social control. Prieto's (2013, 92) explanation is worth quoting at length here:

> ["Representations of space" or "conceived space"] is a top-down mode of knowledge, closely related to Foucault's conception of space as constructed by state power: [i]t involves the social order's ability to regulate behavior by imposing on us a representational framework that both explains and constrains our daily practices, despite the fact that such conceptual abstractions are by definition inadequate to the bodily practices and perceptions they are meant to regulate.

Little could be more top-down than the deity's frequent communication with Abram in this narrative. If Abram's dream is divine in origin, as assumed by Daniel Falk (2007, 80; 83), Crawford (2008, 118), Gevirtz (1992, 241), and Esther Eshel (2009, 52), or if it is at least conceived to be divinely sent by the characters, it could well be described as a "representational framework" that helps regulate the behavior of Abram, and especially Sarai, for several years after the event (19.23). As the landscape and action of the dream put constraints on at least Sarai's daily life, so the broader plot of this section of the Apocryphon is partly explained, if not justified, by the dream's events. But there is an important caveat to these claims: the narrative of the dream only has these powers as it is interpreted, however poorly or incompletely. The dream, as Abram relates it, is certainly conceptually inadequate as an explanation or prompt of many of the bodily events that affect the characters in scenes to come.

Lefebvre's third category, which is somewhat confusingly referred to as "representational spaces/spaces of representation," or "lived space," also has something to contribute here, though Prieto's (2013, 92–93) translation and treatment of Lefebvre's presentation is quite opaque. Prieto contrasts this level of space with the second, top-down category of knowledge by suggesting that it is conceptualized as coming "from the bottom up, from the individual":

> These are still representations, but they are "directly lived," in the sense that the actors and eye witnesses themselves provide these representations.... They are developed inductively, through reflections on lived experience.... The goal of this third level of representation is to cobble together a representation that will make the individual's experience meaningful *to him or her*—not to provide universally valid explanations or definitions. (93)

This is congruent, in a subtle but meaningful way, with some of the dynamics of Abram's relation of his dream and his interpretation(s) of it in the Apocryphon. For all the top-down quality of the sending and reception of the dream itself (if it is indeed sent through divine agency or presented as such), the dream does not, in Abram's telling, contain any key to its meaning. The interpretation(s) related in 19.19–21 are contingent on their context and produced by Abram's own reflection and construction of meaning, a process that infects Sarai in turn. Yet, a basic objection also needs to be lodged here: Prieto's explanation of the "third level of representation" presumes the good faith of the individual, but this may be a risky supposition in the case of Abram.

Media(tion)

Prieto (2013, 90) underlines the "uncertainty of mediation" that impacts any and all of Lefebvre's "moments of the construction of space." Mediation and its multiple effects should be part of any disciplined reflection on narrative, but the Apocryphon, and perhaps this dream section in particular, presents some unusually rich avenues for exploration. In a discussion of the etymology and meaning of the words *medium* and *media*, W. J. T. Mitchell and Mark B. Hansen (2010, xi) note the *Oxford English Dictionary*'s emphasis on a medium's "intermediary" capacity. The physical remains of the Apocryphon provide a provocative case of an intermediary entity. These ink scratches on leather lay for close to two millennia in complete silence in a cave, yet they always possessed the latent power to relate a story known (in its particulars) nowhere else and to introduce living human beings to the characters who dwell there. This potential energy, despite its longevity, did suffer from significant erosion, a process that sadly has accelerated dramatically since the manuscript's discovery (Machiela 2009, 29–30). Its ability to mediate even a visual record of written signs on its sheets of leather has been seriously impaired by wear, decay, and disappearing ink. And while these indignities are, in part, the natural consequences of advanced age, the manuscript was not left whole even in antiquity: the innermost sheet ends in a smooth cut, suspending the text midsentence at the end of column 22. Today, mechanical images of the Apocryphon are, in some sense, more real than the disintegrating and essentially unreadable artifact that sits in the Shrine of the Book in Jerusalem. Photographs and printed editions of the text are the only way into the narrative that still endures. And this is only to speak of the document's physical, visually detectable transmission of signs. Other practical operations of its mediation(s) are also full of difficulties, not least its presentation of a text encoded in a long-dead dialect of a language in which few are competent. Even those who are experts, I would argue, still approach a text such as the Genesis Apocryphon in a strikingly mediated way, through deeply layered strata of photographs, editions, grammars, lexica, and other scholarship, whether physically consulted or resident in memory, that cannot but intervene between text, eye, and brain. And this is not even to mention the meddling of deep and even unconscious knowledge of the canonical Genesis in scholarly readings. That the Apocryphon still manages to entertain and puzzle, despite these barriers, is, I think, genuinely moving.

Furthermore, any "narrative-communication situation," as Seymour Chatman (1978, 147–51) terms it, involves several other intermediaries. These vary in number and name according to the needs of the discussion at hand and the predilections of the commentator: between a flesh-and-blood "real author" and his or her "real reader" there may be conceived an implied author, an implied reader, and a variety of narrators and narratees. I am most concerned here with the narrator, which with Rimmon-Kenan (1983, 86–89) and against Chatman I am prone to say is indispensable to a narrative—there is no tale without a teller. Abram, as the retrospective narrator of this section of the Apocryphon, is one of the media of this tale, an intermediary in a profound and often multifaceted sense. With reference to his dream that he relates in 19.14–17, Abram is just about the only conceivable primary intermediary of his private mental imaging. If I suspend firm resolution of the "nature" of literary characters, can I conceive of Abram's dream as a patterned firing of synapses in his sleeping brain somehow sensually apprehended? Can I then conceive of his words—Aramaic nouns, verbs, and particles arranged in a linear way—as first spoken or thought and then written down? Abram, the character, may be literate according to later narrative evidence (19.25; all this produced, naturally, by Abram himself). In any case, a narrator who repeatedly identifies himself as "I, Abram" (19.14; twice in 20.10-11; 20.33; and 21.15) relays the supposed content of the dream within the context of a larger tale of his and his family's move to Egypt.

Moving the frame outward a bit further, there are actual words and clauses formed out of letters written on leather by a real person and archived in a cave. With training, study, and much intermediary scholarly aid, I can visually apprehend these signs, in the forms in which they are generally agreed to be, and decode them, forming a mental image that is in some way analogous to what Abram said he saw. I must insist on an at least partial transferability of the sensuous impressions "experienced" by Abram that night in his story world and those that I call up in my mind's eye as I sit here writing this. Nothing in this narrative makes sense to me if some pool of human experience doesn't join me to the "concrete semblances of real men and women" that are literary characters.[6] So I, too, have an image of trees, men, and so on in my mind, but what a formidable array of media filters this image must penetrate in order to come to rest there!

In the near context as well—both in his report of his dream as a fellow character to Sarai in 19.17-21 and in his "later" narration of all these events to his narratee—Abram may be a kind of "medium" in the spiritualist sense. In his relation and interpretation of the plot and symbolism of his dream, Abram may be conceived as mediating the communications of a disembodied, or at least ordinarily absent, being. This might hold even if the dream's origin is not (according to the norms of the story world) truly divine, even if Abram has made it up completely. The fallout from the dream's interpretation(s) shows just how seriously its message(s) impacted at least Sarai's daily life (19.23), which suggests that its provenance is implied or presumed to be from a higher authority. Once again, the question of Abram's reliability is a central, insoluble problem.

Lest I be accused of being too hard on Abram, I must also acknowledge my own, unavoidable mediation in this "narrative-communication

---

6. "Concrete semblances" is the formulation of Ronald Crane quoted in Chatman (1978, 137); substance, not fixity, is what "concrete" signifies to me in this phrase.

situation." I make no claims of penetration to original intent or reception. I am the real reader here, and thus about the only element of this transaction to which (I imagine) I have something close to unmediated access. The "representations" in this essay, of characterization, space, and otherwise, are inescapably mine, and I am constructing meaning all along as I write, an activity that Gary Weissman (2016, 7) argues amounts to "rewriting," a project perhaps only different in scale from that of the anonymous real author of the Apocryphon. In his work on setting in narrative, Chatman (1978, 138) says that "characters exist and move in a space which exists abstractly at the deep narrative level, that is, prior to any kind of materialization, like the two-dimensional movie screen, the three-dimensional proscenium stage, the projected space of the mind's eye." Yet, some kind of projection is necessary, and all of this varies, within certain limits, with the projector. When we speak of an image, it seems, we must always ask: whose image? A botanist, a skilled painter, and I presumably all project different images of a date palm. Even a photograph of one specimen of the species is unlikely, I think, to look the same to all three of us.

Abram's Dream as an Image

Mitchell's work (2010, 41) on the nature of images suggests that Abram's dream, as a (highly mediated representation of a) mental process ranked among "psychological phenomena that can be accessed only indirectly, through verbal descriptions or graphic depictions," may itself be properly regarded as an image. More fundamentally, given the context at hand, Mitchell argues that narrative is an entirely legitimate medium for the construction of images (40). In a presentation that has strong affinities with traditional formalist and structuralist distinctions between the what and the how of narrative, often illustrated by the "transposability" of a story among various discourses and media, Mitchell speaks of the "remediation" potential of images: "an image can appear in a narrative or poem as well as in a painting, and be recognizable as 'the same' (or at least a similar) image" (40).

The action of Abram's dream is sympathetic to analysis as a kind of moving image, analogous to the illusory but convincing movement of cinema. The climactic development in the dream's plot, the date palm's cry, is primarily an aural event. Yet this, too, fits comfortably within a cinematic metaphor, as contemporary film is a firmly mixed medium that uses both sights and sounds. Moreover, as Mitchell remarks, boundaries bleed on all sides of traditional media distinctions. "Verbal media," for example, such as books or leather scrolls, must be first taken in by the eye, even if the object is to read them aloud (42).

There may be several elements that are defined more or less absolutely in a motion picture that must remain provisional and ambiguous in a reading of Abram's dream's imagery. In a film, as Chatman (1978, 98) notes, "angle, distance, and so on are controlled by the director's placement of the camera. Life offers no predetermined rationale for these placements. They are all choices." Abram, as a narrator of a "verbal narrative," may have fewer of these choices. Verbal narratives lack a film's absolute "frame," for example, and the absence of visual icons means that the story space of verbal narratives is "doubly removed from the reader," a "mental construct rather than an analogon" (96–97, 101). These claims can all be qualified. As Chatman recognizes, the story space of a film doesn't end at the frame; as with a text, what is not shown or said may be, and often must be, inferred. Mental construction can be crucial to story building in a film. Common wisdom, now often flouted, holds that the scariest movies are those where the monster remains off-screen.

In any case, Abram seems at least to have *made* relatively few explicit choices of detail in his laconic narration; the reader must make them herself, if she is so inclined. From what perspective does Abram "see" the action of his dream? Does his "eye," or the lens of his camera, remain stationary, move about, zoom in and out? His initial urging of his narratee may suggest that he's at some remove, far enough away to regard both trees in their entirety: "Look!—a cedar and a date palm" (19.14–15). Machiela's translation, "there was a single cedar and a single date palm," evokes a certain blankness around the two, which may emphasize a wide-angle or remote perspective. Line 15 is unfortunately very damaged for the space of the next few words. If Machiela's reading, following Klaus Beyer, is correct, this initial "view" of the two trees is succeeded, jarringly, by a reference to a relationship that is completely invisible: "Look!—a cedar and a date palm (they had sprouted together from one root)." So straightaway, under this cinematic metaphor, Abram has turned "aside" and provided information, as in a voice-over, that cannot be detected visually unless through some special effect.[7] Alternatively, Abram has intuited, in dream-fashion,

---

7. More satisfactory for my experiment here (and, to my reading, a more skillfully deployed tale, as the "twist," whether true or not, is left a surprise) would be to read with Fitzmyer (2004, 98–99, 185): "a date palm, (which was) [very beauti]ful." But this

a hidden truth that explains some of the action but blows the punch line in the process.

After this the text clears up a bit and men come into the initial tableau, injecting the first hint of significant motion, save for stirring leaves, into this moving image. These human players enter the frame "seeking to chop down and to uproot the cedar, and to leave behind the date palm to its solitude," as Abram relates it. How the intent of these men might be conveyed is, to me, one of the most enigmatic features of this short film. Is their aim communicated visually, through facial expressions or bodily attitudes? Are they brandishing axes, ropes, and saws? Have they led in a donkey pulling a cart, betraying a plan to haul away fresh lumber? Any of these seem more satisfactory than attributing the detection of their desire to a vague feeling of the dreamer. Supporting the idea of there being some kind of sensuous clue, whether visual or aural, may be the fact that the date palm awakens to the danger and cries a halt. I imagine the axe, poised to strike the cedar's trunk, arrested by an uncanny voice emerging from the date palm. This aural intervention, at home in the cinematic metaphor, brings out further visual questions. How does the date palm speak, that is, vibrate the air to form words? Does a scar on its bark form a suggestion of lips? Does the tree or its foliage tremble a bit, making speech out of dry rattles? Or do the sounds merely emanate from its general direction, as from a hidden speaker? These questions are not idle but evoke precisely the kind of decisions that would need to be made by the director of this film.

Part of what the date palm says, moreover, can be understood as a direct invitation to visualize: "See [ארי]—the two of us are sprouted from one root!" (19.16). Yet this aural urging to "look!" points to something that simply cannot be seen. The men have been guided by appearances and quite naturally so; the trees are completely different above ground. A quick glance at photographs of *Cedrus libani* (the cedar of Lebanon) and *Phoenix dactylifera* (a common date palm) demonstrates the unlikelihood of confusing these species; it would be remarkable indeed if these trees sprouted from one root. The men refrain, apparently, not because of something they see, but because of the date palm's verbal assertion—perhaps, a timely lie. But the behavior of the men is even less well defined at the end of the dream than it was at the beginning, as what is mostly specified is

---

reading is rejected out of hand by Machiela (2009, 71) as fitting "neither the available space nor the ink remains."

what they do not do. Their intention, supposedly, was to chop down the cedar and to leave behind (שבק) the date palm, but they end up leaving behind (שבק) the cedar and chopping down nothing at all (19.15–17). Do they leave, muttering, hauling their tools? Do they simply desist in shock and stand around? Or does Abram wake up suddenly, *ex medias res*, leaving the dream vision before its action is concluded—as suggested, perhaps, by the inadequacies of his interpretations?

Sight, Seeing—and Watching

Abram presents his dream in terms of what he "saw" (חזי), followed shortly by another arguably visual indicator in the presentative particle הא: "I saw ... look!" (19.14: והא ... וחזית).[8] Moreover, Abram's brief recounting of the dream to his narratee is replete with linguistic data that may be visualized. The theme of sight, which first appears here in the narrative, also links much of the narrative action and motivation going forward. Prompted by what Abram sees in his dream (19.14), Sarai lives in fear of being seen by men for five years (19.23). When this happens anyway, a mostly visual description of Sarai in poetic verse inflames Pharaoh's lust, entices him to lay his eyes on her himself, and as a result he abducts her (20.2–9). Finally, Abram prays that God would make God's hand "be seen" (20.14) in punishment of Pharaoh, and the fulfillment of this request eventuates in the king's sight of Abram in another dream (20.22), which sets the resolution of the entire episode in motion.

And there are yet other layers of sight and seeing in Abram's narrative dream complex. I am attempting to see, from my perspective, what Abram said he saw—which may include, in the detail of the root(s), something that cannot be seen. The men who arrive must be conceived as visually apprehending the trees, if only to navigate toward them with the aim of cutting down the cedar, and there may be suggestions that the date palm is a tree of grace and beauty that draws the eye. Whether or not there was an explicit statement of the palm's beauty in Abram's relation of the dream, as Fitzmyer reads, the broader context hints that its attractiveness may motivate the men in their attempt to "leave it behind." Whatever the interpretive or predictive weaknesses of the dream, the date palm is plainly

---

8. Compare Abram's tour guide speech in 19.13, plus the usages of הא in 13.13–14 (the latter a supralinear addition) and, perhaps, 22.27.

presented in the narrative as Sarai's dream analogue. Although Sarai's beauty is not explicitly mentioned (at least in the text that remains) until somewhat later, there it is the subject of prolix praise and the sole stated reason that Pharaoh abducts and "marries" her (20.2–9). Moreover, Sarai seems to intuit, after hearing Abram's report of his dream, that her appearance is a catalyst to danger, as she takes frightened care to avoid the eyes of men (19.23). If the men in the dream, themselves analogues of Pharaoh and his retainers, can be conceived as gazing with covetousness or even lust at the lovely, swaying date palm, there is a multilayered voyeurism built in to the narrative: Abram is watching them watching—and meanwhile, I am watching it all.

This idea meshes with some of the possible psychological underpinnings of the biblical (and retold) "sister-wife" episodes. In a classic article, J. Cheryl Exum (1993, 100–101, 106) argues that these incidents are driven by a male, unconscious fantasy that "the wife have sex with another man" or at least become the object of the desire of another. Observing a rival's lust kindles the husband's own and confirms the wife's sexual draw. Along with Freud, Exum's analysis builds on René Girard's "mechanism of triangular desire," and here we find yet another level of mediation, the middle term between the desiring subject and the desired object, the "mediator of desire," in this case Pharaoh and his courtiers. Tellingly, in keeping with the triangle metaphor, the tie between subject and mediator is as important as that between subject and object, and "the impulse toward the object is ultimately an impulse toward the mediator" (Exum 1993, 106 n. 31), an impulse that aims at coming to resemble the mediator. Here, Abram gains kinglike wealth and grows more powerful than the Pharaoh of Egypt and all of his sages. As the only healer or exorcist capable of alleviating their afflictions, Abram literally holds their fate in his hands (20.16–33). In distinction from Genesis and other retellings, moreover, Abram in the Apocryphon explicitly relates how he watches others watch the lithe date palm, Sarai's analogue, albeit in a dream, a fantasy. Later, he even pens a poem, further fantasy, imagining the lingering, head-to-toe gaze of his powerful mediators of desire on Sarai's body, on the "blossom of her face," her "lovely breasts," her "full thighs" (20.2–8). Like Candaules, immortalized by Herodotus, who fatefully convinces his captain Gyges to spy on his wife as she undresses for bed (*Hist.* 1.8–12), Abram enjoys the confirmation of his wife's desirability by watching her being visually "taken" by another. Unlike the early Lydian king, however, Abram not only retains life and wife but has the better of the swap of wealth and status with his rival.

Conclusion: The Uncertainty of Mediation

In my reading of Abram's dream in its narrative context, I argue that the action of the dream is poorly predictive of much of the coming plot, and that Abram's interpretations fail to foretell serious threats to Sarai. Binding and complicating these are Abram's identity as a first-person, participatory narrator and attendant suspicions about his reliability. Much remains unresolved, including Abram's candor, motive, and interpretive ability.

Considering Lefebvre's moments of the production of space, I contend that the dream mediates a potential or assumed divine warrant that "explains and constrains" the daily life of at least Sarai. But again, this is ultimately only as construed, inadequately, by Abram himself. The dream as related offers no glosses or ciphers.

Reflecting on the underlying problem of mediation, at last, I find mediators stacked up like panes of glass, some mostly clear and some bubbled or crazed, but the final thickness of these layered prisms leaves much that is distorted. Not least among these is the sole, lacunose manuscript of the Apocryphon, but even the welcome discovery of another copy would introduce new interpretive layers without necessarily clarifying events and intentions in the story world. In watching Abram's dream as an image, much of the detail can only be sketched in *by me*, and Abram's motive in this sister-wife tale can only be supposed *by me*. And if I follow Exum, Abram's desire and fear, two sides of the same coin, are unconscious, unknown, or unacknowledged by Abram himself. And so I arrive back at the "uncertainty of mediation … of the individual consciousness," with both Abram and me being uncertain mediums.

Bibliography

Bauer, Jenny. 2019. "Thirdings, Representations, Reflections: How to Grasp the Spatial Triad." Pages 207–24 in *Perspectives on Henri Lefebvre: Theory, Practices and (Re)Readings*. Edited by Jenny Bauer and Robert Fischer. SpatioTemporality / RaumZeitlichkeit 4. Berlin: de Gruyter.

Chatman, Seymour. 1978. *Story and Discourse: Narrative Structure in Fiction and Film*. Ithaca, NY: Cornell University Press.

Crawford, Sidnie White. 2008. *Rewriting Scripture in Second Temple Times*. Grand Rapids: Eerdmans.

Eshel, Esther. 2009. "The Dream Visions in the Noah Story of the Genesis Apocryphon and Related Texts." Pages 41–61 in *Northern Lights on the Dead Sea Scrolls: Proceedings of the Nordic Qumran Network 2003–2006*. Edited by Anders Klostergaard Petersen et al. STDJ 80. Leiden: Brill.

Exum, J. Cheryl. 1993. "Who's Afraid of 'The Endangered Ancestress'?." Pages 91–113 in *The New Literary Criticism and the Hebrew Bible*. Edited by J. Cheryl Exum and David J. A. Clines. Valley Forge, PA: Trinity Press International.

Falk, Daniel K. 2007. *The Parabiblical Texts: Strategies for Extending the Scriptures in the Dead Sea Scrolls*. LSTS 63. London: T&T Clark.

Fitzmyer, Joseph A. 2004. *The Genesis Apocryphon of Qumran Cave 1 (1Q20): A Commentary*. 3rd ed. BibOr 18B. Rome: Pontifical Biblical Institute.

Gevirtz, Marianne Luijken. 1992. "Abram's Dream in the Genesis Apocryphon: Its Motifs and Their Function." *Maarav* 8:229–43.

McDonald, Joseph. 2020. *Searching for Sarah in the Second Temple Era: Images in the Hebrew Bible, the Septuagint, the Genesis Apocryphon, and the Antiquities*. LHBOTS 693. London: T&T Clark.

Machiela, Daniel A. 2009. *The Dead Sea Genesis Apocryphon: A New Text and Translation with Introduction and Special Treatment of Columns 13–17*. STDJ 79. Leiden: Brill.

Merrifield, Andy. 2006. *Henri Lefebvre: A Critical Introduction*. New York: Routledge.

Mitchell, W. J. T., and Mark B. N. Hansen, eds. 2010. *Critical Terms for Media Studies*. Chicago: University of Chicago Press.

Osswald, Eva. 1960. "Beobachtungen zur Erzählung von Abrahams Aufenthalt in Ägypten im 'Genesis-Apocryphon.'" *ZAW* 72:7–25.

Prieto, Eric. 2013. *Literature, Geography, and the Postmodern Poetics of Place*. New York: Palgrave Macmillan.

Rimmon-Kenan, Shlomith. 1983. *Narrative Fiction: Contemporary Poetics*. New Accents. London: Methuen.

Vítek, Tomáš. 2017. "Allegorical Dreams in Antiquity: Their Character and Interpretation." *WSt* 130:127–52.

Weissman, Gary. 2016. *The Writer in the Well: On Misreading and Rewriting Literature*. Theory and Interpretation of Narrative. Columbus, OH: The Ohio State University Press.

Violence and Vulnerability: The Vision of Jeremiah in 2 Maccabees

Richard J. Bautch

This study's point of departure is the literary materials prior to the narrative of 2 Maccabees, which begins at 3:1 and continues to the book's conclusion. Before the narrative there is a first-person preface by the epitomizer (2:19–32), which is preceded by two letters to the Jews in Egypt (1:1–10a; 1:10b–2:18). It is in the context of these letters that the figure of Jeremiah makes a cameo appearance and instructs Babylon-bound deportees to take with them fire that they preserved from the Jerusalem temple (2:1–8). In this historical flashback, Jeremiah is also credited with securing three important fixtures from the temple—the tent, the altar, and the ark—by placing them in a hidden cave on what is ostensibly Mount Nebo. With respect to Jeremiah, the other relevant passage is located near the end of 2 Maccabees, where the prophet dramatically appears in a dream (ὄνειρον) and gives Judas Maccabeus a golden sword along with the command to strike down his adversaries (15:13–16).[1] The subsequent death of Nicanor provides the final resolution to this book. The image of Jeremiah with a sword forms a literary frame with the earlier passage (2:1–8) and so raises the question of this text's relationship to the legendary prophet. Not a major character, Jeremiah is rather a channel of historical consciousness, a role that the prophet plays in other second-century BCE Jewish texts (Fröhlich 1996, 68–90). In 2 Maccabees, however, Jeremiah is more integral to the book's function and purpose, which relate to resistance, than he is in

---

1. Regarding the dream, it is described as "a dream, a sort of vision" (NRSV). The Greek reads ὄνειρον ἀξιόπιστον ὕπαρ, which connotes a veritable dream, i.e., no illusive phantasm but a reality (cf. LSJ, s.v. "ὕπαρ").

Daniel and 1 Enoch.[2] The difference lies in the fact that he is portrayed in a striking image that begets violence, and that the image in turn forms a frame around 2 Maccabees as a narrative of resistance. As a frame, Jeremiah never enters into the narrative tableau but keeps to the margins. Jeremiah does not interact much with Judas Maccabeus or any of his confreres, yet he is never far from the action as a bringer of historical consciousness tasked with inspiring the Jewish resistance against the Seleucids. It is worth noting how "frame" here describes both the literary convention deployed in 2 Macc 2:18 and 15:13–16 as well as the rhetorical notion of cropping around a picture to emphasize certain elements within while creating a border that holds together a constructed reality (Iorgoveanu and Corbu 2012, 92). Jeremian historical consciousness envelops the text rhetorically.[3]

The commentaries on 2 Maccabees (e.g., Schwartz 2008, 160; Goldstein 1983, 182–84; Doran 2012, 55–57) treat the book's introductory section predictably and dwell on issues such as the authorship of the two letters. None, however, deal with the figure of Jeremiah in any depth or address his rhetorical function in either 2:1–8 or 15:13–16. Jeremiah's role is only beginning to come to light (Lange 2017). What follows here is a study of 2 Maccabees that focuses on the martial image of Jeremiah that comes to Judas Maccabeus in a vision or veritable dream and forms a frame around the narrative. The frame clearly serves a rhetorical purpose and contributes to the historical consciousness that orients this account of resistance. In addition, there are two other interpretive tools that may be brought to bear on the functions that Jeremiah performs in this text. First, the prophet's inclusion in the text's catalogue of images raises the question of rhetography, which is the use of imagery for argumentative purposes within a rhetorical context. Coined by Vernon Robbins (2008, 89), "rhetography" combines

---

2. Ancient historiographers wrote 2 Maccabees as an account of resistance, yet, read through one lens, these authors were hegemonic in that they sought a less diversified community in the aftermath of the struggle against the Seleucid empire. To construct a model community, they supplied readers with common symbols, a common story, and a common gender. The common gender was the masculine, with male and female characters alike marked in this way and depicted accordingly. The historiographers' depiction of Jeremiah supports their hegemonic program. See Bautch (2019, 170) and Portier-Young (2011, 395–96).

3. In 2 Maccabees, the rhetorical dimension is built upon the text's genre, historiography. See Gruen (2016, 169–96).

"rhetoric" and "graphic" to describe "the graphic images people create in their minds as a result of the visual texture of the text." Robbins understands rhetography to work conjointly with "rhetology," the art of reasoning, to address the reasoning and the picturing of the situation. In tandem, rhetography and rhetology play a crucial role in authorizing 2 Maccabees as a hegemonic text that promotes strict social order within the community while exhorting its members to resist attacks from without.[4] Second, on an epistemological level, the figure of Jeremiah in 2 Maccabees points to different modes of human cognition. Daniel Kahneman (2011, 10–13) describes the modes as "system 1" thinking and "system 2" thinking. In system 1 thinking, or "fast" thinking, we make snap "judgments and decisions … guided directly by feelings of liking and disliking, with little deliberation or reasoning." While such decisions can be rash and ill advised, experts routinely make system 1 determinations when working in their ken of specialized knowledge. Kahneman (2011, 13) describes system 1 thinking as the primary human approach to life. System 2 thinking occurs when we need to switch "to a slower, more deliberate and effortful form of thinking." Such "slow" thinking is by nature logical, analytical, and critical. It provides answers to problems we cannot solve immediately and connections to ideas related to our current train of thought. When Jeremiah appears in a warrior motif (15:13–16), the image is a call to fast thinking and direct action. Told to put his enemies to the sword, Judas Maccabeus has Nicanor beheaded (15:30). As Kahneman (2011, 108) remarks, images created in the mind are potent enough "to move our bodies into action immediately (e.g., a mob predisposed to riot that is shown the picture of a hated leader)." Or, in the case of 2 Maccabees, a patriot given to zealotry is shown the picture of a hallowed ancestor, Jeremiah, with sword in hand. The weaponized Jeremiah reveals the basis, or rhetorical frame, upon which system 1 thinking is predicated in 2 Maccabees.[5]

---

4. On an image such as that of Jeremiah authorizing a text like 2 Maccabees, see Racine (2015, 5, 9), who develops a rhetoric of visions by asking, "Do visions provide a type of authority to the speaker which the usual telling does not?"

5. Inasmuch as the frame in 2 Maccabees comprises 2:1–8 and 15:13–16, the former also reflects fast thinking because quick-witted Judeans in the process of being exiled secure a portion of fire from the Jerusalem temple, presumably with great haste. The defining parts of the frame both reflect system 1 thinking.

Jeremiah as Framing Device

In 2 Maccabees, Jeremiah first appears in the context of the Jerusalem temple's purification after its defilement by the Seleucids (2:1–8). According to the second of the two letters, a key to the purification is the recovery of a centuries-old fire used for sacrifices in the first temple. Jeremiah is said to have instructed deportees leaving for Babylon to preserve this fire and hold fast to the commandments and the law of the Lord. Jeremiah furthermore saves three fixtures from the temple—the tent, the altar, and the ark—by placing them at Mount Nebo, the peak from which Moses viewed the land of Israel (Deut 32:49; 34:1). Jeremiah is said to have hidden the three sacred objects in the mountain until a later time determined by God, which would explain why the second temple in Jerusalem is the legitimate site of worship even without the ark and other aforementioned objects. The temple in Maccabean times did not have the ark, but it could claim a strong connection to it through the figure of Jeremiah and the cultic fire that *is* reestablished in Jerusalem (2 Macc 1:30–36). The fire's brilliance is brought to the attention of the Persian king, who declares the temple a sacred precinct and bestows additional favors upon the Jerusalemites (1:34–35). As these royal actions confirm, Jeremiah's work in 2 Macc 2:1–8 is authorizing and rhetorical. It is rhetorical in the sense of rhetology, not rhetography. That is to say, the approbation is textual and not visual. The information about Jeremiah comes from records (2:1), and the prophet instructs by his words alone (2:3). There is no image of the prophet or of the venerable fire secured from the first temple, and the only things "seen" are its brilliance (1:32) and God's glory (2:8), neither of which is actually described.[6]

In the story of the temple fire, Jeremiah forms a type of lineage by appearing after Judas Maccabeus (1:10b) and Nehemiah (1:18–36) yet before Solomon (2:9–12) and Moses (2:10–11). Jeremiah is the center and linchpin of a line encompassing leading figures from Israel's past

---

6. In reception aesthetics used in the analysis of ancient Israel, one finds the argument that developments in theology, specifically the emergence of monotheism, brought about changes in media such as the discontinuance of images in literary production. Although the claim of a cause-and-effect relationship between theology and the erasure of imagery cannot itself be evaluated here, it suggests a path for further investigation with regard to 2 Maccabees. See Schaper 2019, 65–159.

and present.[7] The role is not new to Jeremiah. In the beginning of the book of Jeremiah, notes Yosefa Raz (2013, 89), Jeremiah's unique authority is established when he is cast as "a prophet in the shadow of Mosaic and Deuteronomistic leaders."[8] Jeremiah 1, Raz adds, "frames the entire book" inasmuch as it suggests that the lineage and chronology of his life "thematizes an anxiety over the causes and effects of national history." In 2 Maccabees, the character of Jeremiah similarly represents a highly valued historical tradition within which the events of the narrative occur. Jeremiah authorizes and legitimates these events, in particular the temple's rededication and its annual commemoration in the Hanukkah celebration.

As in the biblical book bearing his name, Jeremiah functions as a frame for 2 Maccabees. The frame provides unity and coherence while it extends the authorizing function of Jeremiah across this text. In 2 Macc 2:1–8, Jeremiah is one of five illustrious ancestors. There is, in addition, the second reference to Jeremiah in 2 Maccabees that together with the first creates a framing structure. After 2 Macc 2:1–8, Jeremiah is not seen until 2 Macc 15:13–16:

> Then in the same fashion another appeared [εἶθ᾽ οὕτως ἐπιφανῆναι ἄνδρα πολιᾷ], distinguished by his gray hair and dignity, and of marvelous majesty and authority. And Onias spoke, saying, "This is a man who loves the family of Israel and prays much for the people and the holy city—Jeremiah, the prophet of God." Jeremiah stretched out his right hand and gave to Judas a golden sword, and as he gave it he addressed him thus: "Take this holy sword, a gift from God, with which you will strike down your adversaries."[9]

---

7. The placement of Jeremiah in the center of the line of leaders functions chiastically. Because the chiasm is a rhetorical technique by which ancient authors sought to persuade readers, the words of Elisabeth Schüssler Fiorenza (2014, 183) apply: "A critical rhetorical analysis not only seeks to uncover the means by which authors and interpreters seek to convince and motivate their readers but also asks about the structures of domination inscribed in the text and their function in particular rhetorical situations and particular sociohistorical locations."

8. Raz (2013, 94) elaborates: "[In Jeremiah 1], though Moses is not mentioned by name, there are a number of elements that hint at his phantom presence as Jeremiah's prophetic 'ancestor,' suggesting a prophetic lineage to replace the lost stability of the line of Judean monarchs."

9. Unless otherwise indicated, biblical citations are from the New Revised Standard Version (NRSV).

In antiquity, hairstyle served as a cultural marker. By design, Jeremiah's hair communicates his exalted status, as Brigitte Kahl (2017, 211) writes: "[Hairstyle] can indicate uncivilized, subhuman and near-beastly [status] *or* superior, even god-like status—being assimilated with the distinction between nature/animals (bushy and wild hair) and culture/human (well groomed hair or no hair)."[10] The latter designation of divinity (or better, a demigod) here applies to Jeremiah inasmuch as his gray hair is marked with dignity.[11] The verb ἐπιφανῆναι coupled with the prophet in 15:13 is associated in 2 Maccabees with miraculous appearances by the God of Israel (2:21; 3:24; 5:4; 12:22; 14:15) as noted by Robert Doran (2012, 215).[12] Accordingly, Jeremiah is further described in terms of majesty (μεγαλοπρεπεστάτην) and authority (ὑπεροχήν). When love moves Jeremiah to pray for the holy city Jerusalem and its inhabitants, it echoes Jer 29:7.[13] The scene comes to a climax when Jeremiah hands Judas Maccabeus a golden sword. The sword conjures up images of divine weapons like Zeus's lightning bolt as it strikes straight down from heaven.[14] Presently,

---

10. In addition, there may be a comparison to the divine figure on high in Dan 7:9 LXX, whose hair is described as καὶ τὸ τρίχωμα τῆς κεφαλῆς αὐτοῦ ὡσεὶ ἔριον λευκὸν καθαρ.

11. Racine (2015, 6) notes that when the report of visions conveys a claim of authority, "the speaker assumes a privileged position in relation to the divine realm." In personal correspondence, Racine points out that Onias, who was murdered in 2 Macc 4:35, identifies Jeremiah in 15:13–16. The high priest's role is essential because he is deemed reliable and speaks from beyond the grave with the authority of heaven.

12. Doran (2012, 292) observes, "[The verb's] use here would seem not just to imply a simple appearance [of Jeremiah] … but also to bring with it the connotation of a divine action."

13. Jeremiah 29:7 reads: "But seek the welfare of the city where I have sent you into exile, and pray to the LORD on its behalf, for in its welfare you will find your welfare." To "seek the welfare of the city where I have sent you into exile" has hegemonic overtones. Lundbom (2004, 351) comments: "'To seek the welfare of one's city' would certainly mean not to engage in revolt." The tone of law and order is consistent with Maccabean rhetoric.

14. Earlier in the narrative of 2 Maccabees, emissaries sent from heaven wore golden armor (3:25) and brandished golden weapons (11:8). Moreover, in the book of Jeremiah the sword as weapon is a motif with חרב (sword) attested seventy-one times, typically as the means of chastising God's sinful people. Evidence of this is found in the passages from Jer 11 and 12 cited above. In the final chapters of Jeremiah, however, the sword (50:35–37) signals retribution visited upon the Babylonians, whose misfortune results in their diverse population becoming as women (50:37). On the pejorative portrayal of women in Jeremiah, see Sharp (2013, 39).

with the same golden sword Judas destroys the Seleucids' last hope, that is, Nicanor and his forces. The victory is described as a manifestation of God's power (15:27: τῇ τοῦ θεοῦ μεγάλως εὐφρανθέντες ἐπιφανείᾳ), and rightly so as the sword was a gift from God given by Jeremiah.

The image of Jeremiah completes the frame around the narrative of 2 Maccabees with rapidity. As such, it signals Kahneman's fast thinking, also known as system 1 thinking. The sword appears, and in short time Nicanor is beheaded. Just as quickly, his head is publicly displayed in Jerusalem at a liturgically auspicious moment, when the priests are stationed before the altar (15:31–32). Judas takes pains to show his compatriots the disgraced, dismembered Nicanor, who thus becomes a second image, in addition to that of Jeremiah, capable of motivating the masses. With this graphic scene the book of 2 Maccabees concludes by stating that the rites conducted with Nicanor's severed head would be recalled annually in a celebration on the thirteenth day of the twelfth month. Rather quickly, as Daniel Schwartz (2008, 10) observes, Nicanor's Day would evolve into Hanukkah. This chain of events allows little time for contemplation or consideration of alternatives. As the image of Jeremiah as demigod motivates the troops resisting the Seleucids, it also authorizes their actions. The authorization extends to the subsequent rituals: the priests' ministrations, Nicanor's Day and Hanukkah. Inasmuch as these rituals occur in and around the newly rededicated second temple, whose authorization is first indicated in 2 Macc 2:1–8, the frame of authorization around the book of 2 Maccabees is joined together in all its constitutive parts.

Jeremiah: A Vulnerable Prophet

The events described in chapter 15 signal the conclusion of 2 Maccabees.[15] The frame begun in 2 Macc 2 is completed, and the graphic images of Jeremiah and of Nicanor defeated serve as the final word, victory, to a violent narrative. Throughout the conclusion, fast thinking is relentless, and there is no nuance to God's justice in the face of attacks upon Jerusalem by hostile forces. Yet there are other portraits of Jeremiah beyond that of the prophet advancing a golden sword.

The parallel frames in 2 Maccabees and the book of Jeremiah are a *coincidencia oppositorum* with the emphasis upon *oppositorum*. Readers

---

15. 2 Macc 15:37–39, the compiler's apology, is an epilogue.

of 2 Maccabees will recall that Jeremiah's story begins in the seventh century BCE. He is said to prophesy in Judah and Jerusalem over a period of decades into the following century. This was the time of the exile with the forced migration of scores of Israelites from Jerusalem to Babylon.[16] Jeremiah's biography reflects the vulnerability of the community, and he himself is described as suffering loss, dislocation and injustice.[17] As this motif of vulnerability is not explicitly attested in 2 Maccabees, it would be a stretch to say that the original readers were focused upon it, and it cannot simply be read into the text. The fact remains, however, that in the mid-second century BCE there were different Jeremiah traditions circulating literarily, each contributing to a historical consciousness that the text would impart to the reader. The vulnerable Jeremiah was a distinct channel of historical consciousness. That being said, where is the vulnerable Jeremiah in 2 Maccabees? Derrida (1981, 63) writes that the text hides something in order that it might imply that same thing, which is embodied and represented but not disclosed. That which is implied, in this case Jeremian vulnerability, is not hidden randomly as if it were simply lost. Edward Said (1983, 216) observes that it is the nature of texts to conceal a thing yet imply it, to designate it as a cultural "opposite" so that it may be kept in isolation. In this case, that which is undisclosed yet implied is Jeremiah's stance against brutality and his embrace of vulnerability.[18]

Many biblical interpreters of Jeremiah today focus on this aspect of his story. As Madipoeane Masenya writes (2010, 153): "Exile is experienced today in South Africa by African-South African people.... The experience of African and Judean exiles losing their lands for foreigners was powerful." Jeremiah, like the psalmists, laments that the land has been lost and thus experiences its own suffering (Jer 12:1–4). The prophet asks God,

---

16. See Boda et al. 2015, 77–94.

17. In Jer 11:18 and following the prophet speaks directly to God in a series of laments that are personal in tone while expressing the corporate agony of all the people. The series concludes at 20:18, and in many cases the prophet's lament is followed by a matching response from God. See Holladay (1986, 358).

18. The theory of fast thinking/slow thinking suggests a model of reading that incorporates the martial Jeremiah and the vulnerable Jeremiah; the undisclosed, implied vulnerable Jeremiah would be an effect of slow thinking, which is logical, analytical, and critical. Slow thinking involves solutions to situations that cannot be resolved immediately by making connections to ideas related to the current train of thought (i.e., fast thinking). Jeremiah in a warrior motif (15:13–16) triggers fast thinking and direct action, but slow thinking that critiques the motif is also a factor.

"How long will the land mourn, and the grass of every field wither?" (12:4). The figure of Jeremiah, notes Kathleen O'Connor (2012, 274) "embraces suffering of many kinds. The artistry of the book named after him captures suffering of women across the ages. Although he is God's chosen spokesperson, he meets rejection and pain at every turn. In this way he can encourage and even comfort women and men who suffer in related ways, actual or more distant." The artistry of the book, O'Connor emphasizes, allows for the suffering described therein to reverberate across periods of time, and even the more distant readers can relate to Jeremiah's pain and rejection. In the twenty-first century, Masenya and O'Connor are but two of the many scholars who read Jeremiah in the context of loss and suffering. In the wake of individual and societal trauma, those who search for meaning may employ Jeremiah as a guidepost.

In the book of Jeremiah, suffering sometimes comes at the hands of personal enemies: "I was like a gentle lamb led to the slaughter. And I did not know it was against me that they devised schemes, saying, 'Let us destroy the tree with its fruit, let us cut him off from the land of the living, so that his name will no longer be remembered!'" (11:19).[19] According to the text, the people of Anathoth and of the ancestral houses who oppose Jeremiah and disregard the Lord are punished severely with a consuming sword wielded by God (11:22; 12:12). It appears, however, that divine justice, howsoever swift, is no solace to Jeremiah, who remains a symbol of vulnerability and suffering. The prophet actually tells God "you are acquitted," if one translates Jer 12:1a as does Holladay (1986, 375) by reading forensic vocabulary. Jeremiah pronounces an acquittal of God for wielding the sword, as if the action itself were criminal. Here the biblical text reflects system 2 cognition or thinking that is grounded in something other than either immediate feelings of liking and disliking or facile understandings of pain and pleasure. Divine retribution meted out to his enemies is no consolation to Jeremiah, who is peaceable in the extreme.

The portrait of the prophet Jeremiah as vulnerable yet peaceable has appealed to later generations and allowed them to attribute a certain historical consciousness to this prophet. Masenya (2010) and O'Connor

---

19. Jeremiah gives the impression that he is a sacrificial victim, and Jeremiah's enemies speak in the cohortative "let us destroy." The background of the quotation is the law in Deut 20:19 forbidding the destroying of a fruit-bearing tree as found within a besieged city. Jeremiah identifies with the fruit-bearing tree in Deuteronomy as he relates his struggles with his adversaries. See Holladay (1986, 372).

(2011) offer readers a Jeremian hermeneutics of empathy, and there is no reason to limit such readings to our current era. In the period when 2 Maccabees was written, not long after the Seleucid empire persecuted Jerusalem, readers of this text were doubtless aware of the figure of Jeremiah as a channel of historical consciousness that, unlike the hegemonic powers of the day, was not monolithic. It is plausible that some members of the second-century community identified with Jeremiah in terms of his vulnerability. Although the vulnerable and nonviolent Jeremiah is undisclosed and implicit in 2 Maccabees, it is plausible that its first readers made connections with his other side, which *is* disclosed and made explicit in the book of Jeremiah.[20] The other side of Jeremiah reflects an icon of suffering who finds no relief in a devastating sword (Jer 11:22; 12:12), even when it expresses divine judgment, the justice of God. Across the divide, however, the writers of 2 Maccabees lift up for all to see the prophet who brings a sword authorizing the violent campaign of Judas Maccabeus.

Conclusion: Paradox and Community

Dreams and visions pose a challenge to readers of ancient texts, with 2 Maccabees serving as a special case. Jeremiah appears in a dream and presents the protagonist with a golden sword that figures prominently in the violent narrative's final action. The image of Jeremiah late in 2 Maccabees cannot be interpreted without reference to its earlier description of the prophet, which forms a frame around the narrative for the purpose of authorizing it. Furthermore, if one looks outside of the frame, one sees other faces of Jeremiah, such as the vulnerable and suffering Judean prophet associated with loss and exile. While the vulnerable Jeremiah—who is very much in the view of biblical interpreters in the twenty-first century—is indeed outside the textual framework, he can be located within it, and within 2 Maccabees, as an implicit and undisclosed character. In its fullest expression, the challenge is thus to integrate the very different traditions of Jeremiah that are invoked by this Second Temple period text, or at least to align them in some meaningful way. How can a single text contain two Jeremiahs, one violent and the other vulnerable? One represented in a striking vision, the other

---

20. See in the following section further discussion of the Jerusalem community responsible for 2 Maccabees (i.e., its first readers, in the first century BCE).

invisible and implicit? In terms of literary analysis, the deconstruction of 2 Maccabees into a binary opposition clarifies the issues in the text, violence or vulnerability, but it is hardly a result that satisfies the biblical reader. A narrative such as 2 Maccabees today calls for creative thinking, especially with regard to community. In contrast to the dichotomous reading that precludes new insights into community, Jeremian violence and vulnerability can be explored as a paradox that, in turn, sheds light on emerging models of community. The issue of paradox is a familiar one to postcritical readers of Jeremiah who seek sites of meaning in the book's more difficult passages.

L. Juliana Claassens (2017, 609) has drawn attention to the paradox whereby Jeremiah reports hatred for God because God had violated him (Jer 20:7) and in the same breath professes God "to be the Liberator-Warrior God who delivers the needy from the hands of evildoers" (20:11, 13). These sharply divergent divine metaphors indicate "contestation and contradiction" that is deep within the character of Jeremiah. The prophet's paradox extends to the community that is writing his narrative: "These divine metaphors that are rooted in contestation and contradiction reflect the deep-seated paradox of faith experienced by the prophet that, quite likely, also belonged to the people during the time of the Babylonian invasion and exile" (611). Claassens further demonstrates that in communities under such duress, new language for God sometimes emerges. That is, conflicting images of God, who is "both destroyer and a delivering presence," show how Jeremiah and the people "struggle to make sense of the inexplicable" as they articulate their experience (618). Out of anguish, theological creativity arises.

In the case of 2 Maccabees, the Jewish forces defending Jerusalem experience duress, and loss is looming large. There is, however, a historical gap between when these events occurred in the second century BCE and the writing of 2 Maccabees roughly fifty years later.[21] Thus, the community of 2 Maccabees is no longer the oppressed, but they run the risk

---

21. Since 2 Macc 1:9 refers to the year 188 of the Seleucid era (125/124 BCE), the date provides the *terminus ad quem* for the prefatory letters and for the book as a whole. Schwartz (2008, 11) has suggested a different reading of the date, placing the composition earlier in 143/142 BCE, but even that scenario allows for a generation to have passed since the beginning of institutionalized Hellenism under Jason in 175 BCE.

of becoming the oppressors.[22] They are no longer vulnerable, but at what price would they make themselves invulnerable? They are a conflicted community sorting through their own legacy of trauma and the opportunities newly available to them because they prevailed over the Seleucids. In our world today, this community would be poised for a process of healing and reconciliation.[23] In such a process, the biblical Jeremiah could serve as a resource. A sense of solidarity and shared strength can arise when those who have known suffering meditate on the examples of Jeremiah. At the same time, readers will note how Nicanor's beheading and the subsequent public spectacle serve as the impetus for Nicanor's Day and other national holidays. What is actually celebrated on these occasions? Is it the values of the community or the destruction of those who would oppose it? Are readers invited to envision the future or to indulge themselves with a revenge fantasy? In this context, appealing to Jeremiah means wrestling with the paradox of violence and vulnerability and weighing the moral options that are before the readers of 2 Maccabees, in antiquity and as well today.

With these hermeneutics of community, the sword of Jeremiah remains a touchstone. The bladed imagery found in 2 Macc 15:13–16 and Jer 11:22 and 12:12 recurs again in Jeremiah 20. This chapter begins with the priest Pashur punishing Jeremiah and putting him in the stocks (Jer 20:1–2). Jeremiah responds with an oracle in which Pashur and his allies are either slain by the sword of the Babylonians or taken to exile and there dispatched by the sword (Jer 20:4). The prophet changes the name of Pashur, who is now to be called "terror-all-around."[24] In the words of Claassens (2017,

---

22. In 143/142 BCE, Demetrius II extended to Judea exemption from all taxes. As reported in 1 Macc 13:36–40, this policy signaled that "the yoke of the gentiles was removed from Israel" (1 Macc 13:41). The decree also calls for peace to prevail between the Seleucids and Judeans (13:37, 40) with clemency extended to all in Judea for any "errors or offences" that they had committed (13:39).

23. Although its historicity can be debated, the decree of Demetrius II (see previous note) suggests that armed conflict did not truly end until there was a durable peace based on reconciliation. Hostilities remained until there was reconciliation involving reparations as well as accountability. In the modern era, the systematic crimes of regimes over decades have led to high-profile commissions of truth and reconciliation. See for example Stanley (2001, 525–46); Spooner (2011, 73–94); Arsenault (2015, 15–17).

24. Although the clash with Pashur is distinct from the lament of Jeremiah (20:7–13), both passages are part of the basic stratum of this section of Jeremiah, and there is linkage between them ("terror-all-around" recurs in 20:10). See Holladay (1986, 537).

614): "Pashur's new name thus points beyond the suffering he inflicted on Jeremiah to violent death by the sword and plundering the city's wealth by the Babylonian invaders." In a footnote, Claassens describes Pashur's fate as "ironic" (614 n. 19); Jeremiah's tormentor will himself be subject to violence and incarceration. The oppressor will now be oppressed. Is this twist of Pashur's fate merely ironic? In the biographical context of Jeremiah, who in chapter 20 is highly vulnerable, the language of "suffering-all-around" undermines the sword and indicts those who would use it gratuitously. Wielding the sword to avenge Jeremiah or punish Pashur would be dubious. Anyone who has identified with the vulnerable Jeremiah or developed empathy for the incarcerated would have little appetite for such capital punishment. A community that celebrates the sword would appear to be morally compromised, even if it had previously been aggrieved. The text never states these truths because it does not need to; the paradox of violence and vulnerability speaks for itself.

In 2 Maccabees, the figure of Jeremiah provides a frame, a window through which the considerable violence that is laced throughout the book's narrative is to be viewed and understood. While the ancient authors of this text intended a triumphal reading of the text keyed to the golden sword of the prophet, we have seen that other readings are possible. Other readings, in fact, are encouraged in light of Jeremiah's other legacy as a vulnerable prophet who is himself subjected to violence. Communities that have endured suffering and survived will find in the sword a great challenge. Just as it can be a haunting symbol of their past trauma, it can be a weapon that they take up to define their future. Or it can be something new, a sword marked by contradiction and paradox. Jeremiah, who both implicates God in his suffering and praises God for delivering the needy, shows that in the paradox God is revealed through theological language previously unavailable. But to encounter *that* God, and speak *that* language, a community must make a choice.

Bibliography

Arsenault, Virginia. 2015. "Resistance to the Canadian Truth and Reconciliation Commission." *Swisspeace* 2:1–42.

Bautch, Richard J. 2019. "Reading Judith, Tobit and 2 Maccabees as Responses to Hegemony." Pages 157–73 in *Intertextual Explorations in Deuterocanonical and Cognate Literature*. Edited by Jeremy Corley and Geoffrey David Miller. DCLS 31. Berlin: de Gruyter.

Claassens, L. Juliana. 2017. "Not Being Content with God: Contestation and Contradiction in Communities under Duress." *OTE* 30:609–29.
Derrida, Jacques. 1981. *Dissemination*. Translated and edited by Barbara Johnson. Chicago: University of Chicago Press.
Doran, Robert. 2012. *2 Maccabees*. Hermeneia. Minneapolis: Fortress.
Fröhlich, Ida. 1996. *Time and Times and Half a Time: Historical Consciousness in the Jewish Literature of the Persian and Hellenistic Eras*. JSPSup 19. Sheffield: Sheffield Academic Press.
Goldstein, Jonathan A. 1983. *II Maccabees: A New Translation with Introduction and Commentary*. AB 41A. Garden City, NY: Doubleday.
Gruen, Erich S. 2016. *The Construct of Identity in Hellenistic Judaism*. DCLS 29. Berlin: de Gruyter.
Holladay, William L. 1986. *Jeremiah 1: A Commentary on the Book of the Prophet Jeremiah, Chapters 1–25*. Edited by Paul D. Hanson. Hermeneia. Philadelphia: Fortress.
Iorgoveanu, Aurora, and Nicoleta Corbu. 2012. "No Consensus on Framing? Toward an Integrative Approach to Define Frames Both as Text and Visuals." *Romanian Journal of Communication and Public Relations* 14:91–102.
Kahl, Brigitte. 2017. "*The Galatian Suicide* and the Transbinary Semiotics of *Christ Crucified* (Galatians 3:1): Exercises in Visual Exegesis and Critical Reimagination." Pages 195–240 in *The Art of Visual Exegesis: Rhetoric, Texts, Images*. Edited by Vernon K. Robbins, Walter S. Melion, and Roy R. Jeal. ESEC 19. Atlanta: SBL Press.
Kahneman, Daniel. 2011. *Thinking, Fast and Slow*. New York: Farrar, Straus and Giroux.
Lange, Armin. 2017. "Jeremia in Den Makkabäerbüchern." Pages 209–19 in *Die Makkabäer*. Edited by Friedrich Avemarie et al. WUNT 382. Tübingen: Mohr Siebeck.
Leuchter, Mark. 2015. "Sacred Space and Communal Legitimacy in Exile: The Contribution of Seraiah's Colophon (Jer 51:59–64a)." Pages 77–100 in *The Prophets Speak on Forced Migration*. Edited by Mark J. Boda, Frank Ritchel Ames, John Ahn, and Mark Leuchter. AIL 21. Atlanta: SBL Press.
Lundbom, Jack R. 2004. *Jeremiah 21–36: A New Translation with Introduction and Commentary*. AB 21B. New York: Doubleday.
Maier, Christl M., and Carolyn J. Sharp, eds. 2013. *Prophecy and Power: Jeremiah in Feminist and Postcolonial Perspective*. LHBOTS 577. London: Bloomsbury.

Masenya, Madipoane. 2010. "Jeremiah." Pages 147–56 in *The Africana Bible: Reading Israel's Scriptures from Africa and the African Diaspora*. Edited by Hugh R. Page et al. Minneapolis: Fortress.
O'Connor, Kathleen M. 2011. *Jeremiah: Pain and Promise*. Minneapolis: Fortress.
———. 2012. "Jeremiah." Pages 267–77 in *Women's Bible Commentary*. 3rd ed. Edited by Carol A. Newsom, Sharon H. Ringe, and Jacqueline E. Lapsley. Louisville: Westminster John Knox.
Portier-Young, Anathea E. 2011. *Apocalypse against Empire: Theologies of Resistance in Early Judaism*. Grand Rapids: Eerdmans.
Racine, Jean-François. 2015. "Envisioning Visions in the Bible: Methodological Note on Possible Approaches." Paper presented at The International Meeting of the Catholic Biblical Association of America. New Orleans, LA. 4 August.
Raz, Yosefa. 2013. "Jeremiah 'Before the Womb': On Fathers, Sons, and the Telos of Redaction in Jeremiah 1." Pages 86–100 in *Prophecy and Power: Jeremiah in Feminist and Postcolonial Perspective*. Edited by Christl M. Maier and Carolyn J. Sharp. LHBOTS 577. London: Bloomsbury.
Robbins, Vernon K. 2008. "Rhetography: A New Way of Seeing the Familiar Text." Pages 81–106 in *Words Well Spoken: George Kennedy's Rhetoric of the New Testament*. Edited by C. Clifton Black and Duane F. Watson. StRR 8. Waco, TX: Baylor University Press.
Said, Edward W. 1983. *The World, the Text, and the Critic*. Cambridge: Harvard University Press.
Schaper, Joachim. 2019. *Media and Monotheism: Presence, Representation, and Abstraction in Ancient Judah*. ORA 33. Tübingen: Mohr Siebeck.
Schüssler Fiorenza, Elisabeth. 2014. "Response to John R. Lanci: Transforming the Discipline—The Rhetoricity/Rhetoricality of New Testament Studies." Pages 165–99 in *Genealogies of New Testament Rhetorical Criticism*. Edited by Troy W. Martin. Minneapolis: Fortress.
Schwartz, Daniel R. 2008. *2 Maccabees*. CEJL. Berlin: de Gruyter.
Sharp, Carolyn J. 2013. "Mapping Jeremiah as/in a Feminist Landscape: Negotiating Ancient and Contemporary Terrains." Pages 38–56 in *Prophecy and Power: Jeremiah in Feminist and Postcolonial Perspective*. Edited by Christl M. Maier and Carolyn J. Sharp. LHBOTS 577. London: Bloomsbury.
Spooner, Mary Helen. 2011. *The General's Slow Retreat: Chile after Pinochet*. Berkeley: University of California Press.

Stanley, Elizabeth. 2001. "Evaluating the Truth and Reconciliation Commission." *The Journal of Modern African Studies* 39:525–46.

Dreams of Empire: Pilate's Wife in Matthew

Roy Allan Fisher

The way I direct is always about simultaneity.
For me what is interesting in drama is ...
what Bahktin would call dialogic imagination,
where the truth is never here or here
but it's in the dialogue of these things happening
at the same time, hovering in between.
—Peter Sellars

In a darkened concert hall, a woman dressed in simple black attire with her head bowed and eyes closed slowly rises from among a similarly dressed chorus sitting on a series of nondescript risers. Her arms and head gracefully unfold, expanding outward as she stands, her haunting voice emerging out of this upward opening movement: "Habe du nichts zu schaffen mit diesem Gerechten" (English translation: "Have nothing to do with this righteous man"). Her right arm floats higher, pulling her body upward until her right hand lightly brushes the top of her head where the movement crests then begins to recede, her hands slowly moving in and down sensually caressing her face and neck, gently tracing her body as she folds inward, singing "ich habe heute viel erlitten im Traum von seinetwegen" (English translation: "for today I have suffered much in a dream because of him") before finally sinking back into the chorus whence she came. Thus appears the apparition that is Pilate's wife in Peter Sellars's monumental 2010 staging of Johann Sebastian Bach's *Matthäus-Passion* with the Berliner Philharmoniker and the Rundfunkchor Berlin.[1]

---

1. Bach's *St. Matthew's Passion* BWV 244 (original Latin title: *Passio Domini nostri J.C. secundum Evangelistam Matthæum*) was first performed for the 1727 Good Friday vespers service in St. Thomas Church in Leipzig.

While it may seem strange to begin an analysis of dreams in Matthew's Gospel with a contemporary rendition of the *Matthäus-Passion*, Sellars's staging of this single line from Bach's score embodies Matthew's text in a way that even now continues to bedevil many, if not a majority, of New Testament scholars. At first glance, it might appear that Sellars's staging introduces no new material, but upon closer examination Sellars's staging involves an important interpretative move in reading Matthew's passion narrative. Pilate's wife's words spoken in Sellars's dreamscape are, of course, the very same words attributed to her in Matthew's Gospel. Whereas in Matthew the audience may only hear her words as being mediated through the voice of the narrator, Bach makes the important decision to have the audience hear Pilate's wife speak her words herself.[2] In Sellars's staging, Bach's interpretative move is carried even further by the embodied animation of Pilate's wife. This not only gives her voice but explicitly enshrouds that voice in an animated female body. It is this embodied voice that underscores the active role of Pilate's wife in Matthew's passion narrative. So, while there are no new words in Sellars's staging, his animation of Matthew's text does introduce new material, namely bodies, into the reading of Matthew's passion. The power of Sellars's remediation is that he successfully animates this scene, reintroducing breath and motion in a way that is simultaneously faithful to but not bound by the texts (both Bach and Matthew's). Through this powerful remediation, Sellars renders visible, contra most contemporary scholarly readings of Matthew, the fact that Pilate's wife is not a one-dimensional foil to the obstinate Jews of Matthew's (and Jesus's) day. As I will unpack below, Sellars beautifully captures Matthew's foregrounding of the dialogue between Pilate and his wife so as to draw our attention away from the crowds (e.g., the Jews). It is not insignificant that Pilate's wife is the only woman in the whole of the biblical canon who is said to have had a dream. The intrusion of Pilate's wife into Matthew's narrative is neither gratuitous nor incidental. Something of much deeper significance is afoot. As Sellars makes visible, for Matthew *this woman* and *her words to Pilate* are important. To see this woman, who both dreams

---

2. In his score Bach quotes the 1534 Luther Bible verbatim. I should note that women were not allowed to sing sacred music in St. Thomas Church during Bach's lifetime. Pilate's wife's words would have been sung by a member of the *Thomanerchor*, the boys choir associated with the *Thomaskirche* and directed by Bach (the *Thomaskantor*) from 1723 to 1750.

and speaks, as a foil to the Jews is to miss another instance of Matthew's ongoing critique of imperial power.

This brief vision of Pilate's wife—twenty-seven words in the Greek text—has long provoked a host of questions for interpreters of the passage.[3] From whence comes her dream, and to what end? Does Pilate truly hear and/or heed her warning? Regarding the first question, we must confess ignorance. Matthew gives no clue as to her name or identity apart from her marriage to Pilate. We are simply told that while Pilate was sitting on the judgment seat ἡ γυνὴ αὐτοῦ (his wife) sent word to him. Sellars's animation of Pilate's wife mirrors the phantasmal nature of her role in Matthew's Gospel, appearing suddenly in the opening description of Jesus's judgment before Pilate, uttering her mysterious words, and then just as quickly vanishing back into the chorus. The brief and mysterious nature of her appearance in Matthew led Raymond Brown (1994, 1:294–304) to pair her with the unnamed youth of Mark's Gospel who fled away naked when Jesus was arrested in the garden of Gethsemane (Mark 14:51–52). For Brown, they are two minor characters in the gospel passion narratives who "serve the insatiable desire of interpreters to make whole stories out of one verse." As I demonstrate below, as Sellars's staging of this scene renders so powerfully visible, sometimes one verse alone can indeed signal an important message. As for the remaining two questions, there is much that can and needs to be said about Pilate's wife and her dream.

Dreams and Visions

It should be noted here at the outset that this brief essay does not attempt to psychoanalyze any of the dream reports found in Matthew. As Ernst Ludwig Ehrlich (1953, v) rightly pointed out well over a half-century ago, "The biblical authors who tell us about dreams did not have these dreams themselves. We are dealing with a stylistic device they employed or only with elements of a dream image that they wove into their descriptions." In other words, we do not have any first-person accounts of individual dreams, and thus this analysis will remain at the level of the text itself. As Robert K. Gnuse (1996, 68) puts it, "Dream reports are literary-theological forms, and the attempt to penetrate behind the text is doomed to fail." Simply put, I can neither

---

3. For a summary of the passage, see Brown (1994, 1:803–4) and Luz (2005, 499).

inquire into the mind of Pilate's wife nor can I answer the question of what exactly she may or may not have seen, heard, or experienced.

Sellars's staging is instructive not for any psychoanalytic value but insofar as it renders unambiguously clear the fact that Pilate's wife must be both *seen* and *seen in relation* to the other bodies in Matthew's narrative, including, most importantly, that of Pilate himself. From its opening lines depicting Jesus being bound and brought before Pilate, Matthew's passion account is densely packed with earthy images of bodies (bodies that are bound, hung, buried, standing, sitting, dreaming, suffering, shouting, washed, bloodied, stripped, beaten, spitting, crucified, crying, given, wrapped, placed/laid, etc.). Women in Matthew's Gospel are *women*, that is to say, female bodies and not merely furniture.

As Sellars's staging makes visible, for Matthew Pilate's wife and her dream function as important narrative vectors relative to Pilate. An embodied reading of this dream scene is not a modern imposition on the text, but one that is fully congruent with ancient perceptions of dreams. In the ancient world, as Gnuse (1996, 34) suggests, dreams were understood to be, "phenomena with a special reality of their own" not as "psychological experiences of the mind." Gnuse suggests furthermore that dreams were not considered out-of-body experiences, rather it was understood that "the dream was experienced by the total person in a real fashion" (69). Thus, Pilate's wife's dream cannot be disentangled from the embodied reality of Pilate's wife in the narrative if we are to remain faithful to Matthew's narrative.

Dreams and visions appear throughout the literature of the Greco-Roman world of the first century. John S. Hanson (1980, 1413–14) summarizes the most common function of the dream and/or vision in this period with the following:

> The majority of extant dream-vision reports from Graeco-Roman antiquity are found in narrative contexts: histories, novels, biographies, letters. Despite these various literary contexts, the dream-vision report is frequently understandable in itself; it does not require the literary context for its coherence. Yet the dream-visions are not merely decorative, but often function to direct or redirect the movement of the narrative, and not simply that of the dreamer, though they may coincide.

As we will see below, Matthew likewise situates his dream reports within a narrative context while simultaneously playing with the reader's expectation that a dream would function to (re)direct the movement of the narrative.

Within the traditions of Israel, including New Testament texts, dreams are generally understood to be from God, and as a general rule dreams were not understood to come from either the realm of the dead or demonic powers. For Shaul Bar (2001, 218), dreams serve in much of biblical literature as a medium of communication between humans and God. God is the source of the dreams and the dreamer is passive. This is not to say that dreams are universally seen in a positive light in the biblical tradition. In the postexilic period, there does seem to be a period of time when dreams as a mode of revelation were viewed with suspicion and even hostility (e.g., Num 12:6–8; Deut 13:2–6; Isa 29:7–8; Jer 23:25–32; 27:9–10; Zech 10:2; Sir 34:1–5; 40:5–7).

According to Gnuse (1996, 96–100), dreams appear more frequently and tend to be viewed much more positively in Second Temple Jewish literature (after ca. 250 BCE). This is especially true when it comes to popular folk practices and beliefs attributed to Jews in the Second Temple period. In general, the dreams and visions found in Second Temple Jewish literature do not appear to differ in any significant way from dream and visions in the larger Greco-Roman world. As in the larger ancient world, the purpose of dream reports as literary devices in both the Hebrew scriptures and the New Testament is most often to "advance the plot by divine direction" (Gnuse 1996, 68). In the New Testament, dreams and visions are never attributed to demons or occult powers. Consistent with other Second Temple Jewish texts (e.g., Josephus), New Testament accounts of dreams and visions are best described as a blend of forms reflecting traditional Israelite (e.g., ancient Near Eastern) and Greco-Roman beliefs, language, and styles.

Looking more closely at the New Testament, there do not appear to be any explicit accounts of dreams in the letters of Paul, but there are several references to visionary phenomena of some form (Gal 1:15–17; 2:2; 1 Cor 9:1; 14:6, 26; 15:3–8; 2 Cor 12:1–7). It is only in the Gospels and Acts that we find explicit dream and/or vision reports.[4] Within the Synoptic accounts, these dream/vision reports appear in three general

---

4. There are three proper terms used for visions in the New Testament. The first is ὅραμα, occurring mostly in Acts (Acts 7:31; 9:10, 12; 10:3, 17, 19; 11:5; 12:9; 16:9; 18:9) and one time in Matthew (Matt 17:9; Matthew's description of the transfiguration). The second term is ὀπτασία, found in Luke 1:22; 24:23; Acts 26:19; 2 Cor 12:1. The final term, ὅρασις, occurs only once (Rev 9:17).

clusters.⁵ The first cluster is composed of the dreams/visions in Matthew and Luke's infancy narratives (Matt 1:18–2:23; Luke 1:5–38; 2:8–10). The second general cluster involves the transfiguration pericopes (Mark 9:2–9; Matt 17:1–9; and Luke 9:28–36). The third clustering of dreams/visions occurs at the end of the Gospels beginning with the various accounts of the appearance by a young man at the tomb of Jesus (Mark 16:1–8; Matt 28:1–10; Luke 24:1–9), as well as the various postresurrection appearances of Jesus (Matt 28:26–20; Mark 16:9–20; Luke 24:36–53).⁶ Notably, the account of Pilate's wife and her dream in Matt 27:19 falls outside of the usual clustering of dream/vision accounts.

In spite of these frequent references to dreams and visions in the New Testament, Christian exegetes have traditionally viewed them as subordinate and even inferior literary forms. As A. Oepke (1967, 5:235) writes, "No NT witness ever thought of basing the central message, the Gospel, or an essential part of it, on dreams." Joseph Alexander (1861, 35) went so far as to refer to the dreams in Matthew as "the lowest form of revelation found in Scripture." Such pronouncements however are untenable as we will see in our close examination of the dream report found in Matt 27:19.

Dream Reports in Matthew

As mentioned above, there is some overlap between Matthew and the other Synoptic Gospels when it comes to the clustering of dreams and/or visions in the narrative, but Matthew is unique in the use of ὄναρ to reference dreams. The six occurrences of ὄναρ in the New Testament all occur in the Gospel of Matthew.⁷ Five of the six occurrences of ὄναρ occur in a tight cluster in the infancy narrative (Matt 1:20; 2:12, 13, 19, 22; 27:19) with the sixth and final appearance located in Matt 27. As scholars have long noted, the first five of these Matthaean dream reports not only appear in close proximity to each other, but also share a basic formulaic style.

---

5. This clustering of dream reports refers to their narrative location across the Synoptic tradition, but not necessarily to the actual dreams. While the Synoptics share this narrative schema, the content of the dream reports within the narrative clusters varies.

6. Here I set aside the Apocalypse of John, which is in some sense a single dream-vision.

7. The only other word for "dream" in the New Testament is ἐνύπνιον, which appears once (Acts 2:17).

While the dream report in Matt 27:19 falls outside the basic clustering of dreams in the Synoptic tradition, the appearance of ὄναρ suggests the possibility of relation between this later occurrence and the earlier cluster. In fact, there is good cause for reading the account of Pilate's wife alongside the dream accounts in the infancy narrative, especially those found in 2:12 and 2:22. Following the form-critical work of Gnuse (1996, 104–10), I have set the report of Pilate's wife's dream alongside the earlier Matthean dream reports for the purposes of comparing the sixth occurrence of ὄναρ with those found in the infancy narrative:

1. Situation (provided by the narrative)
    1:18–19 (Joseph's difficult decision)
    2:10–11 (Magi visit the holy family)
    2:13 (Magi leave Joseph)
    2:19 (Herod dies)
    2:22 (Joseph is fearful of Archelaus)
    27:19 (Pilate is sitting on the judgment seat)

2. Introduction to the Dream Report
    2.1. Participle and Postpositive δέ (genitive absolute with full dream reports and aorist participle with simple dream references)
        1:20 δὲ αὐτοῦ ἐνθυμηθέντος
        2:12 χρηματισθέντες
        2:13 Ἀναχωρησάντων δὲ αὐτῶν
        2:19 Τελευτήσαντος δὲ τοῦ Ἡρῴδου
        2:22 χρηματισθεὶς δέ
        27:19 καθημένου δέ [note that here we have present participle]
    2.2. "Behold" ἰδού
        1:20 ἰδού
        2:12 —
        2:13 ἰδού
        2:19 ἰδού
        2:22 —
        27:19 —

3. Theophany: "Angel of the Lord"
    1:20 ἄγγελος κυρίου ... ἐφάνη

2:12 —
2:13 ἄγγελος κυρίου φαίνεται
2:19 ἄγγελος κυρίου φαίνεται
2:22 —
27:19 —

4. Dream Reference
    1:20   κατ' ὄναρ
    2:12   κατ' ὄναρ
    2:13   κατ' ὄναρ
    2:19   κατ' ὄναρ
    2:22   κατ' ὄναρ
    27:15 κατ' ὄναρ

5. Human Recipient
    1:20   αὐτῷ (Joseph understood)
    2:12   — (Magi understood)
    2:13   τῷ Ἰωσὴφ
    2:19   τῷ Ἰωσὴφ
    2:22   — (Joseph understood)
    27:19 ἡ γυνὴ αὐτοῦ

6. Message/Instruction
    1:20b–21 (Joseph told to take Mary as wife)
    2:12   (Warned not to return to Herod)
    2:13   (Joseph told to flee to Egypt with the child and his mother)
    2:19   (Joseph told to return to the land of Israel)
    2:22   (Unspecified warning)
    27:19 (Troubled by the dream)

7. Termination of the Dream
    1:20   ἐγερθεὶς δὲ ὁ Ἰωσὴφ ἀπὸ τοῦ ὕπνου
    2:12   —
    2:14   ὁ δὲ ἐγερθεὶς
    2:21   ὁ δὲ ἐγερθεὶς
    2:22b —
    27:15 —

Dreams of Empire: Pilate's Wife in Matthew   93

8. Fulfillment/Response to the Message/Instruction
   1:24b   (He did as the angel of the Lord commanded him; he took her as his wife)
   2:12   (They left for their own country by another road)
   2:14-15 (Joseph got up, took the child and his mother by night, and went to Egypt)
   2:21   (Joseph got up, took the child and his mother, and went to the land of Israel)
   2:22   (He went away to the district of Galilee)
   27:24   (Pilate's wife warns him to have nothing to do with Jesus)

As this form-critical comparison make clear, the report of Pilate's wife's dream in Matt 27:19 shares a common formulaic structure with the dream reports in the infancy narrative. Additionally, these are the only six instances in Matthew (and in the New Testament period) where we find the expression κατ' ὄναρ. Taken together, the likelihood that Matt 27:19 is unrelated to the five dreams in the infancy narrative is implausible.

This shared formulaic structure does not imply a homogeneity in the six occurrences of κατ' ὄναρ. A careful examination reveals that Matt 27:19 is closer in form to the simple dream occurrences of 2:12 (the warning to the magi) and 2:22 (the warning to Joseph). Only three of the six occurrences (1:18b-24; 2:13-15; 2:19-21) may be counted as full dream reports. The other three occurrences (2:12; 2:22; 27:19) can be described as simple dream reports. This familial resemblance between the simple reports in 2:12, 2:22, and 27:19 accords well with source critical analyses of Matthew's Gospel, particularly in the infancy narrative.

While all five dreams in the infancy narrative occur in Matthew's special material, Brown (1993, 108-9) has convincingly argued that the threefold Joseph dream sequence (1:18-25; 2:13-15, 19-21) is part of preexisting "raw material" that Matthew adapts to his own ends. Brown (1993, 106-7) goes on to suggest that the vague warning via a dream in 2:22 is most likely a Matthean editorial insertion used to explain the additional movement within the narrative of the holy family to Galilee. Likewise Brown (1993, 188-96) observes the narrative involving the magi from the east (2:1-12) is also pre-Matthean in origin with the exception of another vague and unspecified warning via a simple dream in 1:12 that is necessary to unite the preexisting magi narrative to the larger Herod story into which it is inserted. In other words, Matthew uses and creates the first two simple dream reports (2:12 and 2:22) as a way to incorporate preexisting material into his narrative flow.

Key for our discussion is the recognition that the two simple dreams in the infancy narrative (2:12 and 2:22) are unique Matthean compositions. To these we can now add the simple dream found in 27:19, which also seems to be a unique Matthean contribution. Thus while all six κατ' ὄναρ passages belong to Matthew's special material, these six passages may be subdivided into two groupings. The first group includes the earlier pre-Matthean dream narratives (1:18b–24; 2:13–15, 19–21) that were edited by Matthew. The second grouping involves the simple dreams (2:12, 22; 27:19) that were Matthean creations inserted into preexisting narratives.

Pilate's Wife's Dream and the Content of 27:19

Looking more closely at Matt 27:19 reveals that just as we must confess ignorance regarding the specific identity of Pilate's wife, we are just as limited when it comes to the source and specific content and source of her dream. When it comes to the question of origin, we can only note that the larger pattern in Matthew suggests we should read an implied origin of God. The ambiguity in the text does not provide sufficient grounds for suggesting, as some have done, that Matthew had a demonic origin for the dream in mind. Such a reading would go against the grain of Matthew's other dream reports, and in the absence of some compelling textual evidence for a demonic origin we must view such speculation as being improbable.

When it comes to the specific content of Pilate's wife's dream, we find ourselves in a similarly ambiguous state. When she sends word to Pilate, his wife only reveals that she has suffered much because of a dream "about him" (κατ' ὄναρ δι' αὐτόν). Was the dream content auditory in nature? Was it visual? Was it a warning? Did Pilate's wife have a nightmare of some sort, assuming that nightmares may be a sort of message dream (Husser 1999, 160)? While we may find the details a bit sparse, we should note that the form of the narrative is itself not unusual in its first-century setting.

As Helgo Lindner (1972, 52, 69) has shown, dreadful images in dreams and protection via dreams were typical Greco-Roman literary motifs. In Josephus, the recipients of visual symbolic dreams are often described as being "perturbed" or "agitated" (e.g., *Ant.* 2.75: ἀχθόμενος) as well as "troubled" or "disturbed" (e.g., *Ant.* 2.82; 10.269: ταραχθείς). This common motif of dread or terror as being part of the dream experience is also found in the writings of Herodotus, who variously describes folk's reactions to dreams with colorful phrases such as "greatly dreaded the dream" (*Hist.* 1.34), "he feared the vision" (1.107), "fears for himself" (3.30), or "being greatly afraid" (7.14).

Commentators have also noted that Matthew's audience might have heard here an echo to the well-known dream of Calpurnia, Caesar's wife, on the night before his assassination (Plutarch, *Caes.* 63.5-7; Suetonius, *Jul.* 81.3; Appian, *Bell. civ.* 2.115; Cassius Dio, *Hist. Rom.* 44.17.1). Plutarch records that on the night before his death, Caesar observed his wife "uttering indistinct words and inarticulate groans in her sleep; for it seemed that she was holding her murdered husband in her arms and wailing for him" (Plutarch, *Caes.* 63.5). Like with Pilate's wife, aside from being ominous the precise nature of the dream content that causes the dreamer distress is unclear.

Speculation or lament regarding the unspecified origin and nebulous content of Pilate's wife's dream, however, obscures two important aspects of this brief scene. First is the shocking fact that *she*, not *he*, had a dream all. This is the only occurrence in the totality of the biblical record in which a woman is described as having a dream. To my knowledge, Flavius Josephus is the only other Second Temple Jewish writer to record a dream report involving a woman. Out of some thirty-two references to dreams or dream reports in Josephus's collected works, Glaphyra (*War* 2.114–116; *Ant.* 17.349–352) represents the only female who is depicted as having a dream (Gnuse 1989, 360).

Second, the lamentable lack of detail regarding the precise content of her dream obscures not only the content of Pilate's wife's dream, but also the fact that it is not reported as a message. The "word" delivered to Pilate is simply his wife's interpretation of the significance of the dream she has experienced. Thus, Pilate's wife is not only a recipient of a dream but also takes on the added role of interpreter. This is a role accorded to none of the other dream recipients in Matthew. The closest biblical parallel would be to Joseph in the book of Genesis or to Daniel, both of them being receivers and interpreters of dreams.[8]

---

8. The closest Matthean parallel is with the magi pericope in 2:12 where the dream content is similarly vague. In 2:12 however, we are explicitly told that the magi are warned not to return to Herod (χρηματισθέντες κατ' ὄναρ μὴ ἀνακάμψαι πρὸς Ἡρῴδην) and thus the magi are not portrayed as interpreters of dreams.

Jews or Gender?

Recognizing that Matt 27:19 is depicting a female body as both the recipient and interpreter of a dream brings us back round to the significance drawn out by Sellars's staging. To simply say, as Ulrich Luz (2007, 68) does in his magisterial commentary on Matthew, that Pilate's wife is being developed as a "bright foil" in contrast to the Jewish leaders is to completely miss the embodied aspect of the narrative. This misreading of Matthew remains largely without redress and continues to be pervasive in contemporary Matthean scholarship. For example, Derek S. Dodson (2009, 167) writes, "the dream prompts this Gentile woman to send a message to her husband conveying the innocence of Jesus; this is in contrast to the Jewish leaders who are goading the crowd to call for Jesus's death. The reader would be reminded of the Gentile magi who obey a dream and do not participate in the plot to kill the child Jesus, yet the Jewish leaders share culpability in Herod's plot." Lamentably, Amy-Jill Levine's (1988, 4) observation, now more than thirty years old, that "most modern scholarship remains content with the conclusion that Matthaean soteriology is based on the thematic division between recalcitrant Jews and faithful gentiles" could well have been written yesterday.

This casting of Pilate's wife as a foil to the Jews is very much in line with traditional treatments of the magi (going as far back as Augustine), who are also characterized in terms of *good* gentiles versus faithless/obstinate Jews, an opposition brought out in one of John Dominic Crossan's (1968, 131–32) early articles. The contrast drawn out in Matt 2, however, is one of control or authority and not ethnicity (Levine 1988, 99). The gentile magi are aligned with the Jewish Joseph in contrast to the ruler Herod (whose Jewishness was itself contested in certain Jewish circles, a fact Matthew's audience would have known full well). Both the magi and Joseph are in positions of powerlessness, the former as foreigners and the latter as a peasant. As Levine notes, attempts to frame Herod and "all Jerusalem" as faithless Jewish foils to the faithful gentile magi are only possible by ignoring the contexts of the passages themselves (4).

Claims, as for example expressed by Brown (1994, 1:805), that Pilate's wife's dream "stems from the same type of popular narrative wherein God uses extraordinary means to reveal Jesus to the Gentiles since they do not have the Scriptures, and wherein their promptness to accept the revelation is contrasted with the hostile rejection of Jesus by those who do have the Scriptures" must be rejected. As W. D. Davies and Dale C. Allison (1988–

2004, 3:588) astutely note, "We cannot neglect that the very next pericope presents Jesus being tormented by Gentiles." Brown (1994, 1:806) suggests that Matthew's audience would have found in Pilate's wife a parallel to other depictions of noble Roman women who were favorable to Judaism. However, given that Pilate is being asked to adjudicate an intra-Jewish disagreement, it is unclear how any sympathy toward Jews in general on the part of Pilate's wife would have prompted her to takes sides in this debate.

While the ominous nature of Calpurnia's aforementioned dream seems similar to that of Pilate's wife, commentators overlook the fact that the function of these dreams is to signal that the supposed authority (Caesar or Pilate) is in fact not the one in charge. That such a declaration is being made by a woman is likewise significant given the level of authority typically accorded to women in the first century. A far more plausible parallel can be found in the Joseph narrative in Genesis. Like Pilate's wife, Joseph is both a dreamer and an interpreter of dreams. And like Pilate's wife, Joseph is also a marginal figure (he being a Jew, she being a woman) within an imperial power structure. Repeatedly in the Joseph narrative, it is through the use of dreams that the authority of the established power structures is subverted. Importantly, it is first the familial power structure that is subverted via his dreams and then the imperial one in Egypt. In her brief appearance Pilate's wife embodies both of these aspects of the Joseph narrative.

Judgment

This brings us to the next aspect of Matthew's narrative so wonderfully embodied in Sellars's staging, as we see Pilate's wife stand and personally deliver her words to Pilate. Pilate's wife's singular line intrudes into a short pericope common in some form to all four gospels (Mark 15:1–15; Matt 27:15–26; Luke 23:2–25; John 18:28–40). In each Gospel account, Jesus is brought before Pilate for judgment and then delivered up to be crucified. It is only in Matthew's account, however, that Pilate's wife makes an appearance in the narrative. Matthew records that Pilate is καθημένου δὲ αὐτοῦ ἐπὶ τοῦ βήματος "sitting on the judgment seat" when his wife sends word to him. The βῆμα is the place from which Roman justice would be meted out. Sending a message to Pilate while he sits in judgment would have been an unusual action for Pilate's wife to have taken (Nolland 2005, 1170–71).

One might argue that Pilate's wife does not directly speak her words to Pilate. Strictly speaking, the words *are* recounted in the voice of the narrator: "While he was sitting on the judgment seat, his wife sent word to him, 'have nothing to do with that innocent man, for today I have suffered a great deal because of a dream about him'" (Matt 27:19). Such a reading however would be misguided. Once again Bach correctly guides our reading in foregrounding the first-person syntax ἔπαθον "I have suffered," of "her words" by having her personally sing the words rather than merely having them recited by the narrator.[9] That the gospels, including Matthew, were meant to be read aloud (a process that requires the interaction of living bodies) effectively works to shorten the conceptual and temporal gap that one might suppose exists between the written composition of the gospel and Bach's (and Sellars's) staging.

As in the earlier magi pericope, the juxtaposition created in this scene is that of a power differential. Here that differential is embodied as Pilate versus his wife, not as Pilate's wife versus the Jewish leaders or crowd. Diagramming the actual words in Pilate's deliberation regarding what he should do with Jesus reveals that Pilate's wife plays a more central role, especially in relation to the crowd, than often is supposed.

Pilate: τίνα θέλετε ἀπολύσω ὑμῖν (27:17)
Pilate's wife: μηδὲν σοὶ καὶ τῷ δικαίῳ ἐκείνῳ πολλὰ γὰρ ἔπαθον σήμερον κατ᾽ ὄναρ δι᾽ αὐτόν (27:19)
Pilate: τίνα θέλετε ἀπὸ τῶν δύο ἀπολύσω ὑμῖν (27:21)
Crowd: τὸν Βαραββᾶν (27:21)
Pilate: τί οὖν ποιήσω Ἰησοῦν τὸν λεγόμενον χριστόν (27:22)
Crowd: σταυρωθήτω (27:22)
Pilate: τί γὰρ κακὸν ἐποίησεν (27:23)
Crowd: σταυρωθήτω (27:23)

The first thing rendered visible in this diagram is the paucity of words accorded to the crowd. Especially when contrasted with Pilate's wife's words in verse 19. Second, notice the way in which Matthew interposes the warning from Pilate's wife between two very similar questions asked by Pilate. Even as Pilate repeatedly asks the crowd τίνα θέλετε, his wife's statement μηδὲν σοὶ (dative: to you) refocuses our attention on Pilate and the implied authority he assumes in the repeated use of ἀπολύσω (first-person singular aorist active).

---

9. Bach quotes the Luther Bible (1534) which reads: ich habe ... erlitten.

Pilate's twice-asked question would seem to direct our attention to the desire of the crowd, but the insertion of his wife's warning in the center creates a chiasmus that calls attention to Pilate's authority/responsibility:

ἀπολύσω: I will release
μηδὲν σοὶ: nothing to you
ἀπολύσω: I will release

Pilate's wife's words intrude into the threefold interchange between Pilate and the crowds. This is highlighted by the virtual repetition of verses 17 and 21. The question of 27:17 is interrupted and thus must be restated in 27:21. In both Mark and Luke there is also a threefold interchange between Pilate and the crowds and Jewish leaders, but in Matthew the interchange is interrupted by the unique report of Pilate's wife's dream.[10]

If Pilate's wife is more than a foil to the obstinate Jews, then a closer look at her words in terms of imperial rhetoric is warranted. Commentators have rightly noted the odd phrasing of her words to Pilate, μηδὲν σοὶ καὶ τῷ δικαίῳ ἐκείνῳ, which literally mean, "nothing to you and to that righteous one."[11] The closest language in Matthew (and the New Testament) is the declaration of the demoniac in Matt 8:29: τί ἡμῖν καὶ σοί (literally: "what to us and to you?").[12]

John Nolland (2005, 1172) takes this similarity between Pilate's wife's words in Matthew 27 the words of the demoniac in 8:29 to mean that Pilate's wife is denying that Pilate and Jesus have anything in common. From this Nolland concludes that Pilate's wife's comment should be read in terms of Pilate and his wife's self-interest, not in the interest of Jesus:

---

10. Cf. Mark 15:9, 12, 14; Luke 23:14, 20, 22.

11. Pilate's wife describes Jesus as τῷ δικαίῳ ἐκείνῳ, "that righteous one," as opposed to "innocent" as found in most translations. That we should read this dream report in light of the earlier ones is further evidenced by the fact that the very first Matthean dream-vision in 1:20, which is experienced by Joseph, is prefaced in 1:19 by a description of Joseph as δίκαιος ὤν.

12. In the synoptic tradition we find Jesus twice being asked some variant of this question. Only one of the occurrences is found in Matthew, the aforementioned account in 8:29 (cf. Mark 5:7; Luke 8:28) when the demoniac asks τί ἡμῖν καὶ σοί. Here Mark and Luke use τί ἐμοὶ καὶ σοί whereas Matthew uses the minor variant τί ἡμῖν καὶ σοί. A second occurrence can be found in Mark 5:7 // Luke 4:34, another exorcism story this time in Capernaum. Mark is consistent in using τί ἐμοὶ καὶ σοί whereas Luke now uses the minor variant τί ἡμῖν καὶ σοί.

"Should we not detect a rather narrow self-interest in her language of suffering here?" (1173). What Nolland fails to grasp is the explicit link to judgment and authority that occurs in the very next phrase in 8:29. Note that the demoniac's question, ἦλθες ὧδε πρὸ καιροῦ βασανίσαι ἡμᾶς, is fundamentally a question about Jesus's authority. In casting the demons out, Jesus is preempting the final eschatological judgment. In Matt 27, Pilate stands in judgment of Jesus but here Pilate's wife is emphatic that Pilate, even though he sits on the βῆμα, has no authority to judge this righteous one. In John 2:4, Jesus himself uses the phrase τί ἐμοὶ καὶ σοί in response to his mother's observation that there was no more wine at the wedding feast in Cana. While in John 2:4 the phrase is also a distancing mechanism, it creates distance insofar as it is a denial of responsibility relative to the circumstance or time at hand. Significantly, Mary's response, directed to the servants, undermines this distancing claim with an affirmation of Jesus's authority: ὅ τι ἂν λέγῃ ὑμῖν ποιήσατε.

Dodson (2009, 165) sees a closer link to the response of the chief priests and elders to Judas's attempt at returning the thirty pieces of silver along with his admission that he has sinned in παραδοὺς αἷμα ἀθῷον (Matt 27:4). Notice that while their response is indeed one of distancing (Matt 27:4: τί πρὸς ἡμᾶς), it is simultaneously a claim about authority or the lack thereof. In this case, they have no authority to absolve Judas of his sin. Dodson rightly notes that in a similar fashion Pilate's wife is warning Pilate not to involve himself in the judgment of this man. But in failing to see Matt 27 as a mirror story of the magi and Herod pericope in Matt 2, Dodson and other commentators fail to see that this distancing is a covert claim about authority.

Importantly Pilate's wife, unlike the chief priests, elders, and demoniac, does not frame her statement as a question. Her words are a declaration. Pilate is to have nothing to do with this righteous man, because like the case of Herod there is a higher authority in view. This is out of his hands, like it was out of the hands of Herod and like Caesar's fate was out of his hands. The declarative nature of her instruction itself implies authority, which further heightens the sense that this interchange is about authority not ethnicity.

To read the responses of the demoniac and the chief priests and elders as merely "don't bother me" or "leave me alone" is to fail to grasp their association with claims of authority or responsibility. A short excursus by way of the LXX will shed important light on how we might better understand Pilate's wife's warning. The phrase τί ἡμῖν καὶ σοί used by the demoniac in

Matt 8:29 also occurs in Judg 11:12 LXX. Notice the interchange in which the question is raised:

> Then Jephthah sent messengers to the king of the Ammonites and said, "What is there between you and me [τί ἡμῖν καὶ σοί], that you have come to me to fight against my land?" The king of the Ammonites answered the messengers of Jephthah, "Because Israel, on coming from Egypt, took away my land from the Arnon to the Jabbok and to the Jordan; now therefore restore it peaceably."

In 3 Kgdms 17:17–18 the question τί ἡμῖν καὶ σοί surfaces again when the widowed woman effectively asks for the reason or grounds whereby Elijah feels authorized to kill her son. In 2 Chr 35:21 LXX, the Egyptian Pharaoh Neco asks this question of King Josiah while trying to ascertain the motivation behind Josiah coming out to fight him: "But Neco sent envoys to him, saying, 'What have I to do with you [Τί ἐμοὶ καὶ σοί], king of Judah? I am not coming against you today, but against the house with which I am at war; and God has commanded me to hurry. Cease opposing God, who is with me, so that he will not destroy you'" (2 Chr 35:21 LXX). Importantly, in the next verse the Chronicler describes Josiah's failure to heed Neco's warning as a failure to "listen to the words of Neco from the mouth of God" (2 Chr 35:22 LXX). In 4 Kgdms 3:13, the context suggests that when Elisha asks this question of the king of Israel (Τί ἐμοὶ καὶ σοί), he is in effect saying, "why is this my problem/responsibility?"

This question τί ἡμῖν καὶ σοί also echoes David's question to Abishai son of Zeruiah in 2 Kgdms 16:10. In response to Abishai's desire to avenge him, David asks, Τί ἐμοὶ καὶ ὑμῖν (see also 2 Kgdms 19:22). Here importantly the context is not just one of dissociation, but also appears in a context in which the authority of Shimei to curse David is being challenged.

Admittedly, the phrases τί ἡμῖν καὶ σοί and τί ἐμοὶ καὶ ὑμῖν are not technically the same as μηδὲν σοὶ καὶ τῷ δικαίῳ ἐκείνῳ and thus can only be said to approach the words of Pilate's wife. That being said, the construction of τί ἡμῖν καὶ σοί (and to some extent τί ἐμοὶ καὶ ὑμῖν) does provide us with a plausible interpretative possibility for understanding Pilate's wife's words to her husband. This comparison suggests that the reader of Matthew's account should hear in Pilate's wife's words a claim, or more precisely a challenge, regarding Pilate's authority to pass judgment upon Jesus. This reading is not only plausible but as we shall now see, it is also compelling when we bring all the aforementioned elements of this essay together in conclusion.

Dreams of Empire

The words of warning sent by Pilate's wife intrude into Matthew's narrative flow in several surprising ways. Looking closely at Matt 27:19 reveals a sociopolitical intrusion that is mirrored by a literary intrusion into the structure of the brief pericope. First, her words literally interrupt Pilate while he sits on the judgment seat and challenge his very right to pass judgment upon Jesus.[13] This challenge to Pilate's authority is subtly echoed in a series of literary surprises.

As the above form-critical analysis clearly demonstrated, Matthew's account of the dream received by Pilate's wife in Matt 27 clearly belongs to the same form as the dreams in the infancy narratives of Matt 1–2. This shared formulaic structure however works within the Matthean narrative in two directions. In the infancy narrative, all five instances of κατ' ὄναρ are ones where God intervenes in the narrative with directions given via the dream (Matt 1:20; 2:12, 13, 19, 22). George M. Soares Prabhu (1976, 224) describes these infancy narrative dreams as "Heilsgeschichte." As Gnuse (1990, 106) explains, in them "God provides direction to the recipient rather than a prediction of the future." Some of these five divine interventions are explicitly mediated through an angel (1:2; 2:13, 19) and others are not (2:12, 22), but they are all are linked by the repeated presence of the phrase κατ' ὄναρ.

Interestingly, contrary to possible expectations generated by the larger Greco-Roman genre, the dream report in Matt 27:19 does not appear to affect any change in the plot or motion of the narrative. This is also in stark contrast to the previous dreams, which all affect shifts in the narrative to protect the infant Jesus. Dodson (2009, 162) notes that κατ' ὄναρ in 27:19 would evoke the dreams in the infancy narrative (Matt 1–2), but because he sees the earlier dreams as functioning "principally as divine mediums for the protections of Jesus" he misses the significance of the connection. According to this rubric, as a divine medium for protection the dream in 27:19 would be a failure. This leads Dodson (2009, 163) to conclude that there must be "a different quality about the dream of Pilate's wife than

---

13. Jesus's own silence before Pilate is itself a rebuttal of the tribunal's authority to judge him. The only remark Jesus makes is at the opening of the trial when he responds to Pilate's question σὺ εἶ ὁ βασιλεὺς τῶν Ἰουδαίων is the nonanswer σὺ λέγεις (cf. 27:11). Following this terse comment Jesus remains completely silent before Pilate and the judgment seat of Rome.

the dreams of the infancy narrative." Such need not be the case since, as we have seen, the role of dreams in Matthew serves first and foremost to highlight divine sovereignty in the narrative of Jesus's life.

Further support of such a conclusion can be seen in Pilate's actions with respect to Jesus. In Matt 27:24 we find a tacit admission by Pilate that he is not the final authority over Jesus's fate, a marked departure from his earlier claims when the narrative recounts that Pilate saw that he could do nothing and that a riot was imminent. It is then that he washes his hands and declares himself innocent of Jesus's blood. The abrupt entrance of Pilate's wife into the narrative, coupled with the surprising nature of her dream and its apparent failure to change the course of events, serves to provoke the audience to rethink and rehear a familiar story. The audience knows this story. There is difference between meditation and didactic or apologetic text.

The default reading of this text is one that assumes it to be a finished product. Sellars's staging of Bach's score as an inward-looking meditation prompts us to consider how Matthew might be read, and particularly Pilate's wife's warning, if we assume an unfinished aspect to the work. That is to say, Pilate's wife's stunning words are an invitation to reflect and not a didactic absolute. Is her dream report a failure? If nothing changes and Jesus still dies, what was the point of the dream? A curious aside or something more?

Levine (1988, 62) has noted that the women in Matthew's genealogy do more than contrast gentile and Jew. In her reading, these women form part of Matthew's critique of patriarchal power structures (87). Levine identifies the subordination of ethnic divisions to social categories of elites and marginals as a key theme in Matthew. This theme is not only present in the genealogy, but also seems apparent in the account of Pilate's wife. While she only devotes three sentences to Pilate's wife, Levine rightly notes that the fact that she is a woman is what is key in Matthew, not that she is a gentile (264). She also notes the association between her dreams and those of Joseph and the magi as one in which the "marginal and the mobile manifest faith." In Matthew's narrative, Pilate's wife does not function as a polemic against the "Jews" but is part and parcel of his consistent program of dismantling patriarchal power structures (11). Pilate's wife's dream sets her in opposition to Pilate. Her story is a reminder of the importance of women as both witnesses and agents in Matthew's Gospel. This is not "add women and stir." And it does not look like an apologetic. It is a meditation, an expansive reflection. Dreams are fundamentally statements of power, and as the recipient and interpreter of a dream Pilate's wife becomes the voice for an authority that supersedes that of Pilate and, by extension, Rome.

Pilate's wife's dream and subsequently her words are not meant to change Pilate's action, but to render visible the absurdity of Roman claims of ultimate power. The unexpected appearance of a dream in the judgment narrative collapses the distance between infancy and passion in such a way that enables the audience to simultaneously hold multiple critiques of patriarchal power in view simultaneously. Pilate's wife's dream creates a gap through which the audience can enter into the narrative in a reflective or meditative fashion.

The audience already knows the story and this literary feature enables the audience to hold in the present two events that are separated by many years in narrative time. The dream creates a simultaneity in the narrative and temporal flow between the infancy narrative and Jesus's passion. Dreams are often said to provide new information, but here in Matthew 27 it is not so much new information as it is space to reflect on existing information, namely the contrast between earthly and divine authority. Contrary to certain claims that dreams are the lowest form of revelation in Matthew, dreams convey to us one of the central claims of Matthew's Gospel, namely that Jesus's birth, life, and death are all expressions of divine sovereignty. Sellars's genius is his use of bodies-in-motion to operationalize Bakhtin's dialogic imagination and thereby render visible the simultaneity of Matthew's birth and passion narratives. This simultaneity makes evident, as Sellars rightly observes, that the truth of Matthew's Gospel is found in the dialogue of these *things happening at the same time.*

Through the deployment of divinely orchestrated dreams, Matthew creates a co-present tie between a peasant Jew, Eastern magi, and a Roman wife who together subvert Rome's claim to universal authority and salvation. This is a meditation on earthly power structures and their relation to the kingdom of heaven, not a clash of old and new *ethnoi*. Here we must remember Joseph and the magi who similarly call our attention to the contrast between earthly power structures and the kingdom of heaven. Herod did not have the final word on the Christ child, and now Pilate's wife and her dream provide us with a foreshadowing that Pilate, and by extension Rome, do not have the authority to pass judgment on Jesus. They may kill him, but Pilate's unnamed wife provocatively calls us to reflect on the reality that his vindication, his righteousness, is out of Rome's hands.

Bibliography

Alexander, Joseph A. 1861. *The Gospel according to Matthew.* New York: Scribner's Sons.
Bar, Shaul. 2001. *A Letter That Has Not Been Read: Dreams in the Hebrew Bible.* Translated by Lenn J. Schramm. HUCM 25. Cincinnati: Hebrew Union College Press.
Brown, Raymond Edward. 1993. *The Birth of the Messiah: A Commentary on the Infancy Narratives in the Gospels of Matthew and Luke.* Rev. ed. ABRL. New York: Doubleday.
———. 1994. *The Death of the Messiah: From Gethsemane to the Grave. A Commentary on the Passion Narratives in the Four Gospels.* 2 vols. ABRL. New York: Doubleday.
Crossan, John Dominic. 1968. "Structure and Theology of Matt 1.18–2.23." *CJos* 16:119–35.
Daines, Matthew, and Peter Sellars. 1996. "'Nixon in China': An Interview with Peter Sellars." *Tempo* 197:12–19.
Davies, W. D., and Dale C. Allison. 1988–2004. *A Critical and Exegetical Commentary on the Gospel according to Saint Matthew.* 3 vols. ICC. London: T&T Clark.
Dodson, Derek S. 2009. *Reading Dreams: An Audience-Critical Approach to the Dreams in the Gospel of Matthew.* LNTS 397. London: T&T Clark.
Ehrlich, Ernst Ludwig. 1953. *Der Traum im Alten Testament.* BZAW 73. Berlin: A. Töpelmann.
Gnuse, Robert K. 1989. "Dream Reports in the Writings of Flavius Josephus." *RB* 96:358–90.
———. 1990. "Dream Genre in the Matthean Infancy Narratives." *NovT* 32:97–120.
———. 1996. *Dreams and Dream Reports in the Writings of Josephus: A Traditio-Historical Analysis.* AGJU 36. Leiden: Brill.
Hanson, John S. 1980. "Dreams and Visions in the Graeco-Roman World and Early Christianity." *ANRW* 23.2:1395–427.
Husser, Jean-Marie. 1999. *Dreams and Dream Narratives in the Biblical World.* Translated by Jill M. Munro. BibSem 63. Sheffield: Sheffield Academic.
Kittel, Gerhard, and Gerhard Friedrich, eds. 1964–76. *Theological Dictionary of the New Testament.* Translated by Geoffrey William Bromiley. 10 vols. Grand Rapids: Eerdmans.

Levine, Amy-Jill. 1988. *The Social and Ethnic Dimensions of Matthean Social History*. Studies in the Bible and Early Christianity 14. Lewiston, NY: Mellen.

Lindner, Helgo. 1972. *Die Geschichtsauffassung des Flavius Josephus im Bellum Judaicum: Gleichzeitig ein Beitrag zur Quellenfrage*. AGJU 12. Leiden: Brill.

Luz, Ulrich. 2007. *Matthew 21–28: A Commentary*. Translated by James E. Crouch. Hermeneia. Minneapolis: Fortress.

Nolland, John. 2005. *The Gospel of Matthew: A Commentary on the Greek Text*. NIGNT. Grand Rapids: Eerdmans.

Oepke, A. 1967. "ὄναρ." *TDNT* 5:220–38.

Prabhu, George M. Soares. 1976. *The Formula Quotations in the Infancy Narrative of Matthew: An Enquiry into the Tradition History of Mt 1–2*. AnBib 63. Rome: Biblical Institute.

Navigating Dreams and Visions with Affect and Emotion

Why Does Enoch Weep?
The Traumatic Vision of the Book of Dreams

Genevive Dibley

You scare me with dreams and terrify me with visions (Job 7:14)

The fourth book of 1 Enoch, the Book of Dreams, is a sweeping review of sacred history through to the final judgment.[1] The book ends with two vividly opposing reactions to the eschatological vision. God, reviewing his transformative work at the end of the age, is pleased, "the Lord of the sheep rejoiced" (1 En. 90.38c).[2] In stark contrast the prophet, surveying the same scene, despairs. The Book of Dreams concludes with Enoch weeping inconsolably:

> And after that I wept bitterly, and my tears did not cease until I could no longer endure it, but they were running down because of what I had seen; for everything will come to pass and be fulfilled, and every deed of humanity was shown to me in its order. That night I remembered the first dream. I wept because of it, and I was disturbed because I had seen that vision. (1 En. 90.41-42)

It is an arresting ending for a Jewish apocalypse considering the raison d'être of the genre was to assure the oppressed faithful that the justice of God would not tarry indefinitely. As notes Emma Wasserman (2018, 59–107), while acknowledging the injustices suffered by the righteous, apocalypticists nonetheless maintained the God of Israel neither had been deposed nor abdicated his throne and was under no threat from a rival deity. Firmly in control of history, apocalypticists asserted that God would deal with rogue elements of disorder and false belief thus reestablishing the intended, just

---
1. Also known as the Dream Visions.
2. Unless otherwise noted, all translations of 1 Enoch are taken from Nickelsburg 2001.

world order at the eschaton. Though the blessing of the righteous had been demonstratively delayed in the second age, apocalypticists were at pains to reinforce the soundness of the tenets of Deuteronomic theology—those who had remained faithful to the law and YHWH would receive their reward.

At every point in the apocalypse, the sin of angels and humans is met with judgment and destruction. The covenant status of the Jews provides them no exemption. Israel is judged harshly for her apostasy. Enoch's intercessory prayer in the beginning of the apocalypse acknowledges the divine right to execute justice against the wicked and encourages God to do so: "And now, my Lord, remove from the earth the flesh that has aroused your wrath, but the righteous and true flesh raise up as a seed-bearing plant forever" (1 En. 84.6). As the events of the future eschaton unfold before the antediluvian prophet, all seems in good Deuteronomic order: the wicked are judged, the righteous gain ascendency over the remaining gentiles, an unpolluted temple is established, the remaining gentiles turn in respect and fear to God and righteous Israel, and the Jews and gentiles worship together in the remade temple. This certain knowledge of the fundamental stability and fairness of the cosmos permeates the Book of Dreams with one critical exception. The exception comes in the last sentence where the author adds the detail that God's final act in history would be to transform the remaining gentiles into righteous beings but, critically, not into righteous Israel (1 En. 90.38a).

As a prophet, it was arguably Enoch's job to align himself with the priorities and values of the divine. On waking from the vision, Enoch should have been as happy as God was happy. The prophets of the biblical and apocalyptic world were intermediaries between heaven and earth. On behalf of heaven, they called the wayward people back to God and to the covenant. They received and in turn relayed divine chastisement, comfort, and revelation. On behalf of the people, the prophets interceded that God might spare at least a remnant in his righteous anger. They cried the peoples' lament in the midst of judgment and gave voice to the peoples' repentance. Increasingly into the later Second Temple period, the prophets posed the peoples' questions, especially about divine justice, to God. Yet, whatever their sympathies for humanity, the prophets ultimately stumped for God. When the cards were down, the prophet was on the side of the divine.[3] Enoch of the Book of Dreams is therefore jarringly out of step with his patron deity and prophetic tradition.

---

3. The prophet of the book of Jonah proves the rule.

Positioned as the final sentiment of the apocalypse, the redactor purposely unsettles his readers with Enoch's unrelenting sorrow. The apocalypse is left raw, unresolved, and uncomfortable—the exact opposite of the anticipated eschatological sentiment of Isaiah:

> For I am about to create new heavens and a new earth; the former things shall not be remembered or come to mind. But be glad and rejoice forever in what I am creating; for I am about to create Jerusalem as a joy, and its people as a delight. I will rejoice in Jerusalem, and delight in my people; no more shall the sound of weeping be heard in it, or the cry of distress. (Isa 65:17–19 NRSV)

By contrast, the Enoch of the Book of Dreams cannot forget. His grief is such that he cannot stop weeping. He weeps so that he cannot bear it. Something is clearly wrong, but what?

There are indeed many reasons why humans weep. As Tom Lutz (1999) and Flemming Friis Hvidberg (1962) have explained, the act of weeping is itself is a culturally conditioned phenomenon. Within the extant Jewish literary culture of the period, Enoch's tears find many parallels of copious weeping and wasting grief.[4] The *quality* of Enoch's weeping however—bitter and unanswered—finds its closest cognate in the book of Lamentations.[5] Composed in the wake of the destruction of Jerusalem, Lamentations is trauma literature par excellence as remarks Elizabeth Boase (2014). Similarly riddled with lament, the Book of Dreams presents itself as a good candidate to be read in a similar vein as trauma literature. What follows is a reading of the role of emotions in the Book of Dreams attuned to some of the insights offered in the field of trauma studies as a means of unlocking this troubling redaction to the apocalypse.

A Brief Orientation to Trauma Theory

Trauma is a psychological state produced in reaction to an overwhelming experience of catastrophe (Caruth 1996, 11). Situations capable of rendering a psyche traumatized vary widely. Physical violence, mental abuse, systematic oppression, captivity, or acute loss resulting from either a single

---

4. Biblical examples of wasting grief or excessive weeping include 1 Sam 2:33; Jer 8:18; 9:16–19; 13:17; 14:17–18; Pss 69:1–3, 119:28.
5. Lam 1:22; 2:11; 3:48–49; 5:17.

calamitous incident, a series of intermittent injuries, a prolonged state of threat, or a credible threat of harm are all known traumatic triggers (Boase and Frechette 2017, 4). The decisive element in trauma, however, is the perception of threat by the victim. Such perception is highly individualized and conditioned by personal experience and group identity (ethnicity, class, gender, etc.).

Traumatic experiences challenge an individual's core assumptions that the "self has agency and dignity, enjoys solidarity with trustworthy others (human and divine), and inhabits an environment that is relatively safe" (Boase and Frechette 2017, 5). Such assumptions are critical to the maintenance of an individual's identity and their general sense of well-being. Traumatic experiences discredit these assumptions of safety, dignity, and agency thereby fracturing the psychic architecture of the trauma survivor.

Because traumatic experience exists outside the realm of expectation, it often defies linguistic expression in its immediate aftermath (Boase and Frechette 2017, 6). In the wake of such experiences, victims struggle to find the words capable of articulating their experience. They must invent the means of categorizing the trauma, adjusting their previous understanding of the world to encompass misfortune. This critical recategorization allows the victim to invent a kind of comprehension that eventually assigns the trauma meaning. Such an accounting of the event allows for the integration of the trauma into the narrative identity of the victim, thereby enabling them to reestablish their identity in a trauma-adjusted reality.

Increasingly, sociological studies have become attuned to the collective aspects of trauma on societies (Alexander 2004; Erickson 1995). Theorists postulate that social units, made up of individuals capable of experiencing trauma, are equally vulnerable to traumatic experiences capable of fragmenting cultural identities and calling into question a nation's sense of purpose and destiny. As individuals must process traumatic experience, so collectives of people must process trauma to maintain social cohesion, preserve cultural identity and foster resilience in the face of calamity (Saul 2014).

Driven by the work of Cathy Caruth (1991, 1996), Geoffrey H. Hartman (1995), and the Yale School, literary trauma theory understands the production of certain texts to be a reflexive function of trauma. Texts produced in the wake of trauma serve the function of *witness* to and *testimony* of traumatic experience even as they "challenge the capacities of narrative knowledge," as remarks Roger Luckhurst (2013, 79). Shoshana Felman and Dori Laub (1992, 114) have described the performative aspect of such testimony as an *"engagement* between consciousness and history, a struggling act of readjustment between the integrative scope of words and the unintegrated impact of events." The exercise of writing of trauma brings the "trauma within the conceptual bounds of the [collective] psyche—to be managed and understood" (114) rendering it capable of manipulation. As David G. Garber (2013, 2:423) astutely remarks, "If trauma is the wound, literature can be considered the scar."

Trauma theory, as it comes into biblical studies, is less a methodology than a heuristic framework. In its inception, it was largely the prerogative of Hebrew Bible scholars who concentrated their early efforts on the troubling and often disjointed rhetoric of the exilic prophets and particularly Lamentations (Linafelt 2000), Ezekiel (Broome 1946), and Jeremiah (O'Connor 2011). It has since greatly expanded in its application, as shown in the work of David M. Carr (2014) and Shelly Rambo (2010).

What Enoch Saw in the Book of Dreams

The Book of Dreams (1 En. 83–90) consists of two prophetic visions granted to the seer Enoch set in a succinct narrative frame. These two visions (one short in 1 En. 83.3–4; one long in 85.1–90.38, also known as the Animal Apocalypse) are dreams set in a brief narrative frame. The Book of Dreams is widely held to be a composite work, the frame and first dream fitted around the original composition of the Animal Apocalypse. A brief introduction (83.1–3a) establishes the narrator as an older Enoch recounting these two prophetic dreams to his son Methuselah. The first vision Enoch experiences as a youth while staying with his grandfather. In this short and brutal vision, the young Enoch witnesses the world dissolved and wakes terrified (83.3b–4). His grandfather interprets Enoch's dream as a revelation of impending divine punishment for human sin. He instructs his grandson to appeal to God to spare a remnant from the coming destruction (83.5–9). Enoch's subsequent petition is the longest human speech in the apocalypse (84.2–6). Praising God's sovereign power to enact his will, the prophet accepts the wisdom and justice of God's decision to utterly destroy the wicked, asking only that God save the righteous.

Sometime later before he marries, Enoch has a second vision known as the Animal Apocalypse (85.1–90.38). This longer vision grants Enoch's earlier petition—the prophet sees from creation through the apocalyptic flood to the survival of his great-grandson Noah. However, Enoch is made to see far more than just the survival of the remnant for which he pleaded. The prophetic dream continues well past the survival of Noah through the carnage of the second age to its inglorious end in the Maccabean War and eschaton.

The encapsulated vision of the Animal Apocalypse is an allegory in which the created order is demoted a single degree: angels appear as humans and humans as animals. Adam emerges from the earth as a white bull. The heifer Eve bears three bulls in turn: one black indicating wickedness (Cain), one red indicating futility (Abel), and one white indicating righteousness (Seth).[6] Adam, Seth, Noah, Shem, Abraham, and Isaac are represented as white, righteous bulls. This animalistic metaphor for the favored and righteous shifts with the birth of Jacob from white bulls to sheep. At this point the author drops the tricolor scheme. The sheep of Israel are never anything other than white. Among the flock of Israel, from Jacob onward, righteousness is indicated by the imagery of sheep *with their eyes open*. The gentile beasts, in contrast to the bulls and sheep, are aberrant and unintended beings, the product of the unholy mixing of the stars with the herd in the first age and the children of Ham and Japheth in the second. The tricolor scheme is never applied to the gentile beasts because the beasts are categorically profane.

The perpetual whiteness of the sheep is significant as it indicates the flock's innate capacity for righteousness; the sheep need only open their eyes to realize their potential. The drama of Israel's history in the Animal Apocalypse is the flock's struggle to achieve their latent capacity for righteousness. This makes the tale of the flock one of redemption and restoration. By contrast the beasts, being unholy, lack the capacity for righteousness and therefore, the reader must conclude, the capacity for redemption.

The Lord of the sheep (God) engages history in response to the wailing lament of the sheep oppressed by the wolves (the Egyptians). The Lord of

---

6. It needs to be acknowledged that in our modern context the color scheme employed by in the Animal Apocalypse is deeply problematic. Engaged in the work of justice, it is incumbent on modern scholars to stay conscious of the ways in which ancient texts and our conversations about them potentially serve to alienate, devalue, and marginalize historically disenfranchised people in our own time. It is with deep sympathy as to how rightfully triggering the association of *white* with *favor/righteousness* and *black* with *wickedness/evil* is in our modern context that I proceed in an attempt to understand how the author of the Book of Dreams employed this imagery in his own time.

the sheep wars against the wicked wolves, whom he ultimately drowns like the wicked of Noah's generation before them. Here it is critical to note that the mechanism of the flock's liberation is the judgment of their enemies. Emerging from the sea, the flock begins to open their eyes. They arrive at the foot of Sinai and fear the God they meet there. The sheep blind themselves and begin to go astray (89.32). The Lord of the sheep is filled with great wrath and judgment ensues. In keeping with the Deuteronomic modus operandi established in the first apocalypse, the wicked are slaughtered. An ominous cycle is established as the flock enters the pleasant land: "sometimes their eyes were opened, and sometimes they were blinded ... and the dogs began to devour the sheep" (89.41a–42a).

The apex of the second age comes as the house (Jerusalem) is greatly expanded and the tall tower (the temple) is built upon which the Lord of the sheep stands for a time in the midst the flock (89.50). This is the last positive thing that is said of the flock in the apocalypse until the eschaton. The sheep in the next sentence stray from the safety of the house and the tower and murder the prophets (89.53). The Lord of the sheep beats the flock in the hopes they will turn, but when they will not repent the Lord slaughters the flock and then abandons them altogether to be savaged by the gentile beasts (89.55–58). The sheep are said to be blind and unwilling to open their eyes (89.74), and eventually they are blindfolded (89.54). They become the prey of the beasts and abusive shepherds who slaughter the flock. The flock is decimated and all appears hopeless when snow white lambs (Judas Maccabee and his compatriots) are at last born to the flock and begin to open their eyes (90.6–7). Defending the blinded flock, the lambs battle the eagles, vultures, ravens, and kites (the Greeks) tearing at the sheep. Judas cannot be defeated by the gentile hordes, but neither can he win any battles in this apocalypse. For a brief moment a large sword is given to the flock (sans Judas) to kill the beast who flee before them (90.19). Before a proper final battle can commence, however, the throne of God is set up on the battlefield and the judgment suddenly begins (90.20).

The apocalypse traces the outline of Israel's sacred history with a ruthless efficacy. As I have argued elsewhere (Dibley 2013), the dark and reductive historical recounting in the Animal Apocalypse is purposeful. The narrative stresses at every turn the futility of historical processes. There is no messiah, no specially gifted leader, no piety of a righteous minority capable of arresting the desperate trajectory of the age. In this sense the Animal Apocalypse is an exemplar of the genre;

there is no hope for the world as it is, it must be remade through divine judgment.

The apocalypse has been relentlessly driving to judgment. Yet, the world had already endured divine judgment in the deluge, a judgment that was supposed to have eradicated evil by drowning those that embodied it. To be creditable, a second apocalypse with the same agenda as the first needed to have a new solution to the problem of evil. The author of the Animal Apocalypse offers just that. The classic elements of a Jewish eschaton are present: God in his glory is made manifest, the wicked and apostates are judged and destroyed in fire, Jerusalem and the temple are restored, the dispersed and dead are reclaimed returning to Jerusalem, the remaining beasts not directly implicated in the abuse of the flock make their submissive eschatological pilgrimage turning in peace to God and Israel, the remaining sheep are all righteous, and the sheep and beasts worship together in the purified temple (90.20–36). The innovation comes at the very end. The author adds that the final divine act performed in history would be to transform the remaining gentile beasts from their unintended creaturely forms to white bulls returning them to humanity's original, Edenic state of being (90.38a). It is in response to this scene—the transformation of the beasts into white bulls and not white sheep—that God is said to be happy (90.38c) and Enoch wakes and despairs (90.39–42).

Emotion in the Book of Dreams: Who Feels What?

Humans in the Book of Dreams feel principally negative emotions. Primarily humans feel fear (86.5; 89.1, 15, 30–31, 33, 35, 49; 90.37) but also terror (83.5; 86.5), bitterness (85.6; 90.39), grief (89.67; 90.39), and distress (90.42). Against this dirge of negative emotion there is a single exception; the text says the sheep were satisfied as they settle in the pleasant land (89.40). This is the only positive emotion humans feel in the entirety of the apocalypse. Beyond this single example, the best thing that happens to the sheep is they at one point stop crying (89.20).

Humans respond to their emotions in the Book of Dreams by crying out (83.5; 85.6; 87.1; 89.15, 16, 19, 31, 38, 52, 57; 90.3, 6, 10–11, 13), lamenting (89.20, 53; 90.3, 11), weeping (89.69), weeping bitterly (90.41), and grieving exceedingly (89.67). With the exception of Enoch's opening intercessory prayer, every instance of human speech in the Book of

Dreams is weeping lament. Threading the apocalypse, lament emotionally scores the text for the reader. Although angels in the Book of Dreams are not ascribed emotion, the earth feels grief for those slaughtered upon her (87.1). As the author makes clear, the first two ages were an unmitigated disaster.

God, by contrast, feels two emotions in the Book of Dreams, wrath/rage and happiness/joy. Both of these emotions he feels in equal measure as three times he is said to feel wrath and three times happiness. In the first instance, Enoch identifies the deluge as an act of divine wrath in his prayer: "And now, my Lord, remove from the earth the flesh that has aroused your wrath" (84.6). In the second instance, God's wrath is directed against the Hebrews at the foot of Sinai. There this wrath is qualified as great or extreme: "And the Lord of the sheep was filled with great wrath against them" (89.15a). The final installment of divine wrath is directed against the gentile hordes in what amounts to the final battle just before the judgment: "And I saw until the Lord of the sheep came upon them in wrath" (90.15).

God is happy or rejoices on three distinct and telling occasions. The first comes as the flock abandons God and is in turn abandoned by God ahead of the Babylonian destruction of the kingdom of Judah.

> And I saw that he abandoned that house of theirs and their tower, he threw them all into the hands of the lion so that they might tear them into pieces and devour them—into the hands of all the beasts. And I began to cry out with all my might and to call to the Lord of the sheep and to show him concerning the sheep, because they were devoured by all the wild beasts. And he was silent though he saw (it), and he *rejoiced* because they were devoured and swallowed up and carried off, and he abandoned them into the hands of all the beasts as fodder. (1 En. 89.56–58, emphasis added)

It is noteworthy that the destruction of Israel is the only instance of divine joy prior to the final judgment. The second and third cause for divine rejoicing comes post-judgment as eschatological prophecy. The sheep and beasts that survive the winnowing of the final judgment gather together in the temple and worship God together in peace: "And all that had been destroyed and dispersed by all the wild beasts and all the birds of heaven were gathered in that house. And the Lord of the sheep rejoiced greatly because they were all good and had returned to that house" (90.33). The last emotion accorded God in the Book of Dreams is happiness over the transformation of the gentiles: "the Lord of the sheep rejoiced over it and over all the cattle" (90.38c).

Qualifying as Victim

Traumatic experience is reserved for humans in the Book of Dreams. Within the narrative, there are two distinct types of trauma victims: the people who experience the events directly and the prophet who is made to witness them.

By the end of the apocalypse the character of Enoch in the Book of Dreams experiences a vicarious victimization by witnessing the trauma of history unfold. As direct victims of trauma experience a fracturing of their assumptions concerning their safety, society, and justice, so too those unfortunate enough to witness traumatic events can suffer similar psychological repercussions, a function of reflexive empathy for the suffering (American Psychiatric Association 2013, 309.81). Enoch's victimization progresses through the apocalypse. The prophet begins endorsing the divine destruction of the wicked in the flood, an objective reporter at a moral distance from the targets of divine wrath. He records traumatic events and the laments those who endure them, but he does not himself intercede. However, at the point the flock murders the prophets and God hands them over to the Babylonians wolves, Enoch finds himself intimately and emotionally entangled with the outcome of the flock. In an act of selective prophetic countertransference, Enoch reverses his earlier position regarding the wicked and instead becomes an advocate for iniquitous Israel (89.57).[7] Countertransference (McCann and Colletti 1994, 90) in a clinical setting is the redirection of a therapist's feelings toward their client, an emotional entanglement born of empathetic engagement with the client's trauma. Enoch's emotional entanglement and identification with his client Israel is such that the prophet comes down to join the flock prior to the judgment, presumably as a sheep, to share their fate (90.31).

---

7. Thanks to Laura Allman, CLSW, who tipped me to the significance of this problem in the fields of psychology, social work, and public health and thought it might apply to Enoch in this text. "Vicarious traumatization" or "vicarious victimization" denotes traumatization or victimization indirectly transmitted from a victim to a victim-service-provider as a consequence of the provider's empathetic engagement with the victim in the course of offering services..

The case of Israel's victimization is more complicated. As presented by the redactor, the primary trauma in the Book of Dreams is the Babylonian war, the moment in which the flock and God mutually abandon each other and God rejoices in the flock's destruction. This centering of 586 BCE as the moment of primary cultural trauma follows the biblical source material. The Hebrew prophets, in doing the work of absorbing and assimilating the trauma of the war and all its attendant horrors and humiliations into the narrative and identity of the nation, had blamed the people for their tragedy. They argued that Israel's defeat was punishment for profaning God, his sanctuary, and his covenant. It was an apologetic tailored to acquit the divine on the charges of impotency in battle or capricious indifference in the face of the nation's calamity. *Victim* implies *crime* and Israel, the prophets emphatically argued, was the *criminal* and not a *victim*. If there was a victim in this situation, it was God who had been defiled by Israel: "I am profaned in their midst" (Ezek 22:26). The guilty, the prophets imply, cannot be victims of justice although they suffer.

What, then, is the efficacy of a label actively rejected by the people it is meant to describe? It is important to note that trauma differs fundamentally from other forms of self-identification that need to be heard and honored. The abused child who adamantly denies being harmed is no less of a victim for his denial even if he believes the abuse is a form of love. A rape survivor is no less a victim if she faults herself for her assault. It is common for the victims of trauma to blame themselves. Elizabeth Boase and Christopher G. Frechette (2017, 4) see self-blame as a survival mechanism enabling victims to assert agency and self-control over and against the very real threat of overwhelming violence or chaos. Self-blame holds within it the illusion of power. If the victim faults themselves, they can plan future strategies that could affect a different outcome. The abused child might vow to be good so as not to provoke their abuser. The rape victim may vow to wear longer skirts, not set her drink down at a party, or not walk at night. There is comfort in thinking that there is some behavior or action that will prevent an assault. By blaming the people for their destruction, the prophets sought to wrest control of Israel's fate both from the gentiles and from God. If Israel was morally culpable, then her suffering was deserved. Her power, however, lay in the covenant and in piety, fidelity, and correct worship. A self-determining moral agent, Israel, the prophets contended, controlled her own destiny.

For all the prophetic protestations, ancient Israel was a victim of extreme episodic violence and repeated colonization. The redactor does not challenge the prophetic apologia in any way, as the Book of Dreams is Deuteronomic to the core. Yet, he scores his apocalypse with lament and in doing so bifurcates Israel's identity by depicting them as both confessed *offender* and manifest *victim* of gentile aggression and divine wrath. It is a complex presentation of the experience of trauma born of the redactor's distance from the primary injury and the pressing need to explain the historical experience of the nation through the late Second Temple period in his own time.

The Redactor as a Victim

As Paul Ricoeur (1984, 1:170) has noted, the reader of a narrative expects to find resolution to the conflict that has driven the plot. The ending need not be predictable to the reader as long as it resolves, satisfies, or acceptably completes the story arc in accordance to the internal coherence of the narrative. This would seem an obvious point. The redactor of the Book of Dreams does resolve the story arcs of the main characters: God, Israel, and Enoch.

The resolution of the story arc of the flock comes predictably at the eschaton. Through the history of the second age, the redactor presents his dual perception of Israel as simultaneously perpetrator and victim. As expected in a Jewish apocalypse, the eschatological judgment and destruction of the wicked is anticipated to achieve the relief of the tortured suffering of the righteous (the Maccabees and their compatriots). This follows the precedent established in the Noachic flood and Exodus narratives in which the destruction of the wicked and enemy is the salvation of the righteous. In the eschatological absence of the wicked, the people's telos can be realized; the flock is *who* and *how* they were intended to be—a righteous people at peace with God and the gentiles and worshiping in the temple. It was the apocalypticists' fantastical and desperate hope that the justice of the final judgment would resolve the people's trauma and so palliate the history of the second age. Following this hope, the bleak story arc of the flock in Book of Dreams is fully resolved at the eschaton—the flock is "white, and their wool was thick and pure ... and all the sheep were enclosed in that house, but it could not contain them. And the eyes of all were opened, and they saw good things; and there was none among them that could not see" (1 En. 90.32, 34b–35).

The story arcs of God and Enoch are also properly resolved in the envisioned eschaton in the Book of Dreams. The plot of the apocalypse is driven by the divine desire to eradicate the wicked and the prophet's concern to preserve the righteous within judgment. These objectives are complementary. The failure of the first apocalypse (the flood) to achieve its aim is rectified in the second (the final judgment). The intervening series of centuries are indeed gruesome, but the goal throughout the text is clear and unwavering, and both God and the prophet achieve their objectives in the eschaton. Enoch, assimilated into the flock, sees with the flock only *good things* as a new age dawns (90.35). God is happy (90.33, 39). Had the redactor ended with 90.40—"and this is the vision that I saw while I slept. And I awoke and blessed the Lord of righteousness and gave him glory"— the reader would be hard pressed to imagine why the weeping lament of 90.41–42 was missing.

As the character arc of Enoch is properly resolved at the eschaton, commentators have expressed difficulty reconciling the prophet's angst-ridden epilogue. The majority of scholars engaging the Book of Dreams focus on the Animal Apocalypse and leave the epilogue aside in their analysis as part of a later redaction. Those writing commentaries (Nickelsburg 2001, 1:408; Olson 2013, 295; Tiller 1993, 392) on the unified composition of the Book of Dreams unanimously take the lament to be that of the character Enoch and interpret the prophet's weeping as sorrow over the fate of humanity, the sympathies of a righteous man for those doomed to suffer. However, outside the narrative, there is the possibility of a third human trauma victim—the redactor.

There is reason to think that the prophet's tears are in fact those of the redactor. At the epilogue, the narrative pretext thins. The son Methuselah, to whom Enoch has been recounting his visions, drops away. The narrative, which had been tragically harrowing before its great apocalyptic reversal, becomes abruptly raw, frustrated, and wildly disjointed, undoing the resolution achieved only a sentence before, and there it is left, a mess. The final lament is in the mouth of Enoch, but here in these last verses one can hear the redactor's voice just under the surface of the prophet, the redactor weeping out his *nephesh* through the eyes of his character, a victim in his own right.

Identifying the redactor as a voiced victim in the text postulates a high level of emotional correspondence between the redactor and the character of Enoch in the final lament. Also problematic, the redactor is known to us only by the Book of Dreams. To what degree the visible trauma of the text correlates with the redactor standing behind the text is admittedly speculative. It is nonetheless a critical exercise to attempt to distill the redactor from his character. The experience of trauma is intricately and inseparably tied to the victim who perceives the situation as traumatic. Identifying the voice of victim in the epilogue is key to identifying the traumatic trigger. Enoch's final lament appears disjointed and inappropriate because it has been assumed to be a plot point. But is it the character who is weeping, or is it the redactor, expressing his own authorial confession, who is weeping in response to *his* trauma?

Identifying the Redactor's Trauma

In choosing Enoch from the mythic past, the redactor sets his main character in a profoundly different relationship to the events portrayed in the apocalypse relative to himself. For the antediluvian Enoch, the events he witnesses in his visions are entirely in the future, each revelation a fresh trauma as it unfolds before him. For the redactor, writing during or shortly after the Maccabean War, all Enoch saw, save the eschaton, was already in the past—the primary trauma of the fall of Jerusalem lay four centuries in the past.

It does not follow that because the apocalypse was a retrospective on the nation's tragedies that the redactor was not affected by these events. The redactor of the Book of Dreams inherited a world shaped by the trauma of his ancestors. M. Gerard Fromm (2012) has brought attention to the ways in which trauma is passed generationally in the remembering and memorializing of traumatic events within a culture. Israel's historic trauma had been catalogued and canonized. More importantly for the redactor, it had been heavily curated through the lens of Deuteronomic theology. The prophets had scarred the wound of Jerusalem's destruction, but as a scar alters the topography of the skin, so the prophets had altered the psyche of the nation. The strategy of victim-blaming on the national, cultic level ensured that Israel would survive, but also ensured that she could never forget.

The redactor of the Book of Dreams absorbed and reproduced these Deuteronomic constraints. Even though the catalogue of historical tragedies laid out in the apocalypse is presented as a series of traumas for the people living through them, they are, from the perspective of the redactor, both predictable and theologically accounted for. Trauma assaults a victim's core assumptions concerning justice. What is the injustice of the Book of Dreams?

Every instance of lament in the Book of Dreams is triggered by the traumatic event that immediately precedes it. The causes are obvious; Eve laments Abel, the earth laments the murdered, the Hebrews lament the baby boy drowned in the Nile, the Egyptians lament their firstborn sons, and so on. If the lament of the epilogue is read accordingly, and not as a reaction to the totality of the preceding vision as commentators have taken it, then the direct antecedent to the prophet's final lament is the transformation of the gentiles (90.38).

The Injustice of the Eschatological Transformation of the Gentiles

The gentiles without exception are portrayed in the Book of Dreams as murderous thugs, the weapon the Lord of the Sheep deployed against the flock to devastating effect. The flock is punished harshly for their inequities, living or dying under the Deuteronomic prescription. The flock does achieve a final state of righteous purity in the eschaton but only because it is culled in the judgment, with the apostates thrown into the fire.

By stark contrast, gentile beasts, unholy and unworthy, are transformed into righteous beings simply because the Lord of the sheep wills it to be so. This act of divine magic is unsolicited and wholly unmerited; the beasts neither appeal to be made righteous nor do they do anything that would make them worthy of consideration for transformation. The beasts do make peace with the flock and worship in the temple prior to their transformation, but this is a self-interested reflection of their understanding of the shifted power axis in the eschaton. Aligning themselves with the Lord of the sheep and the empowered righteous flock is a survival strategy.

The reader labors with the prophet under the supposition that the violence leveled against the flock throughout the apocalypse was disciplinary, its aim the moral reform of the sheep. Israel's ability to learn through divine discipline and stay the course served as the apocalyptic pretext for the righteous minority's acquittal in the coming judgment. The gentiles of the Book of Dreams, largely undisciplined by God throughout history, are simply granted by God in the eschaton what the flock struggled through the brutal centuries to attain under their own power.

The redactor of the Book of Dreams was not the first Jewish writing to postulate the continued existence of gentiles beyond the judgment. The prophets had imagined a remnant of gentiles serving as witness to Israel's eschatological glory, humbly making pilgrimage to Jerusalem and submitting to the authority and teaching of Israel. This sentiment is perhaps epitomized in Zechariah:

> Many peoples and strong nations will come to seek the LORD of hosts in Jerusalem, and to entreat the favor of the LORD. Thus say the LORD of Hosts; In those days ten men from the nations of every language will take hold of a Jew, grasping his garment and saying, "Let us go with you, for we have heard that God is with you." (Zech 8:22-23 NRSV)

However, the prophets were vague on exactly what gentile repentance and orientation to God would entail beyond the dazzling moment of their turning. Isaiah prophesizes that the gentiles would walk in the ways of the Lord:

> In days to come the mountain of the LORD's house shall be established as the highest of the mountains, and shall be raised above the hills; all the nations shall stream to it. Many peoples shall come and say, "Come, let us go up to the mountain of the LORD, to the house of the God of Jacob; that he may teach us his ways and that we may walk in his paths." For out of Zion shall go forth instruction, and the word of the LORD from Jerusalem. He shall judge between the nations, and shall arbitrate for many peoples; they shall beat their swords into plowshares, and their spears into pruning hooks; nation shall not lift up sword against nation, neither shall they learn war any more. (Isa 2:2-4 NRSV)

The phrase "walk in his paths" presumably means the gentiles would become law-abiding people. Israel was defined by her possession and adherence to the law over and against the law-less gentiles. Whether a law-observant gentile could still be a gentile proper under this definition is unexplored in the prophets. It would not have been much of an extension within the tradition to intuit that the law-abiding gentile would in some fashion become functionally Israelite by default if not ancestral design. Isaiah, however, does not further explore the eschatological contingencies of Torah-observant gentile identity. The great gentile turning was a distant future that the prophets could afford to leave undefined, an injustice borrowed against the future. Yet as the prophets' future slid into the redactor's past, more specificity was required of the timing of divine justice—*when* and *how* the gentile threat would be eliminated.

The transformation of the wicked gentiles in the Book of Dreams corrects the error of the first apocalypse in which righteous Noah was saved along with his unrighteous sons and so reinfected the world (1 En. 89.9). It also accounts for the longevity of gentile supremacy that had stretched centuries beyond Judah's return from exile. Yet, when the gentiles are transformed in the apocalypse, they are transformed from *beasts* into *white bulls* and not into *sighted sheep*.

The scholarly consensus at the present moment understands both the beasts *and* the sheep as being transformed into white bulls in the eschaton as a return to an Edenic/Adamic state. This does not, however, seem to be the most natural reading of the text or narrative more broadly. In the final phrase of 1 En. 90.38 it appears that the rejoicing of the Lord has two clear objects. If the beasts and the sheep have both been transformed into white bulls, why reintroduce a seeming post-transformation distinction when "the Lord of the sheep rejoiced over them and over all the bulls"? God is introduced in the Animal Apocalypse as "their [the sheep's] Lord" in the exodus account (89.15–16) and is ever after called the "Lord of the sheep" without any ambiguity. If the category of *sheep* is dissolved with the category of *beasts* in the eschaton, transformed into white bulls, it is odd the author would continue to refer to God as "Lord of the *sheep*" as opposed to reidentifying God as "Lord of the *bulls*" to fit the new reality. The Lord of the sheep in the post-transformation eschaton in the Animal Apocalypse would in effect be Lord of nothing. The author's retention of God's moniker, "Lord of the sheep," makes perfect sense if the beasts are transformed into white bulls and the Lord of the sheep rejoices over the sheep and the bulls.

As white bulls were the intended form of humanity—Adam, Seth, Noah, Abraham, and Isaac are all white bulls—commentators have stressed the restoration of this transformation and, in the process, have missed an insult to the sheep. The sheep were Israel. Their inheritance was Sinai and the special relationship with God through the covenant. The transformation of the gentiles into righteous beings, but not Israel, represents a decentering proposition at the least and a devaluing one at the worst. It reveals a novel righteousness, one independent of Israel and the law, a righteousness bestowed and not earned, one rule for Israel and another for the gentiles.

If there was always more than one path to righteousness and salvation at the judgment, what was the point of the centuries of striving and suffering through the crucible of the second age if, when given the choice, God makes the gentiles righteous apart from, if not in contradiction to, Israel?

The divine transformation of the gentiles is deeply unfair. The Book of Dreams is Deuteronomic to the core. For Israel, the boundaries were set—submission, repentance, and adherence to the covenant. If Israel desired divine favor, as the apocalypse made absolutely clear, then she must be worthy of it. Predicated on their special relationship, the tortures Israel endured were made bearable because they had theorized that God punished those he loved to save them from the greater fate of apocalyptic destruction:

> Know then in your heart that as a parent disciplines a child, so the Lord your God disciplines you. (Deut 8:5)

> Happy are those you discipline, O Lord, and whom you teach out of your law. (Ps 94:12)

> I know, O Lord, that your judgments are right, and that in faithfulness you have afflicted me. (Ps 119:75)

> My child, do not despise the Lord's discipline or be weary of his reproof, for the Lord reproves the one he loves, as a father the son in whom he delights. (Prov 3:11–12)

> Why should any who draw breath complain, about the punishment of their sins? (Lam 3:39)

What surfaces in the Book of Dreams is the redactor's fear that, in the end, Israel was the only true target of God's justice in the second age. This dystopian vision reveals that the suffering of Israel, deserved though it may have been, was ultimately without purpose—for they who had struggled and borne the identity of the flock in the heat of the day came to the same pass as the beasts who stumbled mindlessly into mercy. The redactor's unrelenting weeping through his character Enoch sounds a jarring tonal dissonance, his tears registering a wordless protest. Like trauma victims the world over, the redactor is left to absorb the wound.

Bibliography

Alexander, Jeffrey C. 2004. "Toward a Theory of Cultural Trauma." Pages 1–30 in *Cultural Trauma and Collective Identity*. Jeffrey C. Alexander et al. Berkeley: University of California Press.

Boase, Elizabeth. 2014. "The Traumatized Body: Communal Trauma and Somatization in Lamentations." Pages 193–209 in *Trauma and Traumatization in Individual and Collective Dimensions: Insights from Biblical Studies and Beyond*. Edited by Eve-Marie Becker, Jan Dochhorn,

and Else Kragelund Holt. SANT 2. Göttingen: Vandenhoeck & Ruprecht.
Boase, Elizabeth, and Christopher G. Frechette. 2017. "Defining 'Trauma' as a Useful Lens for Biblical Interpretation." Pages 1–26 in *Bible through the Lens of Trauma*. Edited by Elizabeth Boase and Christopher G. Frechette. SemeiaSt 86. Atlanta: SBL Press.
Broome, Edwin C. 1946. "Ezekiel's Abnormal Personality." *JBL* 65:277–92.
Carr, David M. 2014. *Holy Resilience: The Bible's Traumatic Origins*. New Haven: Yale University Press.
Caruth, Cathy. 1991. "Introduction to Psychoanalysis, Trauma and Culture." *American Imago* 48:1–12.
———. 1996. *Unclaimed Experience: Trauma, Narrative, and History*. Baltimore: Johns Hopkins University Press.
Dibley, Genevive. 2013. "Abraham's Uncircumcised Children: The Enochic Precedent for Paul's Paradoxical Claim in Galatians 3:29." PhD diss. University of California at Berkeley.
Erickson, Kai T. 1995. "Notes on Trauma and Community." Pages 183–99 in *Trauma: Explorations in Memory*. Edited by Cathy Caruth. Baltimore: Johns Hopkins University Press.
Felman, Shoshana, and Dori Laub. 1991. *Testimony: Crises of Witnessing in Literature, Psychoanalysis, and History*. New York: Routledge.
Fromm, M. Gerard, ed. 2012. *Lost in Transmission: Studies of Trauma across Generations*. London: Karnac.
Garber, David G., Jr. 2013. "Trauma Theory." Pages 421–28 in *The Oxford Encyclopedia of Biblical Interpretation*. Edited by Steven McKenzie. 2 vols. Oxford: Oxford University Press.
Hartman, Geoffrey H. 1995. "On Traumatic Knowledge and Literary Studies." *New Literary History* 26:537–63.
Hvidberg, Flemming Friis. 1962. *Weeping and Laughter in the Old Testament; a Study of Canaanite-Israelite Religion*. Leiden: Brill.
Linafelt, Tod. 2000. *Surviving Lamentations: Catastrophe, Lament, and Protest in the Afterlife of a Biblical Book*. Chicago: University of Chicago Press.
Luckhurst, Roger. 2008. *The Trauma Question*. New York: Routledge.
Lutz, Tom. 1999. *Crying: The Natural and Cultural History of Tears*. New York: Norton.
McCann, Lisa, and Joseph Colletti. 1994. "The Dance of Empathy: A Hermeneutic Formulation of Countertransference, Empathy, and Understanding in the Treatment of Individuals Who Have Experienced

Early Childhood Trauma." Pages 87–121 in *Countertransference in the Treatment of PTSD*. Edited by John P. Wilson and Jacob D. Lindy. New York: Guilford.
Nickelsburg, George W. E. 2001. *1 Enoch 1: A Commentary on the Book of 1 Enoch, Chapters 1–36, 81–108*. Hermeneia. Minneapolis: Fortress.
O'Connor, Kathleen M. 2011. *Jeremiah: Pain and Promise*. Minneapolis: Fortress.
Olson, Daniel C. 2013. *A New Reading of the Animal Apocalypse of 1 Enoch: "All Nations Shall Be Blessed."* SVTP 24. Leiden: Brill.
Rambo, Shelly. 2010. *Spirit and Trauma: A Theology of Remaining*. Louisville: Westminster John Knox.
Ricoeur, Paul. 1984–1988. *Time and Narrative*. Translated by Kathleen McLaughlin and David Pellauer. Chicago: University of Chicago Press.
Saul, Jack. 2014. *Collective Trauma, Collective Healing: Promoting Community Resilience in the Aftermath of Disaster*. Routledge Psychosocial Stress. New York: Routledge.
Tiller, Patrick A. 1993. *A Commentary on the Animal Apocalypse of I Enoch*. EJL 4. Atlanta: Scholars Press.
Wasserman, Emma. 2018. *Apocalypse as Holy War: Divine Politics and Polemics in the Letters of Paul*. AYBRL. New Haven: Yale University Press.

Exploring the Visions in Acts in Their Narrative Context

Deborah Prince

The book of Acts is filled with vision narratives. In the first chapter the apostles watch as Jesus ascends into heaven and they receive a vision of two men in white (1:9–11). In Acts 2 the vision at Pentecost is narrated and Peter provides an explanation for such experience in his speech to those assembled: "In the last days it will be, God declares, that I will pour out my Spirit upon all flesh, and your sons and your daughters shall prophesy, and your young men shall see visions, and your old men shall dream dreams" (2:17). Visions continue at a fast pace through Acts 12, after which their presence becomes more sparing, but they still span the entire book. The final vision is recounted in Acts 27. One cannot read Acts, therefore, without recognizing the centrality of visions. Revelation is the only New Testament book that exceeds Acts in terms of its visionary material. Often the speeches in Acts gain the most attention, but visions are as prominent as the speeches. Word and vision form an interlocking pair. As Brittany E. Wilson notes (2016, 456–81), the author of Acts (hereafter called Luke for the sake of simplicity) clearly values both sight and hearing in the presentation of his story.

The aim of this essay is to explore the visions in Acts more fully not only to gain insight into their role in the narrative itself but also to expand our understanding of the varied nature of vision narratives throughout the biblical tradition. I will examine how Luke narrates visionary experiences and their rhetorical force and I will clarify how visions are described, where and when they are narrated, and ultimately their function. In previous articles I have examined specific vision narratives in Luke and Acts. Here my goal is to provide a broader picture of the visions in Acts as a whole. Several characteristics will be highlighted below, including the relationship between the sensory and spatial elements of the vision accounts, the use of vision pairs and a diverse assemblage of visionaries, and the placement of visions at key moments of transition and conflict within the narrative. These characteristics bolster the authority and reliability of the vision accounts, their revelatory content, and the process of community discernment of their meaning and purpose, all of which are crucial for guiding Jesus's followers (those within the narrative as well as Luke's own community) at pivotal moments of change and conflict.

It will be helpful to begin with a broad picture of the visions in Acts and their placement in the narrative. According to my working definition there are eighteen vision narratives in Acts: thirteen different vision narratives (1:9–11; 2:2–4; 5:19–20; 7:55–56; 8:26; 9:3–7, 10–16; 10:3–6, 10–16; 12:7–10; 16:9; 22:17–21; 27:23–24) and five that recount previously narrated visions (Cornelius and Peter retell their visions in 10:30–32; 11:4–10; and 11:13–14; Paul shares his vision on the road to Damascus in 22:6–10 and 26:13–18).[1] These visions are diverse in regard to their length, style, and visionary elements. My working definition for a vision narrative is: a narrative that recounts a revelatory encounter with the divine in which the divine presence is distinctly manifested to a person or group of people. The vision may be primarily visual, auditory, or engage both senses. The divine may appear or speak directly or through an intermediary.

The aforementioned working definition challenges the attempts of some scholars to more narrowly define and classify biblical dream and vision narratives. Such attempts I have addressed in a prior publication (Prince 2018, 337–59, 339–43). Scholarship ranges from a focus on determining formal parameters for vision accounts to the argument that such classifications limit our understanding of visionary experiences in the ancient world. Adela Yabro Collins (1996, 1195), who is known for her work with the book of Revelation and apocalyptic literature more broadly, emphasizes the visual dimension of visions. She goes as far as to distinguish visions from theophanies and epiphanies because of the emphasis of the latter on the physical presence of the divine figure and the message delivered. The typical formal features she presents are associated with

---

1. I do not include in the count visions mentioned but not narrated (9:12) or the conclusion to the believers' prayer in 4:31. Excluding the latter was a difficult decision. It seems to point back to the Pentecost event, and the shaking of the earth is an indication of divine presence in Jewish scripture, but it is such a fleeting picture that it seems to be closer to the mention of Paul's vision than a narrative of a "distinct manifestation" of the divine.

symbolic and allegorical visions, which are prevalent in apocalyptic literature and even several Old Testament prophetic books. But it quickly becomes apparent that this description is not sufficient for the vision narratives found in Acts. Dennis Hamm (1990, 70–71) has argued that what are commonly called visions in Acts are not actually visions but "auditions." The problem with this language is that Luke clearly identifies even solely verbal encounters as "visions." For example: "Now there was a disciple in Damascus named Ananias. The Lord said to him in a vision [ὁράματι], 'Ananias.' He answered, 'Here I am, Lord'" (9:10). Never does the narrator describe anything that Ananias "saw," if indeed he saw anything. The diversity of the nature of perception described in these visions illustrates the wide range of experiences that the biblical text considers to be visionary. We should not imagine that visions are only about "seeing" the divine in a literal way, nor should we assume that visions are clearly either physical or mental experiences. There is a complex interaction between the senses engaged and their physical and mental qualities. It is necessary, then, to expand common definitions of vision when discussing the book of Acts.

As noted above, the visions in Acts are significantly more numerous in the first twelve chapters than the whole last half of the book. The greatest concentration of visions is found in Acts 9–10, including the longest and most complex vision narratives. It is commonly agreed that Acts 1:8 provides a key to the structure of the book as a whole: "But you will receive power when the Holy Spirit has come upon you; and you will be my witnesses in Jerusalem, in all Judea and Samaria, and to the ends of the earth." Acts 1–5 narrates the activities of the apostles while in and around Jerusalem and Judea. Acts 6–12 narrates the spread of the word beyond Judea and indicates a shift toward diaspora Jews and the gentile mission. Acts 13–28 completes the pattern by narrating Paul's missionary journeys into the gentile world of Greece and Rome, ultimately stretching to the "ends of the earth." This high concentration of visions in the first twelve chapters demonstrates that visions are more frequent during the period of debate and conflict regarding the identity of the growing Jesus movement. Acts 9 and 10 are pivotal in this narrative structure, for it is in these chapters that the gentile mission comes to the forefront of the story and the conflict over the identity of the community comes to a head with visions that provide clarity and authority (Haenchen 1971, 362; Koet 2006, 15–16) for the mission to the gentiles. Once Peter silences his critics among the circumcised believers in Jerusalem and they recognize that "God has given even to the gentiles the repentance that leads to life" (11:18), the visions diminish sharply.[2]

Characteristics of Vision Narratives

Before turning to the relationship between conflict and visions in Acts, I must first discuss how visions are narrated in Acts. There are three characteristics that are particularly significant: the relationship between the verbal and visual elements of the vision, the horizontal or vertical orientation of the encounter, and whether the vision stands alone or is paired with another vision (Hanson 1980, 1395–427; Lohfink 1976, 73–77).

First, the visions in Acts are largely verbal (Wilson 2016, 475–76). Fewer than half of the visions have a significant visual component, and some are purely auditory (e.g., 8:26; 9:10–16). Even when a vision contains strong visual elements, a verbal component exists as well. According to John S. Hanson (1980, 1395–96) this is not unusual in ancient literature. According to Hanson, dream-visions could be auditory, visual/symbolic, or a combination of both (1409–12).[3] In particular, it is essential to recognize the close connection between seeing and hearing in the visions in Acts. This connection between seeing and hearing can be found throughout ancient works on rhetoric, history, and philosophy. Ancient authors regularly emphasized a balance between seeing and hearing as necessary for effective and authoritative communication. This can be seen in the discussion of the narrative technique of *ekphrasis* (Webb 2009, 111–14), which ancient *progymnasmata* (school exercises) claim creates "seeing through hearing," a sentiment invoked by Aristotle and other philosophers who claim that the basis of human thought and language is found in mental images. Similarly historians (Rothschild 2004, 216; Prince 2018, 10–12) have balanced the value of seeing events for oneself (autopsy) with

---

2. Two qualifications must be made: (1) The question of the inclusion of the gentiles is not finally settled in Acts until the Jerusalem Council in chapter 15; (2) There is one more vision in this cluster. Peter's release from prison in 12:6–10 meets the basic requirements for a vision, although this identification is called into question by the narrator's language (12:9).

3. There are often verbal elements present in highly visual visionary narratives in other biblical texts as well. Symbolic visions within the prophetic tradition often contain verbal explanations for what is seen (see Jer 24:1–10; Amos 7–8; Zech 1–6; Dan 7–8).

Exploring the Visions in Acts in Their Narrative Context   133

the need to hear the accounts of others. The fact that the vision narratives in Acts vary in terms of the presence of visual and auditory components does not undermine their status or authenticity as visions. The diversity of terms demonstrates the fluid nature of such experiences and the value of being able to convey multiple sensory experiences as a means for providing support and corroboration for encounters with the divine.

Second, the reader should note that a pattern emerges when the relationship between the visual/auditory elements is compared with the spatial orientation of the narrative. When a vision narrative emphasizes the verbal nature of the encounter, the account is usually oriented horizontally. When a vision has strong visual elements, however, the orientation is vertical. When I describe a vision narrative as horizontally oriented, I mean that the interaction between the divine presence and the visionary occurs in everyday, earthly time and space. Often these visions involve an angel that approaches the visionary and acts or converses as any other human might do (5:19-20; 10:3-7; 12:7-8; 27:23-24). In such cases, there may be no description that specifies the nature of the encounter other than that the visionary has heard a divine voice (8:26; 9:10; 22:18). Vertically oriented visions more clearly present the visionary as engaging a divine reality that exists in the heavenly realm. Either the visionary is described as looking up (1:9-10; 7:55) or the divine presence or visual stimulus is described as coming down from above (2:2; 9:3; 10:11). There appears to be a strong relationship between the senses engaged in the vision and its spatial orientation.

The Relationship between Sensory and Spatial Orientation

A further important theme to explore in terms of the way the vision narratives are presented in the book of Acts concerns the relationship between sensory and spatial orientation. In Acts 5 the apostles have been put in prison by the Sadducees. The narrator announces in a straightforward manner that one night an angel of the Lord came and opened the doors of the prison, led the apostles out, and told them to go and preach in the temple (5:19-20). Even though this event is not explicitly identified as a vision by the narrator, and there is no use of Luke's favorite terminology for visions here, this event meets the criteria set above in that it tells of a distinct encounter with a divine intermediary that provides instruction for the visionary. Similar divine-human interactions in Luke-Acts have been identified in the text as visions (Luke 1:22; 24:23; Acts 8:26; 10:3;

27:23). This vision in Acts 5 is an excellent example of what I refer to as the verbal-horizontal pattern. The angel of the Lord is said to be present, but there is no visual description of him (contra Luke 24:23; Acts 1:10) or any concern to highlight what is being seen or the visionaries' reaction to it. Rather the emphasis is on the actions and the words of the angel. Without any visual description to the contrary, the angel could easily be exchanged with a human actor and nothing would need to be changed to make sense of the account. It is narrated as if it is an everyday occurrence. Another example is Cornelius's vision of the angel of God in Acts 10. Like the previous example, there is no visual description of the angel, although there are more visual elements here than in 5:19–20. First, this encounter is identified as a vision (10:3: εἶδεν ἐν ὁράματι). Second, Acts 10:4 reports that Cornelius "stared [ἀτενίσας] at him [i.e., the angel] in terror." There is some recognition that what Cornelius sees is meaningful, but the emphasis of the interaction is the message that the angel delivers (10:4c–6). One final example is Paul's account of a vision (literally trance: ἐκστάσει) during his defense speech in Jerusalem (22:17–21). He tells of his experience in a way that is difficult to identify, but follows more closely the verbal-horizontal pattern than the visual-vertical pattern. Immediately after he retells his vision on the road to Damascus, Paul also tells the crowd that he had an experience in the Jerusalem temple in which he "saw the Lord saying to me, 'Hurry; leave Jerusalem at once, because they will not accept your testimony about me'" (22:18). Although the words Luke puts in Paul's mouth imply a visual aspect to the encounter (ἰδεῖν αὐτὸν λέγοντά μοι), there is no visual description at all, only the words of the divine voice. Again, if one did not know with whom Paul was speaking, there would be no reason to consider this conversation out of the ordinary.

Less frequently in Acts, the narrative emphasizes the visual nature of the encounter and the visionary's interaction with the heavenly realm. Stephen's vision is the clearest example of the visual-vertical orientation. At the conclusion of Stephen's long speech in Acts 7 he is filled with the Holy Spirit and "he gazed [ἀτενίσας] into heaven and saw the glory of God and Jesus standing at the right hand of God" (7:55). There is no divine speech or message in this vision (quite unusual in Acts!).[4] Only Stephen speaks. After the vision is described by the narrator Stephen repeats in his own words (in similar, but not exact language) what he is

---

4. The only other example is the Pentecost event in Acts 2:2–4.

seeing to the crowd (7:56). Peter's vision on the rooftop shares this visual and vertical orientation. Peter falls into a trance (ἔκστασις) and sees "heaven opened and something like a large sheet coming down, being lowered to the ground by its four corners" (10:11). Stephen also describes seeing "the heavens opened" (7:56). Peter's vision varies significantly from Stephen's, however, in that he sees an object that is lowered to earth and engages in conversation with a voice that tells him to "kill and eat!" (10:13-15). Peter's vision concludes with the object being taken back up into heaven (10:16). While the visual and vertical dimensions of Peter's vision are clearly defined by the detailed description of what Peter saw (10:11-12) and the upward focus of the opening and closing of the vision narrative, there also exists a strong verbal component in the dialogue between Peter and the voice. The voice is not identified, but the description of the heavens opening in conjunction with earlier vision narratives (7:55-56; 9:3-6) certainly indicates that the voice belongs to God or Jesus. This vision has many parallels with the symbolic visions known from the prophetic books of Amos and Zechariah, with the important distinction being that the visionary's dialogue with the divine figure does not explain the symbols seen. As notes Miller (2010, 453-54), Peter will come to understand what he has seen through his interactions on earth with Cornelius and his emissaries (10:17-43). While verbal elements are encompassed by the visual orientation of the narrative, the vision still displays a clear visual and vertical emphasis.

The narrative of the ascension in Acts 1 is more problematic. The first difficulty is determining when the vision begins. Acts begins with a secondary preface and transitions almost seamlessly into an appearance of the risen Jesus to his disciples (Acts 1:1-8). Is this resurrection appearance itself a vision? It meets the criteria established at the outset of this essay and in my previous work (Prince 2005; 2016, 123-39). After Jesus's commission to the apostles to be his witnesses to the "ends of the earth" (commissions are frequently made through visions) Jesus's ascension into heaven is narrated (1:9). Should this be read as the conclusion to the resurrection appearance, or a vision in its own right? Here the orientation certainly fits the visual-vertical pattern as the apostles watch as Jesus is lifted up into heaven. After Acts 1:9 there is a quick and again seamless transition to a vision of two angelic men (1:10-11) whose appearance follows the verbal-horizontal pattern discussed above. Hence, the second difficulty is determining the sensory and spatial orientation of this pericope(s). Certainly, there is a complexity to the opening of the book that I cannot solve here. Sufficient for my purposes is to illustrate the careful interweaving of various narrative elements in this vision(s). Although the appearance of the two men to the apostles parallels other angelic appearances that occur on an earthly plane (e.g., Acts 5:19–20; 8:26; 10:3–6; 12:7–10; 27:23–24), there remains a distinct emphasis on the visual and the vertical that is not found in those visions. First, there is a physical description of the two men dressed in white garments (Acts 1:10), which helps to identify them as heavenly beings (cf. Luke 24:4). Second, the entire account, including the verbal message given, is overwhelmingly oriented toward heaven. The apostles were gazing (ἀτενίσας) at the sky as Jesus ascended when suddenly two angelic figures appeared beside them and instructed them as to the coming and going of Jesus from heaven, in the process using the phrase εἰς τὸν οὐρανὸν three times in the course of their message (Acts 1:11). Yet, this section does seem to create a transition from Jesus's ascension into the heavenly realm to a vision of angels who appear to the apostles within their ordinary space and time and speak of Jesus's ascension and return in such a way as to reorient them to their earthly commission to be witnesses in the world.

The examples above show that, although there is a strong correlation between the sensory and spatial orientations of the visionary encounters, rather than forcing each vision into one or the other pattern, it seems more reasonable to recognize that a continuum exists that ranges from visual-vertical to verbal-horizontal. Some visions fall more closely toward one end or the other, but many display a mixture of characteristics and fall somewhere in between the two extremes.

Vision Pairs

The third characteristic is the use of pairs of visions in the narrative. There are two sets of double visions in Acts. These are clustered at the heart of the vision section in Acts 9 and 10. According to Hanson (1980, 1414), a double dream-vision report refers to a narrative in which a pair of dreams or visions, experienced by two different individuals, connects in some way so that "they produce what may be called a 'circumstance of mutuality' between the two dreamers." Gerhard Lohfink (1976, 75) emphasizes that such visions "work together toward a single purpose or goal." Saul's vision is intertwined with Ananias's vision in Acts 9, as is Peter's vision with Cornelius in Acts 10. In each case, the visions are interdependent. As I have argued (Prince 2017), the meaning or fulfillment of one vision cannot be completed without the other. Not only are these visions paired, but the pairs are paired in adjacent chapters! Each vision pair contains a vision that has a visual-vertical orientation (9:3–7; 10:10–16) and a vision that has a verbal-horizontal orientation (9:10–16; 10:3–6). Saul and Peter's visions, which are more visually and vertically oriented, begin and end each vision pair and so encompass the verbally oriented visions of Ananias and Cornelius. Additionally, each of the four visions in these two chapters is longer than previous or subsequent visions. Each vision ranges in length from five to seven verses, whereas other vision narratives in Acts range from only two to four verses. Add to this the increasing frequency of visions from Acts 1–8 and a crescendo of visionary narratives is evident, reaching its peak in the paired visions of Saul and Ananias and Cornelius and Peter. Looking closely at how visions are narrated in Acts illustrates clearly that they are central to the book's structure and message. Hanson (1980, 1415) does not say much about the function of double visions other than to suggest that they are "generally aimed at a resolution of some sort." More will be said below regarding the function of these double visions in the larger narrative, but first I will turn to a study of the placement of the visions within the wider structure of the narrative.

Transition, Conflict, and Visions

The relationship between conflict and visions is clearest, perhaps, in the double visions in Acts 9 and 10, but almost all visions in Acts are narrated at key moments of transition or conflict. Several visions form an integral part of narratives that describe transitions in the identity of the burgeoning group of Jesus's followers (1:9–11; 2:2–4; 8:26; 10:3–6, 10–16; 16:9). Most, however, occur during times of significant conflict and danger, such as arrests and defense speeches (5:19–20; 12:7–10; 22:17–21), or threats of violence and death whether by human or environmental causes (7:55–56; 9:3–7, 10–16; 27:23–24).

Visions at the ascension and Pentecost assist the narrative in transitioning from Jesus's earthly ministry and leadership to the mission of the apostles under their own leadership. In both cases as Jesus moves heavenward and out of the center of the everyday work of the mission to bring God's kingdom, the apostles receive divine encouragement that will disengage them from their focus on Jesus's departure (1:11) and refocus their minds and actions on their commission to be witnesses to the world around them (1:8), culminating in their reception of the power of the Holy Spirit to bring that mission to fruition (2:2-4).

The vision of the angel who releases the apostles from prison is the first of two prison break visions (5:19-20 and 12:7-10), which together form an inclusio around the most densely packed group of visions in Acts.[5] In fact, after Acts 12 there are only three more new visions narrated in the remaining sixteen chapters.[6] Following the prison break in Acts 5, the situation becomes more dangerous for the followers of Jesus, and this danger culminates in the most violent narrative, the martyrdom of Stephen, which follows immediately after his heavenly vision (7:54-60). Furthermore, as frequently noted by commentators, Stephen's stoning is closely connected to the narrative of Saul (7:58; 8:3), whose violent intentions are made clear at the opening of his visionary account (9:1-2). The serious nature of the danger to Jesus's disciples is reiterated by Ananias when he balks at the command to go and see Saul that is at the heart of his vision (9:13-14). These narratives of intense conflict and the visions that accompany them are interspersed with visionary narratives that reflect internal conflict and the growth and movement of the community in building their own identity. A summary of the persecution of the church opens Acts 8 and provides a setting and explanation for the scattering of Jesus's followers, specifically the expansion of preaching into Samaria and the story of Philip. Although Philip's mission beyond Jerusalem to Samaria (8:5-8) follows directly upon violent conflict, Acts 8 focuses more on the expansion of the believing community and the inclusion of non-Jews

---

5. I have concluded that the prison-break episode in Acts 12 is a vision even though the narrator appears to disqualify the event as an ὅραμα (12:9). The fact that Peter's thoughts indicate that an ὅραμα is distinct from something that is "really happening" does not mean that the author regards visions as unreal or this experience as something other than a vision. It may indicate, however, that this particular term for visions is used for experiences that relay messages from the divine without any accompanying physical action (as in other instances of ὅραμα in Acts 9:10; 10:3, 17; 11:5; 16:9) and so does not properly describe Peter's encounter in the prison. In other words, Peter may have expected to see and hear the angel, but not to have experienced a change in his physical situation, although the angel did the exact same thing in releasing the apostles from prison in 5:19. This is a difficult verse. The author of Acts does use other terms to identify visions (ὅρασις in Acts 2:17; ἔκστασις in 10:10; 11:5; ὀπτασία in 26:19), so rejection of one term here does not disqualify it as a vision, only as an ὅραμα. This question requires further study.

6. Of course, Paul also retells his Damascus road vision in Acts 22 and 26.

Exploring the Visions in Acts in Their Narrative Context 139

through Philip's encounter with the Ethiopian eunuch (8:26-39). Philip's vision (8:26) leads him to travel the road that will put him in the path of the Ethiopian and so continue to expand the sphere of Christian mission into gentile communities. Likewise, after the violent purposes of Saul are overcome by the double vision he shares with Ananias (9:3-19), the witness of the believers is further expanded through the double vision of the Roman centurion Cornelius and Peter (10:1-48). Conflict is present in all of these situations, but in Peter's case the conflict is limited to internal conflict over who should be welcomed into the believing Jesus community and under what circumstances. There is opposition to his interactions with the gentile Cornelius and his household (11:1-3), but this is not a life-threatening conflict as seen in Acts 5, 7, 9, and 12. After the second divinely led prison escape (12:7-10), the remaining visions reflect both types of conflict. The narrator's account of Paul's vision of the Macedonian man (16:9) supports the spread of the mission onto the European continent. Paul recounts another vision during his defense speech in Jerusalem (22:17-21) immediately after he tells the crowd in his own words about his experience on the road to Damascus (22:6-16). Finally, Paul passes on to his shipmates the hope and encouragement that he received in the face of the danger of shipwreck from an angelic vision (27:23-24).

All of the eighteen visions in Acts are included within a narrative of transition or conflict. The visions occur at diverse points in each narrative. They may be found at the beginning, middle, or end of the narrative. A reader may argue that most of the pericopes in Acts revolve around conflict or transition. This is true. However, when one views the book as a whole it becomes evident that the visions are present at key moments, when conflict has reached an apex or transition becomes extreme. The clearest example of this is found in the visions sandwiched between the two prison break narratives. The high stakes of this section is indicated by the clustering of visions that build upon each other at the crucial moment where conflict and transition meet. The conflict between the apostles and the Jewish leaders begins with their first arrest in Acts 4:1-4 as a result of Peter's act of healing and subsequent speech in Acts 3. But when they disregard the order to "not to speak or teach at all in the name of Jesus" (4:18), they are arrested a second time and miraculously freed by the angel of Lord, who commands them to continue to preach (5:19-20). This conflict with the Jewish leadership escalates until it reaches its deadly expression in the stoning of Stephen. Stephen's speech and vision brings both the conflict between the Jewish and Jesus communities and the transition of the community's identity to a climax (7:1–8:1). From this point on through Acts 11 there seems to be a (at least temporary) denouement, as also acknowledged by Gregory Sterling (1999, 216). Both conflict and transition are unraveled; the dangerous Saul reorients his passion from persecution to proclamation of Jesus and the community expands its witness beyond Jerusalem and into the wider gentile world, accepting the inclusion and baptism of gentile believers. Conflict and transition are intertwined throughout the chapter. Stephen's speech highlights the failures of the Jewish community to follow God's commandments and the violence that is perpetrated based upon such failure, as well as the ways in which God has been leading the Jewish people to expand their understanding of the community. Sterling has argued that Stephen's speech removes the focus from the Jewish temple as the center of Jewish identity. To Sterling, this aspect of Stephen's speech parallels the ideas of other Hellenistic Jews who lived outside Palestine and came to build their Jewish identity within geographic locations outside Jerusalem. Sterling asserts that Stephen's speech provides an important foundation for the broadening of the church's mission beyond Jerusalem, Judea, and ultimately beyond Judaism itself (1999, 212–17). Sterling writes, "The speech is not intended to reject the Temple, but to qualify it by arguing that just as Judaism could extend beyond the Temple, so could Christianity" (1999, 216). As Wilson (2016, 469) suggests, Stephen's vision punctuates his speech, confirms its message, and leads into the acts of witnessing outside Jerusalem that reach further and further into the Hellenistic world. This outward expansion is built upon the revelations received in the vision narratives in Acts 9 and 10, which transform a Jewish persecutor (including of Stephen himself; 7:56; 8:1) into a missionary to gentiles and provide a carefully contrived support system for the gentile mission and the inclusive identity of the Jesus community. Finally, this section of the narrative concludes in Acts 12 as the conflict between Jesus's followers and the Jewish leadership is reoriented toward political power, as represented by the persecution under King Herod and the arrest and miraculous escape of Peter (12:1–19). Although the death of Herod is narrated in Acts 12:20–23, conflict with the Roman political order builds from this point in the story. Yet immediately after Herod is struck down, the narrator proclaims that "the word of God continued to advance and gain adherents" (12:24). In fact, the transition outward from Jerusalem is completed in this chapter as Peter makes his final appearance (12:19) and the chapter (and the rest of the book) turns to the work of Paul (12:25).

The presence of three of the five visual-vertical visions in this section (7:55–56; 9:3–7; 10:10–16) also clearly indicates that Acts 7–12 forms a pivotal point in the narrative.[7] The vertical emphasis of these visions implies a more immediate and direct relationship between the divine and the visionary and so heightens the force of the revelation given through the visions. There is no divine intermediary in these visions, and ordinary space and human sensory experience is breached. Furthermore, there are no new visual-vertical visions narrated after Acts 12.[8] My reading of Acts 7–12 as a climax and denouement of conflict and transition does not intend to imply that conflict in Acts ceases after Acts 12. Paul faces opposition, even violent opposition, on several occasions. But again, it is when this opposition becomes most pronounced, at the point of his arrest in Jerusalem and subsequent trials, that Paul reminds his narrative audience of his visionary experiences (22:6–10, 17–21; 26:13–18).

The Function of Visions in Acts: Divine Authorization through Community

The prominence and frequency of visions at crucial points of conflict and transition within the Acts narrative suggests that they function to provide authority for these transitions and the resolution of conflict. Ernst Haenchen (1971, 362) has argued that the force of the vision in Acts functions rhetorically to assert divine authorization for the messages revealed through each vision, even over and above human thought, understanding, or action. According to Bart J. Koet (2006, 15–16), messages conveyed in Acts through dream-visions "cannot be challenged, because they come from God." Divine power is clearly at work and certainly the visions show divine approbation of the actions that will flow out of these revelatory experiences. The narrative placement of the few visual-vertical vision narratives at the opening of the book and in the pivot of Acts 7–12 support the rhetorical force of direct divine encounter on the major issues of tran-

---

7. As discussed above, the first two (Acts 1:9–11; 2:2–4) fall at the opening of the book and mark the transition of Jesus's ministry to his followers and establishes the structure of that ministry through the act of witnessing to Jesus within expanding geographic and cultural circles.

8. Although Paul does retell his vision on the road to Damascus in Acts 22 and 26.

sition and conflict. But if the divine word through visions was undeniable, then why are so many visions clustered and spread throughout the book? Would not just a few suffice?

In fact, there is more at work than divine authorization in the visions. Human discernment and endorsement of what is seen and heard is equally championed by the vision narratives. Some scholars have recognized a more balanced relationship here between divine authority and human decision-making. John Miller (2008) has argued that visionaries in Acts are actively engaged in seeking to understand and interpret what they see and hear. Haenchen and others go too far, Miller states, when they focus "exclusively on the irruptive, exterior facet of dreams/visions," and ignore "the more interior facet of interpretation" (182). Miller provides a helpful correction. Yet he continues to focus on the role of the *individual* visionary in interpreting and discerning the divine message.

What has not been fully appreciated about the function of the visions in Acts—although William S. Kurz (1993, 131) mentions it in passing—is that they provide not only divine sanction and insight into the process of individual discernment regarding the pivotal moments of change and conflict, but that they also function to highlight the corroboration and authorization of the broader community as well. I would assert that the visions in Acts, as a whole, function to reveal how the community discerns and sanctions God's will together. Even personal encounters with the divine are not sufficient to provide full understanding or unmitigated authority. The first few chapters narrate visions experienced by a group. Visions received by individuals in Acts are intentionally and carefully clustered together so that their purpose and meaning are only comprehended fully when the visions of others confirm, corroborate, expand, or explicate them. When discussing the double vision of Peter and Cornelius, Robert C. Tannehill (1994, 131, emphasis added) states:

> This account includes the following elements: divine promptings of persons in a state of receptivity, obedient responses by those persons even though they do not fully understand, and openness to other persons, with mutual sharing of visions. *Indeed, the visions in question here have the specific purpose of opening a relationship between persons of different cultures.* Each is a vision that leads its recipient to be open to a stranger's experience of God.

This holds true for the double vision of Saul and Ananias, although Tannehill and others disagree. Tannehill (1994, 116) holds that the divine commission for Saul that is related to Ananias through his vision (Acts 9:15–16) should not be read as a means of authenticating Saul's mission by the "apostles and the Jewish church before him, through which Paul's commission must be mediated." He argues that the commission is presented to Ananias in order to help persuade Ananias to do what the Lord commands him to do in Acts 9:11–12. Tannehill claims further support for this argument from Paul's second retelling of his vision (26:16–18) where Jesus delivers the commission directly to Paul and Ananias disappears from the narrative. Certainly, Paul's visions in Acts 16, 22, and 27, as well as his final recitation of his encounter on the road in 26:13–18, do not rely on intersecting visions for their authority. Paul has gained sufficient authority in the later chapters of Acts to no longer need support, at least in the immediate vicinity, for his experiences and actions. But this is because the community has already authenticated his divine call and mission through the cluster of divine encounters and human discernment narrated in Acts 7–12.

The cluster of double visions in Acts 9 and 10 also highlights the value of diverse, even antagonistic, visionaries for the promotion of the power and credibility of God's word within community. It is only after members of divergent communities (e.g., a disciple of Jesus and his persecutor; one of the Twelve and a Roman centurion) receive visions that work together to reveal corroborative messages that the audience (both the narrative and rhetorical audience) obtains clarity and certainty regarding the new direction advocated by the visions. The balance between divine authorization and a diverse and widespread communal authorization follows the expectations of an ancient Hellenistic audience, for whom acceptance of visionary encounters as authoritative was not a simple matter. As I discussed in an earlier article on Saul's vision (Prince 2017, 378):

> Ancient audiences were of two minds on the credibility of dreams and visions. On the one hand, the ancient belief that the gods were instrumental in sending dreams and visions certainly lends authority to the event. On the other hand, the vehicle of these divine messages lacks a measurable substance that could call their credibility into question. This ambivalence increased in later Greek thought as the subjective element of vision experiences received greater emphasis. While this change in attitude never overcame the objective view of visions, it did raise questions about the credibility of any particular visionary account. After all, it is human subjects that experience and report dreams and visions, regardless of the authority of their origin or the objectivity of their form.

Indeed, the author of Luke-Acts makes clear in his preface that part of his rhetorical program is to counteract uncertainty (Luke 1:4) regarding the central beliefs and actions of the community. This would certainly include the skepticism that would arise out of the wondrous events that he narrates. Ancient literature (rhetorical and narrative) can be mined for its strategies for assessing and bolstering the reliability of witnesses as well as for how an author or speaker can best organize the presentation of their testimony and other supporting evidence. Many of these strategies are present in Luke's narrative. The clustering and positioning of the vision narratives is just one example.

Conclusion

It is important, therefore, not to lose sight of the human dimension of the visions in Acts when exploring the divine power and revelation that is made manifest through these encounters. As the vision narratives in Acts present God, Jesus, and their intermediaries as directly accessible through the visual-vertical encounters, even more often the divine is present in ways that are experienced in ordinary space and time and in conjunction with the community as a whole, as seen in the verbal-horizontal type of visions and in the clustering of related visions and interdependent double vision narratives. Although it is clear that the visions in Acts function in large part to provide authority for the resolution of crucial points of conflict and transition, this authority is not only divinely ascertained. Authority is also shared and provided by the community. And in the final analysis it is only by this means that God's will is most clearly known.

It is essential to highlight, furthermore, the conjunction of the frequency and variety of vision narratives in Acts. The interplay between the visual and verbal nature of divine communication and the earthly and heavenly orientation of the encounters provides a complex but balanced picture of visionary experience. This picture is further enhanced by the relationship between the diversity of visionaries (whether groups or individuals) and the interdependence of their visions. The vision narratives in Acts are literary devices. Based upon the strong patterns described here and the organization of the visions within the narrative structure, I propose that this conclusion does not, however, disqualify *all* the visions in Acts from having *any* foundation in real human experience. Paul's letters suggest that he experienced visions (Gal 1:12; 2 Cor 12:2-4) and visionary experiences are widely claimed by early Christian and pagan believers alike. The vision accounts in Acts could not serve their purpose if visionary experiences were not known and valued by the audience.

Finally, much more work needs to be done in determining how visions are narrated in Acts and their function in the author's larger program. For example, the significance of the balance and placement of visions received by a group (as in Acts 1, 2, and 5) rather than by individuals, has not yet been considered.[9] It also would be worth examining how the character of the visionaries over the course of the narrative develops, and how this development affects the role of the visions themselves. Considering the authority (both heavenly and community based) granted to the visions of Acts, it is significant that Luke's diverse list of visionaries does not include any women, at least not explicitly.[10]

Bibliography

Haenchen, Ernst. 1971. *The Acts of the Apostles: A Commentary*. Translated by Bernard Noble and Gerald Shinn. Philadelphia: Westminster.

Hamm, Dennis. 1990. "Paul's Blindness and Its Healing: Clues to Symbolic Intent (Acts 9, 22, and 26)." *Bib* 71:63–72.

Hanson, John S. 1980. "Dreams and Visions in the Graeco-Roman World and Early Christianity." *ANRW* 23.2:1395–1427.

Koet, Bart J. 2006. "Why Does Jesus Not Dream? Divine Communication in Luke-Acts." Pages 11–24 in *Dreams and Scripture in Luke-Acts: Collected Essays*. CBET 42. Leuven: Peeters.

Kurz, William S. 1993. *Reading Luke-Acts: Dynamics of Biblical Narrative*. Louisville: Westminster John Knox.

Lohfink, Gerhard. 1976. *Conversion of St. Paul: Narrative and History in Acts*. Translated and edited by Bruce J. Malina. Herald Scriptural Library. Chicago: Franciscan Herald Press.

Miller, John B. F. 2008. "Dreams/Visions and the Experience of God in Luke-Acts." Pages 177–92 in *Inquiry into Religious Experience in Early*

---

9. All other visions are perceived by individuals, but in most cases this "individual" experience is somehow related to the experiences of others (e.g., Stephen, Philip, Saul, Ananias, Cornelius, Peter in Acts 7–12; and Paul's vision in Acts 16:9 which is immediately tied to the "we" passages which begin in 16:10).

10. The exception may be the Pentecost experience, which occurs while they "were all together in one place" (Acts 2:1). The narrator may imply the presence of "certain women" here, as explicitly stated in Acts 1:14.

Judaism and Early Christianity. Edited by Frances Flannery, Colleen Shantz, and Rodney A. Werline. Vol. 1 of *Experientia*. SBLSymS 40. Atlanta: Society of Biblical Literature.

———. 2010. "Exploring the Function of Symbolic Dream-Visions in the Literature of Antiquity, with Another Look at 1QapGen 19 and Acts 10." *PRSt* 37:441–55.

Prince, Deborah Thompson. 2005. "Visions of the Risen Jesus: The Rhetoric of Certainty in Luke 24 and Acts 1." PhD diss. University of Notre Dame.

———. 2016. "'Why Do You Seek the Living Among the Dead?' Rhetorical Questions in the Lukan Resurrection Narrative." *JBL* 135:123–39.

———. 2017. "Picturing Saul's Vision on the Road to Damascus: A Question of Authority." *BibInt* 25:364–98.

———. 2018. "Seeing Visions: The Persuasive Power of Sight in the Acts of the Apostles." *JSNT* 40:337–59.

Rothschild, Clare K. 2004. *Luke-Acts and the Rhetoric of History: An Investigation of Early Christian Historiography*. WUNT 2.175. Tübingen: Mohr Siebeck.

Sterling, Gregory. 1999. "Opening the Scriptures: The Legitimation of the Jewish Diaspora and the Early Christian Mission." Pages 199–217 in *Jesus and the Heritage of Israel: Luke's Narrative Claim upon Israel's Legacy*. Edited by David P. Moessner. Harrisburg, PA: Trinity Press International.

Tannehill, Robert C. 1990. *The Acts of the Apostles*. Vol. 2 of *The Narrative Unity of Luke-Acts. A Literary Interpretation*. Minneapolis: Fortress.

Webb, Ruth. 2009. *Ekphrasis: Imagination and Persuasion in Ancient Rhetorical Theory and Practice*. Burlington, VT: Ashgate.

Wilson, Brittany E. 2016. "Hearing the Word and Seeing the Light: Voice and Vision in Acts." *JSNT* 38:456–81.

Yarbro Collins, Adela. 1996. "Vision." Pages 1194–95 in *The HarperCollins Bible Dictionary*. Edited by Paul J. Achtemeier. Rev. ed. San Francisco: HarperSanFrancisco.

Warning! Cheerfulness Can Be Contagious: A Reading of Hermas's Emotional Spectrum

Jean-François Racine

Dreams and visions frame the whole New Testament. Indeed, the first pages of the Gospel of Matthew include four dreams that successively change the course the story.[1] The final book of the New Testament—Revelation—is a collection of visions. In between, the Synoptic Gospels and the Acts of the Apostles include dreams and visions that impact their respective storylines. These dreams and visions tend to only communicate information. From a formal perspective, one can view them as message dreams and symbolic dreams according to the nomenclature proposed by A. Leo Oppenheim (1959, 47–131) that Frances Flannery-Dailey (2004, 61) considers enduring. Therefore, the emphasis is on message itself and leaves out its emotional impact upon the dreamer or seer.[2] By contrast, an early Christian work, the Shepherd of Hermas, tells much about Hermas's emotions caused by dreams and visions.[3] Information and meaning are essential elements of dreams and visions in the Shepherd of Hermas, but their emotional impact on the work is often explicit. Besides, the range of Hermas's emotions is impressive; it oscillates between deep sadness

---

1. An angel of the Lord tells Joseph in a dream to change his plans about divorcing Mary (Matt 1:18–25). The magi are warned not to return to Herod (Matt 2:12). Joseph is told by an angel to flee to Egypt (Matt 2:13–15). An angel instructs Joseph to return to Israel once Herod is dead (Matt 2:19–21).

2. The exceptions are Pilate's wife's dream (Matt 27:19) that reiterates Jesus's innocence but has no impact on the course of events, and Peter's perplexity following his vision of the animals on the sheet (Acts 10:17). These two passages are treated in this volume in the chapters by Roy Fisher and Deborah Prince, respectively.

3. Throughout this essay, the Shepherd of Hermas (Herm.) designates the book, while Hermas and the Shepherd refer to characters in the book.

(18.6) and cheerfulness (60.1). This paper focuses on Hermas's emotional spectrum, an aspect that has so far received little attention in scholarship on the Shepherd of Hermas, which has mostly focused on questions such as composition, penance, ecclesiology, the relationship between rich and poor, and social setting. The last lines of Philippe Henne's (1992, 167) book on the literary unity of the Shepherd of Hermas and a recent article by Dan Batovici (2015, 161) allude to the range of emotions displayed in the work, but do not pursue the matter further since they study other aspects. Before Batovici, Petra von Gemünden (2009, 321–26) devoted a few pages of a monograph on the affective world in early Judaism and Christianity to the Shepherd of Hermas. Without going into as fine detail concerning Hermas's emotional spectrum as the present essay does, Andrew Crislip (2015) has produced the most extensive study witnessed so far on this topic, arguing that the Shepherd of Hermas promotes happiness as a marker that distinguishes its Christian audience from outsiders.

This essay aims at producing a more thorough map of Hermas's emotions by looking at what causes them and identifying a trajectory of Hermas's emotions through the story, whose terminal point is essentially cheerfulness. Ultimately, the essay argues that two factors explain Hermas's movement toward cheerfulness: being surrounded by cheerful characters and seeing repentance around him. Hermas's journey toward cheerfulness proposes to the audience behaviors that fulfill one's ethical desire, that is, one's desire to have a good life with and for others assuming how biblical narratives contribute to the ethical formation of their audience as Alain Thomasset (2005, 75–76) has argued. This element in particular—the reader's response to Hermas's upbeat emotions—aligns this chapter with others in the volume, which explores how readers respond to dreams and visions in the text.

Since readers may not be very familiar with the Shepherd of Hermas, I begin by providing some introductory notes before diving into the core topic.

Text, Organization, Unity, Genre, Place, Date

The Shepherd of Hermas is part of the Apostolic Fathers, a collection first published in 1672 in Paris by Cotelier. Its length, monotony, and tediousness have deterred many well-intended readers. However, these imperfections did not prevent the Shepherd of Hermas from becoming a widely read work in early Christianity, as indicated by the number of extant manuscripts of the work, especially those in Latin. It may even have been considered sacred scripture in some circles, if one considers its inclusion at the very end of Codex Sinaiticus, a major Greek biblical manuscript that includes portions of the Old Testament and the whole New Testament.

Externally, the Shepherd of Hermas has three sections. Five visions constitute the first section. The second section includes twelve mandates. The third has ten parables (or similitudes). The second and third sections do not mention the name Hermas featured in the first section. Internally though, the Shepherd of Hermas only has two main parts. The five visions that make the first part mostly feature Hermas's encounters with a lady who proves to be the church. The fifth vision provides a transition to the second part. It introduces the Shepherd, its main character besides the narrator, still assumed to be Hermas.

We have no complete Greek text of the Shepherd of Hermas. The current editions mostly rely on two manuscripts: the fourth-century Codex Sinaiticus, which comprises the five visions and the first three commandments (nearly one-fourth of the whole work); and the fifteenth-century Codex Athous, which includes nearly the whole work.[4] Three other Greek manuscripts and various papyrus fragments serve to establish critical editions. About twenty Latin manuscripts are extant as well as fragmentary versions in Ethiopic, Coptic, Persian, and Georgian.

A few phenomena, internal and external, have prompted scholarly discussion on the unity of the Shepherd of Hermas. As mentioned above, the first part of the work mostly features Hermas and the Lady, while the second part mostly features an anonymous intradiegetic narrator and the Shepherd. Also, some Greek manuscripts only preserve the first part of the entire work, and others only contain the second part. These and a few other aporias have served as evidence upon which to formulate multiple authorship hypotheses (e.g., Giet 1963; Coleborne 1969), beginning in the mid-nineteenth century until the mid-twentieth century. However, most scholars have so far assumed single authorship, even though this implies redaction in several stages.

Biblical scholars delight in discussions concerning the literary genre of the documents, assuming that the identification of genre induces certain interpretive assumptions. Hence, one should not be surprised about how much ink has been spilled concerning the genre of the Shepherd of Hermas, especially since, as a whole, the work does not easily fit in estab-

---

4. Only part of the ninth parable and the whole tenth parable are missing.

lished categories. The most common label is nevertheless "apocalypse," even if several scholars acknowledge that it fails in some regards the test of John J. Collins's (1979, 9) paradigmatic definition of the apocalypse genre:

> "Apocalypse" is a genre of revelatory literature with a narrative framework, in which a revelation is mediated by an otherworldly being to a human recipient, disclosing a transcendent reality which is both temporal, insofar as it envisages eschatological salvation, and spatial insofar as it involves another, supernatural world.

Edith M. Humphrey (1995, 120) notes that the Shepherd of Hermas shows little interest in eschatology compared to other apocalypses. Besides, as Michael W. Holmes (1996, 469) remarks, the second part of the work, the Mandates, is devoid of apocalyptic features and aligns itself more with Jewish-Hellenistic homilies. Finally, as Batovici (2015, 154) remarks, at first sight the Shepherd of Hermas does not feature an otherworldly being who delivers revelations and does not picture aspects of a supernatural world; the geography remains mundane. From that perspective, one can understand why the Shepherd of Hermas has been labeled a "failed apocalypse" (Wilson 1995, 41) and a "cooled-down apocalypse" (Joly 1992, 527). Hence, Christopher Tuckett's (2007, 155) warning about the genre of the Gospel of Mary is appropriate when dealing with the Shepherd of Hermas: "Any attempt to specify the genre of a text too precisely may foreclose (or predetermine) interpretive possibilities in relation to a text prematurely."

The Shepherd of Hermas is not unique in the constellation of biblical, parabiblical literature, and Greco-Roman texts from late antiquity. For example, it exhibits a strong resemblance to 4 Ezra in several aspects: the fasting of the seer, a prayer of demand for a revelation, ecstatic manifestations, the appearance of a revelator, the unworthiness, or foolishness of the recipient, and the explanation of revelations. These points of resemblance have even prompted Robert Joly (1992, 527) to speak of "conscious imitation," something that may be an overstatement, as the author of the Shepherd of Hermas may have simply been familiar with traditions also present in 4 Ezra. Patricia Cox Miller (1994, 132) has also highlighted the resemblance between the Shepherd of Hermas and *The Sacred Tales* by Aelius Aristides (117–181 CE) for the following reasons: (1) both works include dreams in which a divine figure—Aelius Aristides's revealer is named Asclepius (i.e., "Lifesaver")—appears to convey some kind of important information to the dreamer; (2) in each work the revealer becomes a permanent companion; and (3) in each work the information gives relief to the dreamer.

The Shepherd of Hermas likely originates from central Italy, as scenes take place by the Tiber (Herm. 1.1) and the Via Campania (22.2). Internal evidence provides no clue about its date of composition. Since Irenaeus alludes to the work (*Haer.* 4.20.2), the text must have been in circulation in some form by 175 CE. The Muratorian fragment mentions the Shepherd of Hermas, but the date of this fragment is debated.

What Are Emotions and How to Approach Them?

Today, psychology has appropriated the study of emotions where it first became an important topic with the 1884 publication of William James's emblematic article, "What Is an Emotion?" Considering the current proliferation of definitions of emotions that have arisen since James's article, anyone located outside the field of psychology who embarks on a study of emotions may feel intimidated by what looks like a jungle. For example, Paul Kleinginna and Anne Kleinginna (1981, 345–79) list and analyze ninety definitions of emotions. As Anke Inselmann (2016, 538) remarks, when studying emotions, the absence of a standard definition is matched by the absence of standard terminology. As Anna Wierzbicka (1999) shows, the understanding of emotion varies across contemporary cultures. There is, therefore, a risk of anachronism when studying a text from another time and culture, which is the case with the Shepherd of Hermas, a late first or early second century CE text from the Greco-Roman world written in Hellenistic Greek, a language that has no dedicated term for emotion.[5] Yet, works in the history of emotions (e.g., Oatley 2004; Matt and Stearns 2014; Plamper 2015) indicate that one should not overemphasize the risk of anachronism. Thus, Jan Plamper (2015, 10–12) argues for continuity regarding emotions across times and cultures, assuming that many emotion concepts are etymologically connected. Besides, cultures that do not have a word for emotion may import it from another language, as the Tibetan language has done. Comparisons among cultures and translations highlight similarities among emotional maps even if they also indicate differences. Finally, Plamper remarks that scholarship without metaconcepts is a random enterprise.

5.. The closest term is πάθη.

James (1884, 189–90) defined emotion as a bodily change that originates from a feeling. Accordingly, James leaves aside emotions that do not have a physiological manifestation. This sorting criterion proves challenging to apply when dealing with a text such as the Shepherd of Hermas. It sometimes mentions a physiological reaction matched with emotion, as in Herm. 9.5: "I was astounded and seized with trembling, and my hair stood on end—terrified because I was alone."[6] In most cases, though, the text mentions no physiological reaction beside the expression of emotion as, for instance, in 47.1: "And when he [the Shepherd] said these things he was so angry with me that I was unnerved and extremely afraid of him." In the latter case, Hermas's fear may come with a physiological reaction (e.g., higher heart rate, blush, dilation of the pupil), but the text does not record it. Should we dismiss this phrase as an expression of emotion because it does not mention a physiological reaction? To adopt James's definition of emotion would result in us leaving out most material that discusses Hermas's sentiments. It would also overlook the fact that the Shepherd of Hermas is a story. Good storytelling, to be manageable and enjoyable, does not include all the information. Following Keith Oatley's (2004, 10–12) suggestion, this study uses a broader definition that considers emotions as a conscious mental reaction subjectively experienced as a strong feeling usually directed toward a specific object.[7] This mental reaction may or may not include a physiological manifestation that the text may or may not record. One should also entertain the possibility that a text records a physiological manifestation but does not explicitly connect it with a mental reaction. If the surrounding context gives some warrant for doing so, this study counts that type of occurrence as the expression of emotion. This definition helps us understand how emotions are evaluative judgments prompted by circumstances. One makes these evaluative judgments based upon norms that are learned rather than innate.[8]

---

6. Throughout the essay, I use Bart Ehrman's (2003) translation published in the Loeb Classical Library.

7. My definition corresponds to the first part of the definition 2c found in the Merriam-Webster Dictionary: "A conscious mental reaction (such as anger or fear) subjectively experienced as strong feeling usually directed toward a specific object and typically accompanied by physiological and behavioral changes in the body."

8. For instance, more than forty years ago, during a funeral at our secondary school presided by the archbishop, a fellow altar boy wiped his sweaty face with the piece of fabric used to hold the archbishop's crozier. Seeing this, a priest got angry at the altar boys. We were fourteen years old and not used to celebrations that included

When approaching emotions in the Shepherd of Hermas, this study adopts principles formulated by Karl Allen Kuhn (2009, 22–27) in a recent work that focuses on the appeal to the audience's emotions in gospel narratives:

1. Emotions are complex phenomena of variable origins.
2. Many emotional responses are instigated and/or shaped by a conscious appraisal of events, objects, or persons and their relationship to what one values.
3. Accordingly, emotions are a gauge of what matters most to someone—they are a window into one's worldview.
4. Emotions are, to some extent, culturally conditioned.
5. Emotions are universal for the most part (e.g., the experience of fear). There is nevertheless diversity across times and cultures in the relation between signifier and signified.
6. Emotions can be evaluated and altered, just as beliefs about the world can be evaluated and altered.
7. Emotions are integrally connected and excited by one's imagination.

In a recent article, von Gemünden (2016) explains the relationship between expressing emotions in a text and its literary genre. Comparing narrative (e.g., the Gospels) and paraenetical sections (e.g., Paul's Letters) of the New Testament, von Gemünden found that narrative texts exhibit a plurality of emotions that are evaluated in various ways, accepted as reality, and often linked to a physiological reaction, as is the case in Mark 8:2 where the phrase σπλαγνίζομαι—translated as "I have compassion" (NRSV and NIV), "My heart is moved with pity" (NAB), and "I feel sorry" (NJB)—literally refers to a gut reaction. By contrast, paraenetic texts mention fewer emotions and frequently display them in a binary mode as, for instance, in the case in Rom 12:15: "Rejoice with those who rejoice, weep with those who weep" (NRSV).

As a genre, narratives combine events, characters, and settings (time and place). Only the characters experience emotions. However, the various events, settings, and interactions among the characters can cause

---

bishops. This altar boy had broken a rule unknown to us. Yet it was the priest, not the altar boy, who experienced the emotion (anger), because the priest alone could make the evaluative judgment.

emotions. Types and ranges of emotions also vary depending on the types of stories. Oatley (2012, 16) has remarked that bookstores often display works of fiction according to the emotions these stories include. Thus, one finds in the sections labeled romance, mystery, and horror various stories that attempt to convey love, puzzlement, and terror.

Plot development also calls for a diversity of emotions. For instance, one of the most common plots is the U-shape journey narrative that has the hero leave on a quest, experience hardships, and return home in a better position. This plot allows for the inclusion of strong emotions caused by the hardships encountered on the road and presupposes some evolution among emotions. Could we imagine and enjoy a story where the only emotion mentioned would be shame from beginning to end?

Finally, some kinds of focalization can let the audience know about emotions beyond physiological manifestations. When studying storytelling, Gérard Genette (1972, 206–11) distinguished three types of focalization: external, internal, and zero focus. When using an external focus, the audience knows the same things as a bystander in the story. For instance, if the narrator says that Hermas was shaking, a bystander close enough could see him shaking. With internal focus, the audience is privy to what is going on in a character's mind. No one would be aware of this if it was not told by the narrator. For instance, the narrator could say that when he saw the Shepherd for the first time, Hermas thought that the goatskin that covered him was filthy. When using "zero focus" to tell a story, the narrator provides otherwise unavailable information to a bystander. The beginning of the Shepherd of Hermas is an excellent example of zero-focus narration: "The one who raised me sold me to a certain woman named Rhoda, in Rome. After many years, I regained her acquaintance and began to love her as a sister" (Herm. 1.1). The audience would be unaware of this background information if not told by the narrator. Genette's theory of focalization contributes to dissociating focalization from the narrator's position as extradiegetic or intradiegetic. An extradiegetic narrator can, for instance, be more prone to internal and zero focus than an intradiegetic narrator who is part of the story. For example, one notes that Hermas, an intradiegetic narrator, often describes his emotional state to the audience differently than does the intradiegetic narrator of Revelation, who rarely does so.

The Shepherd of Hermas has oneiric qualities, not unlike some stories by modern authors Charles Nodier (1780–1844) and Jorge Luis Borges (1899–1986). As one has experienced, it is difficult to include all the inconsistencies of a dream when telling it. The Shepherd of Hermas includes some of these inconsistencies typical of dreams. Here are three examples. First, when Rhoda appears to Hermas in a dream (or alternatively referred to as Rhodalternate), she tells him that God is angry at him because of his evil desire toward her (Herm. 1.6). When the Lady shows up for the first time a few lines after, she tells Hermas that the real reason God is angry at him is because of his incapacity to govern his household properly (3.1). One would expect more consistency from God when it comes to reasons for anger. Second, in Hermas's fourth vision, the Lady, who is the church, shows him the construction of the tower, which is also the church. Third, in the fifth vision, the Shepherd asks Hermas: "Do you not recognize me?" How could Hermas recognize him? He has not met the Shepherd thus far in the story and is even unaware of his existence. However, Hermas notes that his appearance changed while he was speaking, and then he recognized him.[9]

A study of the Shepherd of Hermas as oneiric literature can take several directions. For example, Carl Gustav Jung (1960, 239–49) considers that Hermas repressed his erotic feelings for Rhoda. This repression changed his subconscious, and then his consciousness's reduced intensity led to a somnambulant or ecstatic state that was an intense fantasy that captured his unconscious mind. Cox Miller (1994, 51) criticizes modern psychological interpretations of the dreams. In late antiquity, she argues, most people viewed dreams not as fantasies of the psyche or the subconscious but as an instrument to connect with the realm of spiritual beings that populated the world but were otherwise invisible when awake. This perspective coheres well with Hermas's dealing with the Shepherd. Nevertheless, Cox Miller is not above psychologizing as she considers the Shepherd of Hermas as an autobiographical therapy of consciousness about his adulterous desires (128, 147).

In the last book he published before his death, Ernest Hartmann (2011, 1–47, 107–41), a psychiatry professor at Tufts University whose research was devoted to dreams, suggests that dreams are born of emotions. They are just one form of mental functioning that allows the dream to connect material as we do while being awake. The difference is that dreaming allows us to connect material more broadly and more loosely.

---

9. Everyone has likely experienced shiftiness of characters, places, and events in dreams.

Dreaming integrates new material with older material, guided by emotion since emotion tells what is important to someone. The integration can happen throughout a period through recurring dreams. This integration would help establish one's emotional being. Hartmann's hypothesis is a useful heuristic tool to interpret the emotional component of the Shepherd of Hermas.[10]

The Story

This section summarizes the storyline and notes how it mentions emotions in each section. The story is long and includes an abundance of details that help identify a few intradiegetic narrator traits. Indeed, throughout the whole book Hermas proves to be relentlessly inquisitive, continually asking questions to the Lady, the Shepherd, and the young men who show up between the encounters with the Lady.[11] Hermas also tirelessly notes everything he is told including his emotional reactions to what he hears and sees.

As a story, the Shepherd of Hermas begins with autobiographical notes. The narrator introduces himself as the former slave of Rhoda in Rome. After many years, he was reacquainted with her and began to love her as a sister. In the first scene, Hermas gives Rhoda his hand to help her out of the Tiber where she was bathing. In doing so, he thinks how fortunate he would be to have a wife of such beauty and character (1.2).[12]

---

10. Discussions of the rhetorical aspect of emotion within a Greco-Roman context and the map of emotions in the Greco-Roman world are beyond the scope of this paper. While these are valid angles of approach, one must be careful not to assume that Greco-Roman culture was monolithic. The paper is not so much interested in knowing how Hermas's emotions would have been perceived by its initial audience as to see how they can be relevant in a twenty-first century North American milieu.

11. The Shepherd can be harsh on Hermas. For instance, he calls him a foolish man (40.2: ἀσύνετος; repeated in 41.1 and 47.2 although said gently and cheerfully). He also calls him exceedingly arrogant/brazen (57.2: αὐθάδης λίαν) and then arrogant and sly/crafty (58.2: πανοῦργος). The Shepherd continues by telling Hermas that his stupidity/foolishness (ἀφροσύνη) is persistent. Interestingly this "name calling" prompts no emotion with Hermas.

12. At first, one can be hesitant about calling an emotion Hermas's thought about Rhoda. It is nevertheless soon labeled as "evil desire" and is therefore morphed into an emotion.

Later on, Rhoda appears to him in a dream after he falls asleep on the road in the countryside.[13] She accuses him of sins before the Lord, more precisely to have conceived an evil desire (ἡ ἐπιθυμία τῆς πονηρίας) for her. After Rhodalternate, the dream version of Rhoda, has spoken and left the scene, the narrator describes himself as trembling all over and being upset (2.1), asking himself how he can be saved if this sin is recorded against him. Soon after Rhodalternate has disappeared, an elderly lady shows up and greets him by name. At the moment, the narrator indicates that he is still upset and weeping (2.2) from his previous meeting with Rhodalternate. The Lady perceives something of Hermas's emotional condition, for she asks: "Why are you sad Hermas—you who are so patient, slow to anger, and always laughing? Why are you so downcast and not cheerful?" (2.3). Hermas explains to the Lady his encounter with Rhodalternate. She replies that some thoughts likely arose in Hermas's heart that could lead to sin. She continues by saying that this would be unlike Hermas, "the self-controlled, who abstains from every evil desire and is full of simplicity and great innocence." (2.4).[14] She also tells Hermas that the sin that makes God angry at him is instead his failure to admonish his household, whose members have been acting lawlessly against God. The Lady then reads to him from a book. Hermas does not say what the reading was about, but only tells about the impression it made on him: "All the words were terrifying, more than a person can bear" except the last words that were "beneficial to us and reassuring" (3.3). As the Lady leaves, she is cheerful (ἱλαρά) and tells Hermas to be a man (4.3).

A year later at the same place, the Lady appears again and gives Hermas a book to copy, the words of which he does not understand. Two weeks later he realizes that what he copied speaks of the sins of his household whose members he has not correctly admonished (Herm. 5–7). After these first two encounters with the elderly Lady, a young man appears to Hermas in a dream and asks him whom he thinks she is. Hermas wrongly guesses that she is the sybil. The young man corrects him by saying that she is the church. The Lady appears again to Hermas, asks him to add a few words to the book that he copied, and then sends one copy to Clement

---

13. From now on, I will use the name "Rhodalternate" to refer to the Rhoda who appears to Hermas in his dream.

14. The Lady has a favorable perspective, which at the moment does not really cohere with what the audience knows of Hermas. In fact, the qualities and virtues that she attributes to Hermas look more like goals set before Hermas.

for foreign cities and another to Grapte who will read it to the widows and orphans. She also instructs Hermas to read his copy to the leaders of the local church (8).

The account of the fourth encounter with the Lady is the most elaborate (9–21). Hermas fasts a great deal and asks the Lord to show him a revelation through the Lady. She then appears to him in a dream and makes an appointment with him: he shall meet her in the field where he farms around 11:00 a.m. When he arrives at the field, he sees an ivory couch on which are a pillow and a piece of linen. His reaction when seeing these objects is extreme: "I was astounded and seized with trembling and my hair stood on end—terrified, because I was alone" (9.5).

This time, the Lady comes with six young men she commissions to build, but without being specific about what they are supposed to build. Once they are gone, she invites Hermas to sit on the couch with her. As he is about to sit on the right side, she indicates that he should sit on the left side. Her directive makes him upset (9.9). The Lady detects his emotion and inquires about it before explaining why she makes him sit on the left side. She then shows him a tower being built on the water by the young men. The tower stands for the church (11.3). She then explains to him in detail the process of selecting and rejecting the stones used for the construction. The various types of stones correspond to the various types of believers and unbelievers. Some need extra carving to fit in the tower. The Lady then teases Hermas's curiosity by asking him whether he wants to see more (16.1). This offer makes him excited (περιχαρής). She therefore draws Hermas's attention to seven women standing around the tower who personify faith, self-control, simplicity, knowledge, innocence, reverence, and love. The Lady explains that they are all daughters of each other.

Hermas is puzzled by the changing appearance of the Lady; each time he meets her, she seems younger (18.2–5) and even more cheerful (ἱλαρωτέρα) than before (18.4), so much that he considers her to be "completely cheerful" (18.5). By contrast, Hermas's ignorance about the reasons for these different appearances makes him very sad (18.6). A young man eventually comes to him in a vision to explain that, as the church, the Lady is rejuvenated by the good news of having many people undergo *metanoia* (conversion/repentance; 18.7–21.4).

Twenty days later, as Hermas is walking and praying on the Via Campania, a disembodied voice commands him not to be double-minded. As he is telling himself that double-mindedness does not apply to him, he sees a hundred-foot-long wild beast looking like a sea monster with locusts coming from its mouth encrouching upon him on the road. Hermas's first reaction is to weep (22.7) and pray for deliverance, but he then remembers the command not to be double-minded and courageously faces the beast. At that moment, he is surprised to see it flatten itself on the ground and stay still as he passes by. The Lady, now looking like a young woman, appears at the scene of his encounter with the beast. Seeing her makes Hermas cheerful (23.2). She tells him that the Lord, after seeing Hermas's faithful composure, sent the angel Thegri, the one in charge of the wild beasts, to make the beast inoffensive. This episode ends the cycle of encounters with the Lady. Immediately after the Lady has departed, Hermas hears a noise which makes him turn around in fear (φοβηθείς) because he thinks that the beast is coming back (24.7).

Back home and sitting on his bed, Hermas sees a man come to sit next to him. The man wears shepherd's clothing: a goatskin wraps his waist, he has a bag on his shoulder, and a staff in his hand. The Shepherd introduces himself as being sent by the most revered angel to live with Hermas for the rest of his life (25.1–2). Hermas does not recognize him at first—no wonder as he had never met him before—but as the Shepherd speaks, his appearance changes and Hermas recognizes him. As he recognizes him, Hermas has another extreme reaction: "I was suddenly thrown into confusion, seized with fear, and entirely broken up by grief because I had given him such a wicked and foolish response" (25.4). The Shepherd simply reassures him and immediately puts Hermas to work, asking him to write down all the mandates and parables he is about to tell him for his edification. The mandates aim at inspiring a desire for *metanoia* as it becomes clear at the end of the series when the Shepherd calls himself the "angel of *metanoia*" (49.1).[15] Soon after Hermas has begun taking dictation, he weeps bitterly because of what he is writing (28.3). Later on, while he is still writing under dictation, Hermas comments that these commandments may be too hard to keep (46.4). The Shepherd replies that keeping these commandments is necessary for the salvation of Hermas and his household. Hermas adds that the Shepherd was so angry at him when he said these things that he became unnerved and extremely afraid, for the Shepherd's appearance had become different "so that no one could possibly withstand his anger" (47.1). The Shepherd notices Hermas's condition:

---

15. Hermas also refers to the Shepherd as the angel of *metanoia* in 78.1, who also refers to himself by this title in 110.1.

"he saw me so upset and unnerved." (47.2). As a result, he adopts a more gentle tone. Ultimately, Hermas expresses his resolution to keep all these commandments (49.4).

Hermas initiates the next section on parables with a reflection on the relation between an elm tree and a vine growing on it (51.1). The Shepherd allegorically explains it as similar to the parable about the rich and the poor in the church (51.2–10). The next parables also unpack observations on various trees (52–53) and include a story about an overachieving slave rewarded by his master (55–60). Hermas expresses his gladness for the Shepherd's interpretation of the last parable (60.1). The Shepherd also shows Hermas a deceitful shepherd whose appearance and manners are cheerful, but who turns his sheep to a punishing angel (61–65). Hermas describes the appearance of the punishing angel as "bitter." His appearance makes Hermas afraid of him (62.5). Hermas grieves for the sheep who have fallen under the punishing angel's control (63.1). He later finds out that he has moved into his place and afflicts him to prompt his household's *metanoia* (66). This concern was introduced early in the story and remains unresolved.

The next parable returns to the arboreal theme (67–77) as it revolves around a willow tree. This time, it brings Hermas on location and makes him an actor in the story, as he and the Shepherd take the angel of the Lord's place by distributing and collecting branches of the tree to people. Hermas's marvels regarding all the branches cut from the willow (67.4). The state of the collected branches illustrates the degree to which the recipients of branches have converted or not. *Metanoia* makes the angel of the Lord "extremely cheerful" (67.16–17). Those who brought back branches in good condition (i.e., green, sometimes with buds) are cheerful. This makes the angel of the Lord even more cheerful. The Shepherd even joins in the cheerfulness (67.18). This section is long since everyone can have two chances with the branches they have received. During the second tour, Hermas and the Shepherd are responsible for the collection of branches. Once again, the Shepherd is repeatedly joyful (68.7; 71.1, 6) when the returned branches are in good shape.

The final parable, longer than the other ones (78–110), pursues a trend inaugurated in the parable of the willow branches by bringing Hermas on-site and making him an actor. This parable returns to the theme of the construction of the tower already visited with the Lady. As in the previous telling, the selection of the stones is a long and tedious process. This time the Shepherd and Hermas end up being involved in the decision-making process (84.7–87.4). As in the previous telling, six men work at building the tower, and there are also women on-site. While there were seven women in the first telling, the parable now includes twelve virgins who wear linen tunics. Their names are Faith, Self-Control, Power, Patience, Sincerity, Innocence, Purity, Cheerfulness, Truth, Understanding, Harmony, and Love. Twelve women dressed in black are also on site. Their role is to take away the discarded stones from the tower. The Shepherd instructs Hermas about their names, which position them in opposition to the twelve virgins: Unbelief, Self-Indulgence, Disobedience, Deceit, Grief, Evil, Licentiousness, Ill-Temper, Falsehood, Foolishness, Slander, and Hatred. Hermas has no interaction with them in contrast to the twelve virgins with whom he later spends the night in prayer at the tower after the Shepherd entrusts him to them before leaving momentarily.

During the episode at the tower, Hermas experiences another marvel, this time from all the great and glorious things he sees (79.5). However, he is perplexed by the virgins (79.5) who cheerfully participate in constructing the tower (86.6). Seeing how well the tower was built, the Shepherd becomes very cheerful (86.7), a sentiment that Hermas echoes with desire (86.7). Finally, as he makes a final tour of the construction site with the Shepherd, Hermas becomes cheerful as he sees these things (87.1). When he is left alone with the virgins, Hermas notes their cheerfulness (87.7). He is nevertheless embarrassed (Holmes 1996 has "ashamed") to remain with them (88.3). As the virgins kiss and hug Hermas, who soon starts playing with them, he remarks that he feels young again and happy (88.5).

The story ends happily as the Shepherd and the twelve virgins move into Hermas's house to remain forever with him, given that Hermas keeps his house clean (113.2). The Shepherd and the virgins cheerfully welcome the command to remain with Hermas permanently (113.5).

Hermas's Emotional Spectrum

This section lists and classifies Hermas's emotions. It also includes the narrator's mentions of emotions exhibited by other characters of the story and their view of Hermas's emotional state. This study is especially interested in the factors that cause Hermas's emotions and the emotions' overall evolution.

After each word or phrase, I offer a short definition taken from the Bauer lexicon; the following line(s) lists a reference and some elements of context.

ἀγγαλιάω: to be exceedingly joyful, to exult, to be glad, to be overjoyed
   67.18; the angel of the Lord at the willow tree

αἰσχύνω: to have a sense of shame, to be ashamed
   88.3; Hermas when told that he would stay that night with the virgins

ἀπορέω: to be in a confused state of mind, to be at a loss, to be in doubt, to be uncertain
   79.5; Hermas when observing the virgins working at the tower

γινόμαι νεώτερος: to become younger
   88.5; Hermas spends time with the virgins

ἔκθαμβος: being utterly astonished
   9.5; Hermas sees the ivory couch on the field

ἔκρικτος: frightening
   3.3: Hermas's reaction to the Lady's words

πιθυμέω: to have a strong desire to do or to secure something, to long for
   86.7; Hermas's reaction before the tower

ἐπιθυμία τῆς πονηρίας: evil desire
   1.8 [2x]; Rhodalternate about Hermas

εὐφραίνω: to be glad, to rejoice, to cheer up
   60.1; Hermas after he has heard an explanation

ἥμερος: kind, reassuring
   3.3; Hermas about the words told by the Lady

θαυμάζω: to wonder, to marvel, to be astonished
   67.4; Hermas reacts to the branches cut from the willow tree; 79.5; Hermas about the tower construction and the presence of the virgins

ἱλαρός: cheerful
   2.3, with negation, the Lady describes Hermas; 4.3; Hermas describes the Lady; 18.4; comparative form, Hermas describes the Lady; 18.5; Hermas describes the Lady as being extremely cheerful; 20.1; Hermas

describes the Lady as being more cheerful than before; 23.2; comparative form; Hermas about himself when he realizes that the Lady is the Church; 61.6 [2x]; Hermas describes the deceitful shepherd; 67.16; with the adverb λίαν, the angel of the Lord; 67.18 [2x]; with the adverb λίαν, people whose willow branch turned green; Shepherd, when he sees people whose willow branch turned green; 86.7 with the adverb λίαν; Shepherd when he sees the tower completed; 87.1; Hermas walks with the Shepherd and sees the tower completed; 87.7; comparative form, virgins; 88.5; Hermas while he is with the virgins; 113.5, adverbial form, when the Shepherd and the virgins are told that they are going to stay at Hermas's home

κατηφὴς τῇ ἰδέᾳ: downcast
2.3; the Lady about Hermas

κλαίω: to weep, to cry
2.2; Hermas about himself when he meets the Lady; 22.7; Hermas about himself when he sees the beast; 28.3; Hermas about himself when he hears the Shepherd

λυπέω: to experience sadness, distress
2.1; middle-passive form; Hermas about himself from the episode with Rhodalternate; 2:2; middle-passive form, Hermas about himself from the episode with Rhodalternate; 9.9; middle-passive form, Hermas about himself when he is not allowed to sit where he wanted; 9.9; the Lady asks Hermas about his state; 63.1; Hermas about himself about the sheep led by the punishing angel

λυπή: grief
25.4; Hermas about himself after he fails to recognize the Shepherd

ὀργίλως: angrily
47.1 Hermas about the Shepherd's tone when he addresses him

περίλυπος: very sad, deeply grieved
18.6; Hermas about himself as he wants to know more about the Lady

περιχαρής: very glad
16.1; Hermas is offered by the Lady to see something else

στυγνός: gloomy, sad
   2.3; the Lady inquires about Hermas's state

συγχαίρω: to rejoice with, to express pleasure about one's good fortune, to congratulate
   68.7; Shepherd about the condition of the willow branches

συγχέω: to be confused, dismayed, to be troubled
   25.4; passive form, Hermas about himself after he fails to recognize the shepherd; 47.1 passive form; Hermas about himself because of the Shepherd's angry tone; 47.2, passive form; Hermas about himself because of the Shepherd's angry tone

ταράσσω: to agitate, to disturb, to unsettle, to throw into confusion
   47.2; passive form; Hermas's reaction to the Shepherd's angry tone

αἱ τρίχες μου ὀρθαι: my hair stood on end
   9.5; Hermas's reaction when seeing the ivory couch

τρόμος: trembling, quivering
   9.5; Hermas when seeing the ivory couch

φοβέω: to fear
   24.7; passive form, Hermas about himself when he thinks that the beast is returning; 47.1; passive form with adverb λίαν, Hermas about himself because of the Shepherd's angry tone; 62.5 Hermas's reaction when being showed the punishing angel

φόβος: fear
   25.4, Hermas's reaction after failing to recognize the Shepherd

φρίκη: trembling caused by fear, shuddering
   9.5; Hermas's reaction when seeing the ivory couch

φρίσσω: to tremble, to shudder
   2.1; Hermas's reaction after the episode with Rhodalternate

χαίρω: to rejoice, to be glad
   67.16; with adverb λίαν, Hermas's description of the angel of the Lord;

Warning! Cheerfulness Can Be Contagious   165

71.1, Shepherd's reaction about the condition of willow branches; 71.6, with adverb μεγάλως, Shepherd about the condition of the willow branches

To help interpret these data, one should consider their distribution among characters with a special attention to Hermas's emotional range.

Hermas's Unpleasant Emotions and/or Physiological Reactions (listed by order of appearance)

λυπέω (to experience sadness) 2.1, 2; 9.9; 63.1
φρίσσω (to shudder) 2.1
κλαίω (to weep) 2.2; 22.7; 28.3
ἔκρικτος (frightened) 3.3
αἱ τρίχες μου ὀρθαί (my hair stood on end) 9.5
τρόμος (trembling) 9.5
φρίκη (shuddering) 9.5
περίλυπος (very sad) 18.6
φοβέω (to fear) 24.7; 47.1 with adverb λίαν (very); 62.5
λυπή (sadness) 25.4
συγχέω (to be confused) 25.4; 47.1; 47.2
φόβος 25.4
ταράσσω (to disturb) 47.2
ἀπορέω (to be confused) 79.5
αἰσχύνω (to be ashamed) 88.3

Hermas's Unpleasant Emotional State as Assumed by Other Characters

ἡ ἐπιθυμία τῆς πονηρίας (evil desire) 1.8 [2x] (Rhodalternate about Hermas)
κατηφὴς τῇ ἰδέᾳ (downcast) 2.3 (Lady about Hermas)
οὐχ ἱλαρός (not cheerful) 2.3 (Lady about Hermas)
στυγνός (gloomy) 2.3 (Lady about Hermas)
λυπέω (to be sad) 9.9 (Lady about Hermas)

Hermas's Pleasant Emotions

ἐπιθυμέω (to long for) 1.4; 86.7
ἥμερος (kind) 3.3

περιχαρής (very glad) 16.1
ἱλαρός (cheerful) 23.2 comparative form; 87.1; 88.5
εὐφραίνω (to rejoice) 60.1
γίνομαι νεώτερος (to become younger) 88.5

Other Emotional States

ἔκθαμβος (being utterly astonished) 9.5
θαυμάζω (to wonder) 67.4; 79.5

Hermas's Assumptions about Other Characters' Emotions

ἱλαρός (cheerful) 4.3; 18.4; 18.5; 20.1; the Lady; 61.6 [2×] the deceitful shepherd; 67.16 the angel of the Lord; 67.18 [2×] the Shepherd and people whose willow branch turned green; 86.7 Shepherd; 87.7 virgins; 113.5 Shepherd and virgins
ὀργίλως (angrily) 47.1 the Shepherd
ἀγγαλιάω (to exult) 67.18 the angel of the Lord
χαίρω (to rejoice) 67.16 the angel of the Lord; 71.1 the Shepherd; 71.6 the Shepherd
συγχαίρω (to rejoice with) 68.7 the Shepherd

The Shepherd of Hermas is a narrative based on visions and dreams. As a narrative, all the essential components of the story (i.e., events, characters, and settings) have the potential to provoke some emotions. Besides, as visions and dreams, this narrative depicts extraordinary and unsettling events, characters, and settings that can prompt strong emotions. One can compare the rich possibilities of dreams and visions to prompt emotions to the situation of finding oneself alone in a completely different geographical and cultural situation where language, customs, schedule, social behaviors, smells, and landscape are different. In such a situation, one may end up being emotionally hypersensitive. These extraordinary situations may explain some of the narrator's emotional range in the book.

The next step looks at moments of the story that mention emotions and identifies what narrative elements prompt them. While doing this, the study assumes that if emotions are evaluative judgments, and if dreams are born of emotions and say something about what is important to someone, emotional situations in the Shepherd of Hermas can say something about what makes Hermas react and what is important to him.

The sight of Rhoda bathing in the Tiber (1.2) provokes a desire, as acknowledged in the next episode (1.4, 8).	Combination of event and character.
Rhodalternate's accusation of Hermas provokes trembling, grief (2.1), more grief, and crying (2.2).	Event
The words read by the Lady (not conveyed to the audience) generate at first terror (3.3), although the final ones are beneficial and reassuring.	Event described using an internal focus.
The ivory couch's vision in the field provokes astonishment, trembling, and makes Hermas's hair stand on end (9.5).	Setting
Not being able to sit on the right side of the elderly lady on the ivory couch makes Hermas upset (9.9).	Combination of character and setting.
Being offered by the Lady, the possibility of seeing something else besides the construction of the tower makes Hermas happy/excited (16.1).	Event
Not having all his questions answered by the elderly lady about the meaning of his visions make Hermas very sad (18.6).	Character
The coming of the beast makes Hermas weep (22.7).	Combination of event and character
A noise provokes Hermas's fear as he thinks for a moment that the beast may be back (24.7).	Combination of event and character
Hermas makes an error by not recognizing the Shepherd. Once the Shepherd tells him about this error, Hermas is "thrown into confusion, seized with fear, and entirely broken by fear" (25.4).	Event
Hermas weeps after hearing the Shepherd speak about those who reject the Lord and defraud him by not taking care of the spirit that dwells in them. 28.3 When the Shepherd asks Hermas why he weeps, he replies that he is unsure about his salvation.	Event

Hermas is afraid of the Shepherd because of his angry tone and changed appearance. Hermas describes his condition as confused and very afraid (47.1) and then as upset and confused (47.2).	Character
The Shepherd's interpretation (57–59) of a parable/allegory that features a field, a master, a vineyard, and a slave who builds a fence around the vineyard (55) makes Hermas glad (60.1).	Event
Hermas is afraid of the appearance of the punishing angel (62.5).	Character
Hermas feels grief for the sheep beaten by the punishing angel (63.1).	Event
Hermas is astonished/marvels from seeing the giant white rock surrounded by the virgins and, at the same time, perplexed/confused at their appearance (79.5).	Characters
Hermas's desire to see the tower (86.7).	Setting
Hermas is cheerful while walking with the shepherd and from seeing the tower that has been built (87.1).	Combination of event and character
Hermas is embarrassed/ashamed to stay with the virgins (88.3).	Characters
While being with the virgins, Hermas has the impression to become younger again and is cheerful (88.5).	Characters

Looking at all these data, we find that throughout the book the number and range of Hermas's unpleasant emotions and physiological manifestations are much greater than definitely pleasant ones or more neutral ones (e.g., astonishment). By contrast, the range of the other characters' emotions (as Hermas assumes them) is narrow, and these are practically always pleasant except in one case when the Shepherd's voice and appearance convey anger (47.1). Hermas is almost equally sensitive to events and characters. In two cases, he even becomes emotional because of a spatial setting.

Warning! Cheerfulness Can Be Contagious   169

The range of events and characters that provoke Hermas's emotions is impressive. One could say that almost nothing or no one leaves Hermas emotionally indifferent even if most characters may not notice it except Rhodalternate and the Lady.

The most often mentioned emotional manifestation is clearly cheerfulness present among a broad cast of characters: the Lady, the angel of the Lord, the Shepherd, those whose willow branch express *metanoia*, the virgins, and even the deceitful shepherd. All these, except the deceitful shepherd (seen from far away), interact with Hermas. Yet, cheerfulness rarely applies to Hermas except toward the end of the book, even though the Lady described him as the ever-cheerful Hermas at their first encounter. Cheerfulness is, therefore, important to Hermas, and it practically takes the whole book for him to achieve it.

When Hermas's emotional range evolves toward cheerfulness, what is the catalyst? It may seem that Hermas catches cheerfulness as an infectious disease by hanging around cheerful characters. This would be partly true: Even after several encounters with the cheerful Lady, Hermas still displays unpleasant emotions. His first dealings with the Shepherd are also rocky. I consider that two major turning points put Hermas on a track toward cheerfulness. The first one is his encounter with the beast that he faces courageously by controlling his negative emotions. This exercise of self-control is his response to the Lady's injunction to be a man (4.3). When they meet again, the Lady confirms to him that the Lord commanded the beast to cease and desist once Hermas exhibited a faithful composure. This meeting is also the first time that Hermas is described as being cheerful. Yet, unpleasant emotions soon return as he hears a noise that makes him think that the beast is coming back, and emotions of dismay continue during his initial dealings with the Shepherd. So far, all Hermas's dealings have taken place as one-on-one encounters with Rhoda, Rhodalternate, the Lady—she has helpers, but she sends them away during the meetings— the young man, and with the Shepherd. Hermas is always portrayed as being on his own. For instance, his wife and children, although frequently mentioned, are never brought on stage. When Hermas is brought on the construction site of the tower and begins to help the Shepherd, as he had been at the willow tree, his emotional state definitely takes a turn for the better. At the willow tree, he finds himself among a vast crowd of people, is asked to help, and, in doing so, becomes a witness of *metanoia* taking place around him. His transfer at the construction site of the tower more clearly establishes a new trajectory for Hermas's emotions as he again helps out and sees *metanoia* around him. This time, the context is expressed more clearly as being the construction of the church. Cheerfulness is, therefore, indeed contagious, but will not jump on Hermas unless he is seriously exposed by taking a few "crowd baths" and becomes involved in a construction project.[16]

Toward the end of the book, Hermas's cheerful attitude when staying with the virgins indicates that he has also undergone *metanoia* and has finally become a man, as suggests Wudel (2004, 39–49). He can enjoy spending a night in prayer with twelve merry virgins without losing his self-control and conceiving evil desires.

Conclusion

After discussing what emotion is and what possibilities narrative dreams and visions offer when displaying characters with a broad emotional range, this paper examined Hermas's emotional spectrum in the Shepherd of Hermas. The paper shows that Hermas's emotional state evolves in the story from displaying mostly unpleasant emotions toward a more narrow emotional range where the dominant emotion is cheerfulness. This evolution is prompted by five factors: (1) being surrounded with cheerful characters; (2) witnessing *metanoia* around him; (3) being brought into large companies; (4) helping out in a building project of the tower (the church); and (5) experiencing *metanoia* himself.

The relevance of the Shepherd of Hermas diminished in early Christianity when churches developed more sophisticated penitential practices. There is nevertheless more to this book than the question of second penance. As a fictional work, it contributes to the ethical formation of the audience, a phrase that I owe to Thomasset (2005, 73–94). Thomasset argues that narratives serve the purpose of ethical formation. On the one hand, they expose audiences to characters who show certain dispositions, behaviors, and patterns of action that convey or collide with one's ethical desire, that is, a deep desire to have a good life with and for others. On the other hand, narratives allow one to evaluate the effect of such dispositions, behaviors, and patterns of action through time—the whole narrative— instead of relying on an isolated action to make a judgment. Hermas begins

---

16. "Crowd baths" is the literal translation of the French phrase "bains de foule," which means to mingle with the crowd.

the story in an emotional state that mostly comprises unpleasant emotions and progressively journeys toward cheerfulness through the encounters made on the journey. In the course of events, the audience perceives what dispositions, behaviors, and actions lead to better or worse living conditions. As a moral tale, the Shepherd of Hermas may seem simplistic, as Burnett Hillman Streeter (1929, 209) sarcastically remarked:

> The Shepherd of Hermas and the Apocalypse of John are of special interest as being the chief survivals in literary form of that outburst of prophet which was a conspicuous feature in early Christianity the one representing Rome, the other Asia. ... But, though both write as prophets, *no contrast could be greater than that between the pottering mediocrity of the timid little Greek and the fiery brilliancy of the impassioned Jew. Hermas is the 'White Rabbit' of the Apostolic Fathers.* (emphasis added)[17]

However, we are bombarded on a daily basis with far more simplistic moral tales embedded in Hollywood movies, video games, and advertisements. By contrast, the Shepherd of Hermas begins with an intriguing situation that would normally have little consequence. Instead, it prompts a series of dreams and visions where even once familiar places become fantastic locations. It also clearly pictures Hermas's complex emotional life, a rare depiction in contemporary early Christian works.

Bibliography

Batovici, Dan. 2015. "Apocalyptic and Metanoia in the Shepherd of Hermas." *Apocrypha* 26:151–70.

Borges, Jorge Luis. 1962. *Ficciones*. Edited and translated by Anthony Kerrigan. New York: Grove.

Coleborne, W. 1969. "A Linguistic Approach to the Problem of Structure and Composition of the Shepherd of Hermas." *Colloq* 3:133–42.

Collins, John J. 1979. "Introduction: Towards the Morphology of a Genre." *Semeia* 14:1–19.

---

17. In the corresponding footnote, Streeter quotes Lewis Carroll's own definition of the White Rabbit from an article published in *Theatre* magazine: "Call him 'elderly', 'timid', 'feeble', and 'nervously shilly-shallying' and you will get *something* of what I meant him to be."

Cox Miller, Patricia. 1994. *Dreams in Late Antiquity: Studies in the Imagination of a Culture.* Princeton: Princeton University Press.
Crislip, Andrew. 2017. "The Shepherd of Hermas and Early Christian Emotional Formation." StPatr 9:231–50.
Joly, Robert. 1986. *Hermas. Le Pasteur.* 2nd ed. SC 53bis. Paris: Cerf.
Ehrman, Bart D., ed. and trans. 2003. *The Apostolic Fathers.* 2 vols. LCL 24–25. Cambridge: Harvard University Press.
Flannery-Dailey, Frances. 2004. *Dreamers, Scribes, and Priests: Jewish Dreams in the Hellenistic and Roman Eras.* JSJSup 90. Leiden: Brill.
Gemünden, Petra von. 2009. *Affekt und Glaube: Studien zur historischen Psychologie des Frühjudentums und Urchristentums.* NTOA 73. Göttingen: Vandenhoeck & Ruprecht.
———. 2016. "Emotions and Literary Genres in the Testaments of the Twelve Patriarchs and the New Testament: A Contribution to Form History and Historical Psychology." *BibInt* 24:514–35.
Genette, Gérard. 1972. *Figures III.* Collection Poétique. Paris: Seuil.
Giet, Stanislas. 1963. *Hermas et les pasteurs. Les trois auteurs du Pasteur d'Hermas.* Paris: Presses Universitaires de France.
Hartmann, Ernest. 2011. *The Nature and Functions of Dreaming.* Oxford: Oxford University Press.
Henne, Philippe. 1992. *L'unité du Pasteur d'Hermas. Tradition et rédaction.* CahRB 31. Paris: Gabalda.
Holmes, Michael W. 1996. "Hermas, Shepherd Of." Pages 469–71 in *Dictionary of the Later New Testament and Its Developments.* Edited by R. P. Martin and P. H. Davids. Downers Grove, IL: InterVarsity Press.
Humphrey, Edith M. 1995. *The Ladies and the Cities. Transformation and Apocalyptic Identity in Joseph and Aseneth, 4 Ezra, the Apocalypse and The Shepherd of Hermas.* JSPSup 17. Sheffield: Sheffield Academic Press.
Inselmann, Anke. 2016. "Emotions and Passions in the New Testament: Methodological Issues." *BibInt* 24:536–54.
James, William. 1884. "What is an Emotion?" *Mind* 9:188–205.
Joly, Robert. 1992. "Le milieu complexe du 'Pasteur d'Hermas.'" *ANRW* 27.1:524–51.
Jung, Carl Gustav. 1960. *Psychologische Typen.* Edited by Marianne Niehus-Jung, Lena Hurwitz-Eisner, and Riklin Riklin. 9th ed. Gesammelte Werke 6. Zürich: Rascher.

Kleinginna, Paul R., and Anne M. Kleinginna. 1981. "A Categorized List of Emotion Definitions, with Suggestions for a Consensual Definition." *Motivation and Emotion* 5:345–79.

Kuhn, Karl Allen. 2009. *The Heart of Biblical Narrative: Rediscovering Biblical Appeal to the Emotions*. Minneapolis: Fortress.

Matt, Susan J., and Peter N. Stearns, eds. 2014. *Doing Emotions History*. History of Emotions. Urbana, IL: University of Illinois Press.

Nodier, Charles. 1980. *Smarra, Trilby et autres contes*. Edited by Jean-Luc Steinmetz. Paris: Garnier-Flammarion.

Oatley, Keith. 2004. *Emotions: A Brief History*. Blackwell Brief Histories of Psychology. Malden, MA: Blackwell.

———. 2012. *The Passionate Muse: Exploring Emotion in Stories*. Oxford: Oxford University Press.

Oppenheim, A. Leo. 1959. *Le rêve et son interprétation dans le Proche-Orient ancien*. Translated and edited by Jeanne-Marie Aynard. Paris: Horizons de France.

Plamper, Jan. 2015. *The History of Emotions: An Introduction*. Translated by Keith Tribe. Emotions in History. Oxford: Oxford University Press.

Streeter, Burnett Hillman. 1929. *The Primitive Church: Studied with Special Reference to the Origins of the Christian Ministry*. The Hewett Lectures. New York: Macmillan.

Thomasset, Alain. 2005. "Personnages bibliques et 'formation' éthique des lecteurs." Pages 73–94 in *Analyse narrative et Bible. Deuxième colloque international d'analyse narrative des textes de la Bible, Louvain-la-Neuve, avril 2004*. Edited by Camille Focant and André Wénin. BETL 191. Leuven: Leuven University Press.

Tuckett, Christopher, ed. 2007. *The Gospel of Mary*. Oxford Early Christian Gospel Texts. Oxford: Oxford University Press.

Wierzbicka, Anna. 1999. *Emotions across Languages and Cultures: Diversity and Universals*. Studies in Emotion and Social Interaction. Cambridge: Cambridge University Press.

Wilson, J. Christian. 1995. *Five Problems in the Interpretation of the Shepherd of Hermas: Authorship, Genre, Canonicity, Apocalyptic, and the Absence of the Name Jesus Christ*. Mellen Biblical Press Series 34. Lewiston, NY: Mellen.

Wudel, B. Diane. 2004. "The Seduction of Self-Control: Hermas and the Problem of Desire." *R&T* 11:39–49.

Response

Is There a Reader for this Text?

Rodney A. Werline

In the latter part of the twentieth century, the limitations of historical-critical methodology began to become apparent. The method had especially focused on the history of the development of texts and the redactors that brought together traditions and edited them for their own—and their respective communities'—agendas. Interest in the communities behind the texts had led to attempts to reconstruct their memberships and the special challenges that they faced. Alongside this interest, interpreters sought to reconstruct the opponents of the various communities. These investigations were not without merit, and they brought fascinating insights to the foreground. The questions interpreters raised seriously considered the cultural and sociological milieus of the Greco-Roman world. Still, the nature of the evidence and the millennia of distance between us and the original authors could allow us to get only so close to the original historical and social settings.

Around the mid-1980s, biblical scholarship began to experiment with postmodern literary approaches to texts. In general, scholarship in Second Temple Judaism lagged behind biblical studies' adaptation of these methodologies. Among those new methodologies stood reader-response criticism. In New Testament studies, for example, the books by David Rhoads and Donald Michie (1982) on Mark, Norman Petersen's (1980) work on Mark and to some extent Philemon (1985), Culpepper's (1983) analysis of John, and Jack Dean Kingsbury's (1986) treatment of Matthew represent the major works that employed this critical approach. To some extent, these books paralleled developments among British literary critics such as Northrop Frye (e.g., 1982) and Frank Kermode (see Alter and Kermode 1987), the American critic Seymour Chatman (1978), and the German theorist Wolfgang Iser (1978). While one might contest the degree to which the New Testament interpreters departed from historical—or historical-critical—questions, there was no doubt that a shift had taken place. The locus of meaning in the interpretive process moved away from the historical development of texts and communities and historical authorial intent to the interaction between text and reader. As some might remember, a few reader response critics collapsed all meaning into the reader as the text slowly evaporated. Theorists like Stanley Fish (1980) argued that readers are part of a community themselves and are formed by that community, and this comes to bear in the act of reading. New literary criticism, represented, for example, in Terry Eagleton's (1983) popular book *Literary Theory: An Introduction*, noted the way in which ideologies form readers and, thus, the interpretations that they propose. Despite the great variety in all these theories, they all shared a basic interest; they emphasized *how* meaning happens instead of *what* the true meaning is.

The essays in this volume join the stream of reader-centered approaches to texts, but clearly from the position of how the interpreting community receives and works out the meanings of the texts. Thus, this collection avoids the somewhat untethered-to-history dispositions of the early forms of reader-response criticism. Some manifestations of that early form of reader-response displayed a synchronic tendency that neglected, or seemed unaware of, the forces that formed the text or those that were forming the reader. Nevertheless, reader-response took the shape of the text seriously along with the pursuit of the question about *how* the reader and text were being engaged and *how* meaning emerged in the encounter. Sharing the passion for exploring that phenomenon, these essays take up the reader-centered approach with a whole new bag of highly developed theoretic tools that prop up the weaknesses of the earlier manifestation of the approach.

As the introduction states and several of these essays show, the engagement between text and reader is not without its own tensions and struggles. In some ways, one might say that the community wrestles a meaning out of the text. The editors' introduction characterizes the process like this: "It is intriguing that, in many of these cases, a close reading of the text suggests that the response of the reading community destabilizes or decenters the intended effect of the revelatory experience and challenges the text's authority." However, there is the moment when text's "authorizing function" and community "interpretation" meet— "the *Mitte*." The revelatory experience to which the previous quote refers is a vision or dream—the phenomenon at the center of this collection of essays. This volume collapses these two categories together. Dream and vision texts have received much attention among scholars and rightfully so. References to the phenomena are ubiquitous in the literature and other material remains from throughout the ancient Near East and the Greco-Roman world. Interestingly, in the New Testament, dreams and visions are located primarily in Matthew, Acts, and Revelation. The Hebrew Bible includes many dreams, and the literature of Second Temple Judaism is filled with dream texts. Dreams and visions provide a perfect testing ground for these current essays that emphasize a reader's reception. They offer a kind of Rorschach test for the reader. The odd features of dreams—the ways in which they can defy space, time, physics, their naturalistic oddities, and their general defiance of logic—open them up to a variety of interpretations. When inserted into religious texts, the potential myriad of superfluous details invites the possibility of numerous interpretations. Undoubtedly, some of these would go completely against authorial intent, but we no longer have the authors to confirm what is legitimate and what is not. Even a living author, though, cannot prevent readers from establishing their own meanings in a work—once released into the world, texts take up a life of their own.

The internal inconsistencies or tensions within a vision or dream, as well as its inconsistencies with the reminder of the text or its interpretation within the text, might also generate problems. Nebuchadnezzar's dream of the statue of different materials in Dan 2 provides a famous example of these problems. In the narrative, Nebuchadnezzar demands that someone in the court supply both the content of his dream and its interpretation; the king never recounts the content of the dream himself in the scene. After some court drama, Daniel steps forward and supplies both. He has received both because he prayed to the Lord for these and God delivers these through a revelation. Despite the fact that Daniel supplies both the content of the dream and its interpretation, there are oddities between the two, especially the interest in the toes in the interpretation, which are not mentioned in the recounting of the dream. Further, the interpretation suddenly becomes interested in kings instead of kingdoms or eras (see Collins 1993, 159–75). We also know that the reinterpretation and reappropriation of the dream continued into the Middle Ages and the Reformation, as the various features and materials of the statue stood for continuously differing sequences of kingdoms (see Cohn 1961). As Norman Cohn (1961, 238–39) demonstrates, a violent reapplication of Dan 2 can be found in the preaching of Thomas Müntzer. Each reinterpretation reflects the process mentioned by this volume's editors in their introduction. New communities of readers in different eras challenged the text's authority, wrestled with the text, and arrived at their own mediated interpretations. Thus, the text itself supplies evidence of the reader-centered process as does the long history of the dream's reception, with each interpreting community producing meaning.

Joseph McDonald's essay on Abraham's dream in the Genesis Apocryphon also notes that the dream report displays multiple inconsistencies with the remainder of the story. Going against scholarly consensus, McDonald argues that the dream does not accurately map out or predict the narrative that follows. He also lays out for us how Abraham reports on events in the story for which he is not a firsthand witness. The accumulation of inconsistencies and tensions between the dream, the narrative, and Abraham's character leaves McDonald with no option except to view Abraham as unreliable. Once again, as McDonald states in a footnote, this conclusion places him at odds with most of the scholarly attitude about first-person narration in the Genesis Apocryphon and many pseudepigraphical texts. Most interpreters understand the first-person narration as a strategy employed to lend authority to the text. Thus, the narrator and the narration should be trusted. However, breaking with this consensus, McDonald draws on Shlomith Rimmon-Kenan's theory about unreliable narrators to understand Abraham in the text. To my knowledge, the tactic of an unreliable narrator might be more of a modern phenomenon than ancient. However, McDonald argues that Abraham's story has almost as many lacunae as the manuscript itself and that the layers of mediation might be almost as impenetrable as the manuscript is impossible to read with the naked eye. As McDonald leaves the manuscript with "uncertainty of mediation ... of the individual consciousness," I was also left wondering how we might know the frames of suspended disbelief when reading a story? Or is it even possible? Or is it legitimate to expect this of the reader? Would the reader walk away in a better state if we had an answer to these questions?

Another inconsistency: What happens when a widely acclaimed spiritual hero actually displays clear weaknesses? What if those weaknesses become obscured by the traditions that grow about him, even when the text contradicts traditional presentations? This is the question Gina Hens-Piazza asks about the Elijah traditions. The prophet holds places of renown in Judaism, Christianity, and Islam. However, from that pedestal the prophet's "elevated traditional status can obscure the struggles" the hero encountered and the weaknesses he exhibited. She argues that idealized figures run the risk of distancing and flattening the figure, which might compromise the personality's power to have a spiritual or moral impact on the reader. Hens-Piazza's close reading of the scene of Elijah on Mount Horeb brings fascinating results. There, Elijah turns out not to be the heroic character often imagined. She concludes: "The poetics of his answer [of why he is there] disclose a contradiction surrounding the idealized portrait of Elijah as faithful follower of the Lord. He professes his extreme zeal for the Lord at the beginning of his reply. But the conclusion of his response betrays his ongoing concern for himself." Further, one has to wonder if his trip to Mount Horeb is a quest to be Moses-like and, if so, what that says about Elijah's character. After reviewing the scene on the mountain, Hens-Piazza departs with respect for Elijah in place, but that admiration is of a different nature. The prophet, having been subtly rebuked and chastised for his departure from his work and self-concern, must return and carry out a three-pronged commission, one part of which is to appoint his successor, and in the process becomes more human. Elijah not only exposes his vulnerabilities and weaknesses but also has to face them and then return to society—the actual domain of a prophet—to correct his course. This, Hens-Piazza maintains, provides the kind of humanized exemplar with whom the reader can and should identify. Elijah no longer stands at a distance in heroic, unapproachable grandeur; he is like the reader, and readers recognize themselves in him.

It has become clear over the past several years that the experience of trauma and the cultural memory of trauma played a larger role in the people's experience and the production of texts than we previously considered or imagined. David Carr's (2014) work on formation of the Hebrew scripture has helped us take an important step forward. Israel's experience of pain and devastation mark much of the organizing principles in the collection of texts. For many Second Temple period authors and their communities, the ongoing reality of the dispersion vividly conveys the lingering effects of the centuries of loss, dispersion, domination, and exile. Thus, in the midst of instructions about how to live the moral life and properly navigate the sociocultural landscape, Ben Sira suddenly includes a prayer for Israel's return (Sir 36:1–22). If one reconsiders the literature of the Second Temple period from this perspective, the amount of literature that reflects on the lingering cultural memory of trauma or responds to a recent trauma is quite astounding. So much of it, or at least its significance and role, has been somewhat overlooked. On a theological and literary level, the ongoing, widespread application of Deuteronomic theology also testifies to this cultural memory of trauma.

In light of this, Genevive Dibley's essay on the Book of Dreams in 1 En. 83–90 makes an important contribution to this collection. Dibley zeros in on what is generally understood as Enoch's inconsolable weeping in 1 En. 90.41–42, at the end of the Animal Apocalypse. The vision in the Animal Apocalypse, as Dibley characterizes it, is "Deuteronomic to the core." The people of Israel, represented by white sheep, are "punished harshly for their inequities, living or dying under the Deuteronomic prescription." Those commentators who identify Enoch as the one weeping assert his tears are a response to Israel's and humanity's great suffering. Dibley, however, attributes the weeping not to the prophetic activity of Enoch but to the redactor. But why? The Animal Apocalypse ends with the transformation of all humanity, which includes the gentiles, into white bulls—not even sheep!—which was the animal form that represented Adam, Seth, Noah, Abraham, and Isaac. Thus, while God rejoices, Enoch becomes filled with despair (90:38c). The decentering action of transformation threatens to render Israel's suffering as without purpose. Dibley's own words best summarize the mourning: "The redactor's unrelenting weeping through his character Enoch sounds a jarring tonal dissonance, his tears registering a wordless protest. Like trauma victims the world over, the redactor is left to absorb the wound."

We might be justified in placing Richard J. Bautch's essay about Jeremiah's two appearances in 2 Maccabees, a generally overlooked feature of the work, in a conversation about trauma, though this is not his primary methodology. As he reminds us, the prophet's appearances come in 2:1–8 and 15:13–16. Bautch proposes that the two scenes provide a "frame" for the narrative, and he follows Vernon Robbins's (2008) concept of "rhetography, which is the use of imagery for argumentative purposes within a rhetorical context." The two images in 2 Maccabees significantly differ from the depiction of Jeremiah in the Hebrew Bible book bearing his name, where he is vulnerable, harassed, and persecuted. Yet, Bautch maintains, Jeremiah is always peaceable. That Jeremiah would find "no relief in a devastating sword" (Jer 11:22; 12:12), even if this involved God's divine justice. That image of the prophet lingers in the shadows of the community's memory and produces a paradox for its members, the first readers of 2 Maccabees. Which Jeremiah should the community embrace? How will Jeremiah frame their experience? How will they process their trauma? If I have understood correctly, the paradox Bautch notices does not simply lie in the image of the prophet, but in how the community conceives of God and the paradox of the God who brings judgment and the God who consoles. The framing structure calls on the audience to mediate between the two.

The matter of framing also surfaces in Roy Allan Fisher's essay "Dreams of Empire: Pilate's Wife in Matthew." Fisher begins his essay with a description of the ghostly appearance of Pilate's wife in Peter Sellars's 2010 presentation of Johann Sebastian Bach's *Matthäus-Passion* with the Berliner Philharmoniker and the Rundfunkchor Berlin. Fisher's choice for his opening scene proves fruitful, for he assists the reader in seeing anew the appearance of Pilate's wife in the story. She emerges from out of the shadows, says her haunting and obscure lines, and then disappears as mysteriously as she entered. According to Fisher, her voice does not provide a foil to the crowd and the Jewish leaders of Matthew's scene. To some degree, the basic structure of this essay reminds us of Bautch's investigation into Jeremiah as a frame in 2 Maccabees. In Matthew, the framing device again centers on dreams, for dreams appear at the beginning and near the end of the gospel (Matt 1:20; 2:12, 13, 19, 22; 27:19). He limits his analytical approach according to Robert K. Gnuse's (1996, 68) assertion that "dream reports are literary-theological forms," and any attempt to press beyond the text for a psychoanalytical meaning or the nature of the experience is illegitimate. However, complicating the interpretation of Pilate's wife's dream is the fact that she does not report the content, only that she has had the dream and has "suffered a great deal" because of it. Notably, Fisher, as do many of the essayists, carries out his interpretation with occasional assistance from traditional methods like form criticism and redaction criticism, but he recognizes their limits and finds a way to supplement them. Recognizing that dreams function in the birth narrative to give direction and not to predict the future among other potential functions, he suggests that Pilate's wife's dream is meant to accomplish the same. However, Pilate ignores her advice and apparently believes that he can wash his hands of the situation. The scene, consequently, calls Rome's power into question, for just as Herod was unable to bring an end to Jesus, neither will Pilate have the final word. God will vindicate the righteous one. The framework of dreams collapses the distance between the narrative's opening scenes and this scene near the conclusion as the audience is invited to meditate on the limits of Rome's authority in the gospel story.

Besides visions providing a space to reflect or meditate within a text, or somewhat force one to reconsider the community's shared traditions, they might also have a rhetorical function that seeks to persuade or convince the audience. Of course, this kind of function for a vision—to persuade a third party—requires that a person reports the vision either in an address or in a narrative. This role for visions raises many questions about the intended audience for the visions and the assumptions that the person reporting the vision might also have about the doubters or opponents. In other words, do such vision reports work on people who already share the author's perspective? In this case, the visions function to confirm what the group already holds to be true; they become a way for the community to validate or reinforce its already held positions. As a modern reader, I question how persuasive vision reports would be in convincing outsiders. These are the questions and issues that I bring to the consideration of visions in Acts.

As Deborah Thompson Prince notes in her essay, the first twelve chapters in Acts contain the highest numbers of vision reports. Interestingly, throughout these chapters, the church addresses several defining issues for the fledgling movement, or as she states: "This high concentration of visions in the first twelve chapters demonstrates that visions are more frequent during the period of debate and conflict regarding the identity of the growing Jesus movement." Certainly, the visions in Acts 9 and 10 hold a crucial place in the narrative because these chapters establish the community's position on the inclusion of the gentiles into the church. It is not that the latter chapters of Acts lack visions, but rather that these visions have much less to do with setting the agenda for the community. As Prince explains, once Peter has confirmed the manner of acceptance of the gentiles into the church, the number of visions in the book begins to decline. She maintains that visions in Acts tend to arise in scenes in which conflict intensifies or a transition is required or is imminent. Further, in the overall structure of Acts, the visions leading to the most crucial turn in the book, the gospel going to the gentiles, incorporates visions of what she labels as the "visual-vertical" type rather than the "verbal-horizontal" type. The latter contains fewer visual elements and tends to include more auditory features that, in a way, become part of the action within the narrative. The former contains more visual features and emphasizes the "more immediate and direct relationship between the divine and the visionary and so heighten the force of the revelation given through the visions."

I return to my earlier question about whom Luke is trying to persuade. It is difficult for me to imagine that the author of any New Testament text could have actually expected a wide Greco-Roman readership. Thus, the text must relate more to the formation of Luke's community and the bodies within the community. Still, persuasion always has in mind a real opponent or an imagined or characterized incorrect position, the perspective that threatens community cohesion or existence (cf. Newsom 2004, 190–208 on "counter-discourse"). Thus, Prince correctly states that she has opened up for us many new questions and issues, and we look forward to how she might enlighten us about these.

If a collection of essays explores the way in which texts engage the reader, we should expect an essay on the impact of emotions in a text. The phenomenon has become quite popular in biblical and Second Temple Judaism studies, and a consideration of these aspects of a text is essential. Thus, Jean-François Racine's treatment of emotions in the Shepherd of Hermas is an important contribution to this discussion. As Racine indicates in the early stages of his essay, a treatment of emotions sits well with an assessment of readers' responses. The key questions center on how the emotions in the text affect the implied reader or any reader. An assessment of the emotions in an ancient text is fraught with more complications than one might expect. Anthropologists and cognitive scientists have informed us that emotions are culturally constructed. Thus, we cannot assume that the emotions found within an ancient text convey or evoke the same meaning that we attach to such emotional displays today. Here is another example of the way in which the essays in this volume avoid an approach detached from history and are instead quite mindful of historical considerations. As Racine reminds readers, one must also remember that Shepherd of Hermas is a story, and as a story it intends to evoke a reaction from an audience. Shepherd of Hermas is a long, sometimes tedious and complicated text. Scholars have debated its genre, noting that the text lacks features typically assigned by modern scholars to the modern categorical construct of the apocalypse, though some have noticed a few similarities between characteristics of the book and 4 Ezra. Further, as Racine notes, the visions in the text display the inconsistencies and peculiarities that often occur in dream or vision texts. Unlike Fisher, who avoided an attempt to move beyond the text to the experience of dreams, Racine draws on the work of Hartman to connect dreams more closely to the experience of emotion. While Hermas exhibits a wide spectrum of emotion in the book, the character moves more and more towards a cheerful disposition. Racine lists five factors that move Hermas toward this emotional state. Overall, the purpose of the Shepherd of Hermas includes a reflection on repentance and penance. Beyond this, Racine concludes, the work uses emotions to encourage and direct the audience to consider the emotions and dispositions that contribute to or construct an ethical life.

Perhaps Andrea Spatafora's essay preserves the most features from the early forms of narrative criticism. His work focuses on Rev 12, the famous scene of the woman who gives birth while the dragon is waiting to devour the child. Spatafora recognizes the importance of interpreting the symbols and metaphors throughout the chapter in light of the entire context of the book. While he does not exclude the possibility that a real revelation lies behind the text, he asserts that the pericopes are now carefully constructed literary pieces "that translate into words this ineffable experience of the divine word." Applying the categories of characters, space, and point of view, he examines how the text seeks "to persuade God's people that they are involved in the cosmic struggle between God and Satan. John's rhetoric invites his readers to choose to fight alongside God and the lamb." If I have correctly understood his argument, the author of the text hopes that the readers come to understand that the struggles that they are enduring form part of a much larger cosmic battle between God and Satan. Thus, his assessment of the purpose of the narratival aspects of the text is to convince the audience of the validity of a particular perspective of the current situation and to act. This position departs from interpretations of Revelation that understand the text's goal as encouragement or as catharsis, though he does briefly refer to consolation as an aspect of the text. Nevertheless, the strength of a reader-centered approach lies in how it identifies the way in which a text engages the reader so that the reader takes a place within the drama and inhabits the imaginative world of the narration.

This particular return to reader-oriented interpretation in this collection is a welcomed addition to our various disciplines. Equipped with a host of new methodologies to assist our return, we can avoid the overly synchronic approach and limits that plagued some of the early applications of the methodology. Recently, I also returned to a reader response approach—at least at its skeletal foundations—in reading 1 En. 1–36 (Werline 2015). Carrying ritual theory with me in my tool box, I asked a simple question: how do rituals in the text help audiences to locate themselves in the story? Apocalyptic texts like 1 Enoch are packed full of a variety of ritual actions. Often, ritual actions lead to the revelation that the visionary receives, and they assist the visionary in recounting and exiting the moment. Visionaries might encounter divine beings, observe divine beings in action, and see malevolent beings in action, and any rituals performed by these characters in the scenes might affect the well-being, situation, and future lives of an audience. The audience might even witness angelic beings addressing the struggles facing humans through a ritual performance. Thus, rituals become a literary device that authors can employ to place the reader into the story, and because rituals pack potent social and cultural power, the effect on the reader might be quite profound.

For a brief example of this outside of 1 Enoch and apocalyptic literature, consider Jesus's prayer in John 17 when he suddenly includes this petition: "I ask not only on behalf of these, but also on behalf of those who will believe in me through their word, that they may all be one. As you, Father, are in me and I am in you, may they also be in us, so that the world may believe that you have sent me" (17:20–21). A scene already packed with emotion, intensity of the plot, and complicated characters and themes now delivers a ritual performance in which the author nearly breaks the fourth wall and speaks directly to the audience. Judith Newman pointed out this final feature to me. However, many authors make a similar play with the potent rhetorical, persuasive power that ritual in a text can deliver. At least at those moments, we might all remember that, indeed, the author has a reader in mind, and that the author has crafted the text to engage that reader and to convince that imagined reader of something.

The reappearance or reemergence of the methodology at this moment in the history of scholarship fits quite well with the interest in reception criticism. What is reception criticism other than a careful look at how later readers received the text, engaged and connected with it, and reappropriated it so that it contributes and nourishes the lives of other readers in a completely different situation? In a way, the power of and respect for the original authors and editors does not become lost in the methodological inquiry. Rather, they might garner admiration for their ability to craft a text that has the power to engage generations. Further, the new interpreting communities might find respect in their dedication to preserve, engage, and appropriate the text. Speaking from my area of the academic world—Second Temple Judaism—this kind of approach has promise as we enter into a new stage of interpreting pseudepigraphical texts and the communities that preserved them. With every observation we make, we gain a better appreciation and understanding of readers and perhaps a greater knowledge of ourselves as readers. In the process, we also must not miss the amazing time-defying and culture-defying potency of texts and the act of reading.

Bibliography

Alter, Robert, and Frank Kermode, eds. 1987. *The Literary Guide to the Bible*. Cambridge: Harvard University Press.

Carr, David. 2014. *Holy Resilience: The Bible's Traumatic Origins*. New Haven: Yale University Press.

Chatman, Seymour. 1978. *Story and Discourse: Narrative Structure in Fiction and Film*. Ithaca, NY: Cornell University Press.

Cohn, Norman. 1961. *The Pursuit of the Millenium: Revolutionary Messianism in Medieval and Reformation Europe and Its Bearing on Modern Totalitarian Movements*. New York: Harper.

Collins, John J. 1993. *Daniel: A Commentary on the Book of Daniel*. Hermeneia. Minneapolis: Fortress.

Culpepper, R. Alan. 1983. *Anatomy of the Fourth Gospel*. Philadelphia: Fortress.

Eagleton, Terry. 1983. *Literary Theory: An Introduction*. Minneapolis: University of Minnesota Press.

Fish, Stanley. 1980. *Is There a Text in This Class? The Authority of Interpretive Communities*. Cambridge: Harvard University Press.

Frye, Northrop. 1982. *The Great Code: The Bible and Literature*. New York: Harcourt, Brace.

Gnuse, Robert K. 1996. *Dreams and Dream Reports in the Writings of Josephus: A Traditio-Historical Analysis*. AGJU 36. Leiden: Brill.

Iser, Wolfgang. 1978. *The Act of Reading: A Theory or Aesthetic Response*. Baltimore: Johns Hopkins University Press.

Kingsbury, Jack Dean. 1986. *Matthew as Story*. Philadelphia: Fortress.

Newsom, Carol A. 2004. *The Self as Symbolic Space: Constructing Identity and Community at Qumran*. STDJ 52. Leiden: Brill.

Petersen, Norman. 1980. "When Is the End not the End: Literary Reflections on the Ending of Mark's Narrative." *Int* 34:151–66.

———. 1985. *Rediscovering Paul: The Sociology of Paul's Narrative World*. Philadelphia: Fortress.

Rhoads, David, and Donald Michie. 1982. *Mark as Story: An Introduction to the Narrative of a Gospel*. Philadelphia: Fortress.

Robbins, Vernon K. 2008. "Rhetography: A New Way of Seeing the Familiar Text." Pages 81–106 in *Words Well Spoken: George Kennedy's Rhetoric of the New Testament*. Edited by C. Clifton Black and Duane F. Watson. StRR 8. Waco, TX: Baylor University Press.

Werline, Rodney A. 2015. "Ritual, Order and the Construction of an Audience in 1 Enoch 1–36." *DSD* 22:325–41.

Contributors

Richard J. Bautch is Professor of Humanities at St. Edward's University, Austin. He previously held the Gregorian Foundation Chair at the Pontifical Biblical Institute in Rome. He has written, edited, or coedited seven books, including Semeia Studies 73, *Beauty and the Bible: Toward a Hermeneutics of Biblical Aesthetics*, coedited with Jean-François Racine (Society of Biblical Literature, 2013).

Genevive Dibley (PhD, University of California at Berkeley and the Graduate Theological Union) is an Associate Professor of Religious Studies at Rockford University. Her publications include *Abraham's Uncircumcised Children* (2013), "Rhetorical Audience as a Perception of Self in the Pauline Epistles." (2015), *Uncovering Theologies in Genesis* (2019), "The Making and Unmaking of Jews in Second Century BCE Narratives and the Implication for Interpreting Paul" (2021), and "Was Gentile Reclamation an Apocalyptic Apologetic?" (2022).

Roy Allan Fisher (PhD, University of California at Berkeley and the Graduate Theological Union) is a faculty member in the Theological Studies Department at Loyola Marymount University in Los Angeles, where he is also an affiliated faculty member in Jewish studies and bioethics. His trans-disciplinary work takes place at the intersection of cultural anthropology and classical biblical studies.

Gina Hens-Piazza is the Joseph S. Alemany Professor of Biblical Studies at the Jesuit School of Theology of Santa Clara University and Graduate Theological Union in Berkeley, California. She received her PhD from Union Theological Seminary in New York City and recently is one of the editors for and a contributor to *The New Jerome Biblical Commentary for the Twenty-First Century* (Bloomsbury, 2022). A frequent lecturer at national and international events, her most recent monographs include

Lamentations in the Wisdom Commentary Series (Liturgical Press, 2017) and *The Supporting Cast of the Bible: Reading on Behalf of the Multitude* (Lexington/Fortress Academic), 2020.

Joseph McDonald is affiliate faculty at Brite Divinity School and Texas Christian University in Fort Worth, Texas, where he teaches languages and biblical and related literature. He earned his degree at Brite in Hebrew Bible and early Jewish literature. He is the author of *Searching for Sarah in the Second Temple Era: Images in the Hebrew Bible, the Septuagint, the Genesis Apocryphon, and the Antiquities* (T&T Clark, 2020) and the editor of *Exploring Moral Injury in Sacred Texts* (Jessica Kingsley, 2017).

Deborah Thompson Prince is an associate professor in the Theology and Religious Studies Department at Bellarmine University, Louisville, Kentucky. She received an MDiv from Louisville Presbyterian Seminary and a PhD in New Testament from the University of Notre Dame. She has published several journal articles on vision narratives in Luke-Acts in the *Journal of Biblical Literature, Journal for the Study of New Testament*, and *Biblical Interpretation*. She has also contributed to the commentary series *Feasting on the Gospels: Luke, Volume 1* (Westminster John Knox, 2014).

Jean-François Racine is an emeritus associate professor of New Testament at the Jesuit School of Theology of Santa Clara University and Graduate Theological Union in Berkeley, California. He received his PhD from the University of St. Michael's College in Toronto. Among other works, he is the author of *The Text of Matthew in the Writings of Basil of Caesarea* (Society of Biblical Literature, 2004) and coedited with Richard J. Bautch Semeia Studies 73, *Beauty and the Bible: Toward a Hermeneutics of Biblical Aesthetics* (Society of Biblical Literature, 2013).

Andrea Spatafora, MSF is a priest of the Congregation of the Missionaries of the Holy Family. His doctoral thesis, obtained at the Pontifical Gregorian University in 1997, is entitled "From the 'Temple of God' to God as the Temple: A Biblical Theological Study of the Temple in the Book of Revelation." He is the author of *Symbolic Language and the Apocalypse* in 2008. A revised edition, *Langage symbolique et Apocalypse*, was published in 2016. Father Spatafora is associate professor at the Faculty of Theology of Saint Paul University, Ottawa, Canada, and was dean from 2008 to 2014.

Rodney A. Werline received his PhD from the University of Iowa (1995) and is now the Leman and Marie Barnhill Endowed Chair in Religious Studies and the director of the Barton College Center for Religious Studies at Barton College in North Carolina. His most recent book is *Whenever They Prayed: Dimensions of New Testament Prayer* (Lexington/Fortress Academic, 2021). He coedited *Early Judaism and Its Modern Interpreters*, 2nd ed. (SBL Press, 2020).

Modern Authors Index

Alexander, Jeffrey C.	112	Dobroruka, Vicente	42
Alexander, Joseph	90	Dodson, Derek S.	96, 100, 102
Allison, Dale C.	96–97	Doran, Robert	70, 74
Allman, Laura	118	Eagleton, Terry	178
Alter, Robert	177	Ehrlich, Ernst Ludwig	87
Arsenault, Virginia	80	Ehrman, Bart D.	152
Bar, Shaul	89	Erickson, Kai T.	112
Batovici, Dan	148, 150	Eshel, Esther	57
Bauer, Jenny	56	Ewen, Yosef	34
Bautch, Richard J.	70	Exum, J. Cheryl	50, 65–66
Bennema, Cornelis	34–36, 41	Falk, Daniel K.	57
Boase, Elizabeth	111–12, 119	Farkaš, Pavol	37
Beyer, Klaus	62	Felman, Shoshana	112
Borges, Jorge Luis	154	Feuillet, André	37
Boring, M. Eugene	37	Fish, Stanley	178
Broome, Edwin C.	113	Fitzmyer, Joseph A.	52, 62, 64
Brown, Raymond E.	87, 93, 96–97	Flannery-Dailey, Frances	1, 6–7, 147
Carr, David M.	113, 181	Forster, E. M.	34
Caruth, Cathy	111–12	Frechette, Christopher G.	112, 119
Chatman, Seymour	59–62, 177	Fretheim, Terrence E.	15
Claassens, L. Juliana	79–81	Fröhlich, Ida	69
Cohn, Norman	179	Fromm, M. Gerard	122
Coleborne, W.	149	Frye, Northrop	177
Colletti, Joseph	118	Garber, David G.	113
Collins, John J.	150, 188	Gemünden, Petra von	148, 153
Corbu, Nicoleta	70	Genette, Gérard	154
Cox Miller, Patricia	150, 155	Gevirtz, Marianne Luijken	51, 57
Crane, Ronald	60	Gibbons, Patricia	42
Crawford, Sidnie White	52, 57	Giet, Stanislas	149
Crislip, Andrew	148	Girard, René	50, 65
Crossan, John Dominic	96	Gnuse, Robert K.	87–89, 91, 95, 102, 183
Culpepper. R. Alan	177		
Davies. W. D.	96–97	Goldstein, Jonathan A.	70
Derrida, Jacques	81	Gray, John	15
Dibley, Genevive	115	Gregory, Russell	15

Gruen, Erich S.	70	Luz, Ulrich	87, 96
Gunkel, Herman	1, 7	Machiela, Daniel A.	50–51, 59, 62–63
Haenchen, Ernst	131	Masenya, Madipoeane	76–78
Hamm, Dennis	131	Matt, Susan J.	151
Hansen, Mark B.	58	McCann, Lisa	118
Hanson, John. S.	6, 88, 132, 136–37	McDonald, Joseph	50
Hartman, Geoffrey H.	112	Merrifield, Andy	56
Hartmann, Ernest	155, 185	Michie, Donald	177
Hauser, Alan J.	15	Miller, John B. F.	135, 142
Henne, Philippe	148	Mitchell, W. J. T.	50, 58, 61–62
Hens-Piazza, Gina	33	Newman, Judith	187
Holladay, William L.	76–77, 80	Newsom, Carol	185
Holmes, Michael W.	150, 161	Nickelsburg, George W. E.	109, 121
Humphrey, Edith M.	150	Nodier, Charles	154
Husser, Jean-Marie	94	Nolland, John	97, 99–100
Hvideberg, Flemming Friis	111	Oatley, Keith	151–52, 154
Inselmann, Anke	151	O'Connor, Kathleen M.	77–78, 113
Iorgoveanu, Aurora	70	Oekpe, A.	90
Iser, Wolfgang	177	Olson, Daniel C.	121
James, William	151–52	Oppenheim, A. Leo	1, 6–7, 147
Joly, Robert	150	Osswald, Eva	51
Jones, Gwilym H.	15	Petersen, Norman	177
Jung, Carl Gustav	155	Plamper, Jan	151
Kahneman, Daniel	71, 75	Portier-Young, Anathea E.	70
Kahl, Brigitte	74	Prabhu, George Soares	102
Kermode, Frank	177	Prévost, Jean-Pierre	29
Kingsbury, Jack Dean	177	Prieto, Eric	56–58
Kleinginna, Anne M.	151	Prigent, Pierre	28, 37
Kleinginna, Paul R.	151	Prince, Deborah Thompson	130, 132, 135–36, 143
Koet, Bart J.	131, 141		
Kuhn, Karl Allen	153	Rabatel, Alain	41
Kurz, William S.	142	Racine, Jean-François	74
Lange, Armin	70	Rambo, Shelly	113
Laub, Dori	112	Ratzinger, Joseph	42
Lefebvre, Henri	50, 56–58, 66	Raz, Yosefa	73
Leuchter, Mark	76	Resseguie, James	29–30, 32–34, 41
Levine, Amy-Jill	96, 103	Reymond, Eric D.	22
Linafelt, Tod	113	Rhoads, David	177
Linden, Sander van der	3, 19	Richards, I. A.	30
Lindner, Helgo	94	Ricoeur, Paul	120
Lohfink, Gerhard	132, 136	Rimmon-Kenan, Shlomith	53, 59, 180
Long, Burke O.	1, 16	Robbins, Vernon K.	70–71, 182
Luckhurst, Roger	112	Rotschild, Clare K.	132
Lundbom, Jack R.	74	Rowland, Christopher	42
Lutz, Tom	111	Russell, D. S.	44

Said, Edward	76
Saul, Jack	112
Schaper, Joachim	72
Schüssler Fiorenza, Elisabeth	73
Schwartz, Daniel R.	70, 75, 79
Sharp, Carolyn J.	74
Sister, Moses	1
Spatafora, Andrea	30
Spooner, Mary Helen	80
Stanley, Elizabeth	80
Stearns, Peter N.	151
Sterling, Gregory	140
Sternberg, Meir	35
Stone, Michael E.	42
Streeter, Burnett Hillman	171
Sweeney, Marvin	15
Tannehill, Robert C.	142–43
Thomasset, Alain	148, 170
Tuckett, Christopher	150
Tiller, Patrick A.	121
Vani, Ugo	30, 37, 40
Vitek, Tomáš	51
Wasserman, Emma	109
Webb, Ruth	132
Weissman, Gary	61
Wierzbicka, Anna	151
Wilson, Brittany E.	129, 132, 140
Wilson, J. Christian	150
Wudel, B. Diane	170
Yarbro Collins, Adela	130

Subject Index

Abram, 3, 49-60, 62-66
Acts of the Apostles, 5-6, 8, 89-90, 111, 113, 117-18, 123, 129-47, 178-79, 184, 186-88
  double visions, 5, 129, 136-37, 130, 142-43
  Paul's visions, 143, 145
  vision, 5, 129-46, 184
  vision narratives, 130, 133, 140, 144
Ananias, 131, 137-39, 142-43, 145
angels, 19, 28-30, 32-33, 38-42, 114, 117, 133-34, 136, 138-39, 147, 159-60, 162-64, 166, 169
Animal Apocalypse, 113-15, 121, 125, 128, 182
apocalypse, 44-45, 83, 110-11, 113, 115-18, 120, 122-23, 125, 128, 150, 171-72, 185, 190
Apocryphon, 50-51, 56-59, 61, 65-66, 171
approaches, reader-centered, 178, 186
authority, 3, 5, 33, 71, 73-74, 96-97, 100-101, 104, 123, 130-31, 141, 143-46
beasts, 27-28, 38, 114-17, 123, 125-26, 159, 163-64, 167, 169
  wild, 117, 158-59
birth, giving, 30, 36-37, 41
bodies, 37-38, 71, 85-86, 88, 152, 185
characterization, 34-36, 39, 43, 61
characters, 5, 7-8, 27-28, 31, 33-36, 39-41, 43-44, 53, 57-58, 60-61, 121-22, 153, 155-56, 165-70, 185-87
  flat, 34
  literary, 34, 59-60

characters (cont.)
  minor, 31-33, 42, 87
cheerfulness, 5, 147-73
child, 29-30, 34, 37, 42, 92-93, 126, 186
Christ, 27, 31, 35, 37, 40-42
church, 5, 33, 37, 40-43, 149, 155, 157-58, 160, 163, 170, 184
conflict, 5, 23-24, 29, 120, 130-32, 137, 139-42, 144, 184
conflict and transition, 139-41, 144
desert, 23, 28-29, 31-32, 34-35, 37-39, 43
dragon, 3, 28-34, 37-40, 42-43, 186
dreamers, 7, 9, 63, 88-89, 97, 136, 147, 150-51, 172
dreaming, 9, 25, 88, 155-56, 172
dream reports, 4, 18-19, 87-91, 93-95, 99, 102-3, 105, 180, 183, 188
  simple, 93-94
dreams, 2-9, 13-25, 49-60, 62-66, 69, 78, 85-98, 102-5, 109-11, 113-14, 116-26, 145, 147, 155, 157-58, 166, 178-80, 182-83, 185
  experience, 18, 55, 94
  narrative, 64, 102, 170
  prophetic, 113-14
  simple, 93-94
  veritable, 69-70
dreams and visions, 2, 4-9, 56, 64, 67, 87-90, 105, 109, 141-43, 145, 147-48, 166, 179
  analysis, 2, 56
earth, 29-32, 35, 37-40, 42, 54-56, 110, 114, 117, 130-31, 135
earthquake, 21-23

Elijah, 5, 13–15, 17–18, 20–25, 101, 181
  theophanic vision, 3, 15
emotions, 3–4, 8, 111, 116–17, 148, 151–56, 158, 161, 166, 168–70, 172–73, 185–87
  Hermas, 147–48, 156, 161, 169
  history, 151, 173
  unpleasant, 168–71
Enoch, 2, 4, 70, 109–11, 113, 117–18, 120–22, 128, 182, 186–88
evil, 5, 30–31, 33–34, 38, 41–43, 116, 155, 157, 161–62, 165, 170
eyes, 30, 35, 38, 59, 62, 64–65, 85, 114–15, 120–21
fear, 18, 22, 24, 49, 53–54, 64, 66, 110, 115–16, 152–53, 159, 164–65, 167
gentiles, 4, 80, 96–97, 103, 118–20, 123–25, 131–32, 140, 182, 184
God, 3–5, 13–17, 20–21, 23–24, 27–37, 39–44, 55, 72–77, 79, 81–82, 89, 101–2, 109–10, 113–17, 119–21, 123–26, 134–35, 140–45, 183, 186
heaven, 29–31, 35–36, 38–40, 42, 55, 74, 110, 117, 129, 134–36
Hermas, 2, 5–6, 147–73, 185
  emotions, 5, 147–48, 161
  Shepherd of, 2, 5–6, 147–56, 166, 170–73, 185
household, 139, 155, 157, 159–60
Israel, 21, 23, 32–33, 36, 72–74, 89, 92–93, 101, 109–10, 114–17, 119–20, 122–26, 146–47, 182
Israelites, 20–21, 23, 28, 76, 124
Jeremiah, 2–4, 69–83, 113, 128, 182–83
  vulnerable, 76, 78, 81
Jerusalem, 16–17, 59, 72, 75–76, 111, 115–16, 122–24, 131, 134, 138–41
Jesus, 13, 37, 39–40, 43, 86–88, 90, 93, 96–104, 129, 135–41, 143–44, 146
Jews, 69, 86–87, 89, 96–97, 103, 110, 124, 189
John, 13, 25, 27, 29–32, 36–38, 41–44, 97, 100, 145, 171, 177, 187–88
Joseph, 6, 44, 67, 91–93, 95–97, 99, 103–5, 147, 172

journeys, 17–21, 24, 55, 171
Judas Maccabeus, 4, 69–72, 78
judgment, 39, 43, 71, 97, 100, 104, 110, 115–18, 121, 123, 125–26
  final, 109, 117, 120–21
lady, 149, 155–60, 162–67, 169, 172
  elderly, 157, 167
lamb, 3, 27, 30–31, 35, 38–40, 186
Maccabees, 2–4, 69–76, 78–83, 120, 182–83
magi, 91–93, 95–96, 100, 103–4, 147
Matthew, 2, 4, 85–104, 147, 177, 179, 183, 188, 190
Matthew's Gospel, 4, 86–88, 93, 103–4
narrative context, 49–50, 66, 88, 129–45
Paul, 37, 89, 128, 134, 138–39, 141, 143, 173
Pilate, 86–88, 91, 94–95, 97–100, 102–4, 183
Pilate's wife, 2, 4, 6, 85–104, 183
  dream, 88, 94–96, 99, 104, 147, 183
  words, 86, 98–99, 101
prophecy, 24, 41, 82–83
  power, 82–83
prophet, 3–4, 13–24, 69, 72–79, 81, 109–10, 113, 115, 118–19, 121–24, 171, 180–81, 183
punishing angel, 160, 163–64, 168
readers, 3–6, 8–9, 27–29, 31, 34, 36–37, 41, 43–44, 73, 75–76, 78, 80, 120–21, 148, 177–87
reading community, 2–5, 7–9
redactor, 109, 119–23, 126, 177, 182
Sarai, 3, 49–55, 57–58, 60, 64–66
sheep, 33, 114–18, 120, 123, 125, 160, 163, 168, 182
Shepherd, 33, 147, 149, 152, 154–56, 159–61, 163–69, 172
space, 27, 54–58, 61–63, 104, 133, 183, 186
stars, 29–31, 33, 36, 38, 40, 114
theophanic visions, 6, 16–17, 20–21
tower, 5, 115, 117, 155, 158, 160–63, 167–70
trauma, 2, 4, 80–81, 111–13, 118–20, 122, 126–28, 181–82

trauma (cont.)
   events, 4, 118, 122
   experiences, 112, 118
vision accounts, 5, 129–30, 145
visionary encounters, 15, 17, 136, 143
visionary experiences, 15, 45, 129–30, 141, 144–45
visions, 2–9, 13–45, 56, 69–71, 74, 78, 87–90, 109–10, 121–23, 129–39, 141–49, 166–67, 170–71, 178–79, 182–85
   apocalyptic, 27, 42, 45
   reports, 16, 89, 184
   texts, 179, 185
wilderness, 6, 16, 18–24, 31
woman, 3, 28–34, 36–43, 85–86, 95, 97, 103, 154, 186